AF560004

NEW DIRECTIONS IN RURAL DEVELOPMENT

NEW DIRECTIONS IN RURAL DEVELOPMENT

Edited by

Mr. Bishnu Mohan Dash
Assistant Professor & Chief Editor
Dept. of Social Work
Dr. Bhim Rao Ambedkar College
(University of Delhi)
Delhi (India)

&

Dr. Sanjoy Roy
Ph.D., M.Phil, MSW (UGC-NET)
Associate Professor
School of Social Work
IGNOU
New Delhi (India)

DISCOVERY PUBLISHING HOUSE PVT. LTD.
NEW DELHI-110 002

Published by:

Tilak Wasan

DISCOVERY PUBLISHING HOUSE PVT. LTD.

4383/4A, Ansari Road, Darya Ganj
New Delhi-110 002 (India)
Phone : +91-11-23279245, 43596064-65
Fax : +91-11-23253475
E-mail : parul.wasan@gmail.com
discoverypublishinghouse@gmail.com
web : www.discoverypublishinggroup.com

First Edition: **2012**
ISBN: 978-93-5056-108-9

New Directions in Rural Development

© 2012, Editors

All rights reserved. No part of this publication should be reproduced, stored in a retrieval system, or transmitted in any form or by any means: electronic, mechanical, photocopying, recording or otherwise, without the prior written permission of the author and the publisher.

This book has been published in good faith that the material provided by authors is original. Every effort is made to ensure accuracy of material, but the publisher and printer will not be held responsible for any inadvertent error(s). In case of any dispute, all legal matters are to be settled under Delhi jurisdiction only.

Printed at:
Shree Balaji Art Press
Delhi

Preface

The First Chapter on Rural Marketing Initiatives in India: Challenges, Opportunities and Strategies, jointly authored by Dr. S.P. Aggrawal and Dr. Rajiv Nayan argues for a new role for rural marketing initiatives in India for delivering a better standard of living and quality of life for the rural people. They have highlighted that marketing is the pivot of economic development in rural areas. It is an essential component in income and employment generation in farm and non-farm sectors. Since marketing is one of the pre-requisites for income generation, this article attempted to throw some light both on marketing of rural produce to other areas and improving marketing environment within the rural areas.

The Second Chapter on Panchayats in India: A Historical-institutional Perspective by Dr. G Ram has discussed the evolution of the panchayats in India using the historical-institutional approach in its varied forms. The paper has highlighted that from the hoary past, the notion of *panch parameshwara* has signified the existence of panchayats in India. Almost defunct under the thrust of the British Empire, these panchayats were resuscitated, later, through statutory efforts under the empire and strengthened in the post-Independence period. After a great debate in the Indian parliament, the panchayats were included in India's Constitution as local governance system in the directive principles of policy for the state which direct the state to make efforts for decentralization of power and for establishment and promotion of the panchayats at all levels of rural self government. The Balvant Rai Mehta Committee recommended a three-tier system, and this model attained constitutional status through the Constitution (73rd) Amendment Act, 1992. Though the Panchayati Raj Institutions have been in existence for a long time, they could not acquire the status and dignity of viable and responsive people's bodies due to a number of reasons. Therefore, the 73rd Constitution Amendment Act has enshrined in the Constitution certain basic and essential features of Panchayati Raj Institutions to impart certainty, continuity and strength to them, by adding Part IX relating to Panchayats in the Constitution.

The Third Chapter on Role of NGO's in Marketing Self Employment—A Case Study of RUDSETI (Rural Development and Self Employment Training Institute), jointly authored by Dr. Y.S. Siddegowda and Dr. K.G. Parashurama Sree Dharmasthala Manjunatheshwara College, Ujire, Karnataka has attempted to conceptually analyze the problems of unemployment and the importance of self employment. It has also highlighted the role of NGO's in marketing self employment and also presented a case study of RUDSETI, an NGO, in marketing self employment programme. The paper has also discussed that the problem of unemployment is rapidly assuming dangerous proportions in many countries as their economies and educational systems are unable to accommodate unemployed youths. In many developing countries even low levels of economic growth are not predicted, and thus limit their labor absorptive capacity. Indeed shrinkage of their economies, and related livelihood opportunities are expected. Economists advise that the current system will not meet the supply of labor available. Thus, youth unemployment is an urgent global issue that has repercussions in demographic, social, economic, health, and environmental spheres. These impacts will be felt at the individual, familial, national and global levels if not addressed, and this is a prescription for disaster. This clearly indicates the need for promoting self-employment entrepreneurial ventures among the unemployed. Of late, Government and Non-Government agencies have taken certain initiatives and implementing many schemes to promote self employment programmes and micro enterprises activities. However, the efforts seem to be inadequate against the gigantic unemployment problem. It is under these circumstances that Rural Development and Self-Employment Training Institutes (RUDSETI) came into being and making concerted efforts to promote entrepreneurship especially among rural youths.

The Fourth Chapter on Essential Techniques for Social Work Practice in the Fields of Community Development by Professor Mukul Srivastava discussed that community practice techniques have been neglected by social work educators and authors, reflecting a lack of fit with real world practice needs. To sharpen the debate, the different Social Work Professionals identify five techniques that are helpful, if not essential for community practice: (1) Force Field Analysis; (2) Program Evaluation Review Technique; (3) Nominal Group Technique; (4) Delphi; and (5) Q-Sort. He views that the analysis of these could spark a dialogue leading ultimately to a universally accepted set of community practice techniques in social work curricula. Social work educators who interact with practitioners will confirm what practitioners demand from educators or what students demand from their practicum guide: to place greater emphasis on teaching what social workers do to affect change.

The real world of practice demands competencies in what social workers actually do, rather than how much theory they know. Competent community practice necessitates a repertoire of skills and techniques to effect change along a continuum of system from individuals through family, groups, organizations, to community. However, classroom textbooks and journal articles are dominated by discussion of theories, value dilemmas, and case studies, creating a disconnect between what educators, students and practitioners want and need, and what they get.

The Fifth Chapter on Self-help for chronic poor—an assessment of microfinance as a policy choice' by Dr. Chittaranjan Das Adhikary highlighted that one of the major challenges which keep us ceased is the large scale poverty that we inherited since the time of independence. The development efforts started immediately after World War II did affect our approach to the poverty question. This paper has critically examined the evolution of our approach towards poverty alleviation over the years through trickle down to *'Garibi Hatao'* and beyond. Then it seeks to expose the gaps in our poverty measurement and the inadequacy of income poverty or calorie intake to capture all dimensions of the poor. In conclusion it argues that we need a shift in the poverty paradigm and consider the merit of microfinance as an alternative.

The Sixth Chapter on Rural Development Planning: Theoretical Reflections by Dr. Manish Dwivedi is a critical review/appraisal of strategy of rural development programmes as reflected in post-independence India's planning and development experience. The appraisal is in the nature of a theoretical and methodological critique of the strategy and programmes of rural development. This follows from the basic premise that a strategy essentially presupposes a "theory". The inter-relationship between Theory, strategy and programmatic action/implementation through complex, imply an integral relationship. A critical appraisal of a policy programme and implementation in isolation or de-linked from the strategy and its contextual dependence on theory is not only not likely to be illuminating but oftentimes misleading. The basic methodological approach of the critique in the present study here, is to lay bare the "Internal" links between theory, strategy and programmatic action.

Dr. Anoop Singh in his chapter titled Towards Reform of land acquisition framework in India discusses various instances in which projects have faced delays and interruptions owing to disputes over land acquisition like Nandigram and Singur in West Bengal, the Reliance Special Economic Zone (SEZ) in Raigad, Maharashtra and the Bhushan Steel Plant in Jharkhand, Yamuna and Ganga Expressways in U.P. are recent examples in this regard. One key factor that contributes to these problems is the absence of effective communication between promoters and affected communities, resulting from little or no community involvement in the acquisition process. Very often, promoters provides only promises to community involvement by holding a few inconsequential community consultations—just to prove that the community of project affected persons (PAPs) has been taken on-board. This leads to mistrust among PAPs, which is reinforced when the promoters fail to honour their commitments relating to rehabilitation and resettlement. In addition to the basic land acquisition laws, special enactments related to land acquisition exist in many states, which separately empower the relevant authorities to acquire land for designated purposes. An examination of the implication of these legislations indicates a possible scope for rationalisation of the multiple legislations. Social Impact Assessment (SIA) and Environmental Impact Assessment (EIA) are key component for establishing and sustainability of any project.

The Eighth Chapter on Present value paradigm and rural development contributed by Dr. Brajesh Kumar in his contribution highlights that rural development needs comprehensive treatment using knowledge from across the subjects touching different aspects of the rural life in general and sociology, economics and politics in particular. The question of development has been examined from different angles by the scholars and thinkers in the respective field of investigation. Therefore, development requires multidisciplinary examination of finding ways and means of material and spiritual upliftment in development. In this paper the problem has been examined from demand side management of the rural development within the domain of socio-psychological complexities of rural life determining the characteristics of socio-political demand for development in the country side where the same has been investigated from supply side angle of the problem as reflected in majority of the studies in this regard. The paper finds that the Rural Development lies in our ability to induce thought in the mind of the people, faith in the heart that their efforts will yield for them in time and reality. Fear of losing their rights and welfare, if they fail to remain vigilant and united, also play a vital role for enhancing work culture and productivity of human resources in rural India.

The Ninth Chapter on Static and Dynamic Gains of Micro Finance: An Empirical Study in West Bengal contributed by Dr. Debashis Sarkar has mentioned that despite the persistence of top-down bureaucratic process in the administration of micro-finance by the commercial banks, the static and dynamic benefits are quite visible and tend to benefit the hitherto disadvantaged sections and vulnerable groups of the rural economy. The benefits accruing to those covered by different programmes and there is a pro-poor bias built into the credit system and it needs to be strengthened, if the fight against extreme poverty is to be a success. Micro-finance as an instrument of fighting poverty has come of age and international micro-credit summits are regularly held for dissemination of knowledge and replication of successful experiments like that of Grameen Bank of Bangladesh.

The Tenth Chapter on Land Reforms for alleviation of Rural Poverty jointly contributed by Dr. K. Somasekhar and Dr. G. Venkata Naidu have highlighted that even after 63 years of independence still more than one-forth of rural population lives in below poverty line. Evaluation studies conducted by research institutions identified that the root cause for not being elimination of poverty due to the people does not possess land. This paper examines implementation of rural development programmes and progress of distribution of land. Further it also describes the hurdles for poor progress of land reforms and finally strategies to be adopted to implement land reforms effectively for elimination of rural poverty.

Mr. Trilochan Dash in his chapter Politics of Rural Development has highlighted that since independence, different policies and programmes were introduced in order to uplift their socio- and economic-status of their living by different governments both at centre and states. The most alarming worry is that all the noble policies were in the air due to high bureaucratic in nature, change of government and their shifting of the ideologies, external pressures from the supra-national agencies and most important one is lack of understanding of the masses in the rural India. Many vested interested people took advantage out of it. The slogan *'Garibi Hatao'* remained immortal in Indian soil. The present paper tried to analyze the certain important arguments in this regard which may give further investigation in the field of research.

Mr. Gurupada Saren in his chapter 'Involvement of Women in Panchayati Raj Institutions (PRIs) in India has argued that Panchayati Raj has ensured the better accountability and more transparency in the local affairs of the community and increased the self-sufficiency of women representatives. The noteworthy factor is that Non-Governmental Organizations (NGOs) often provide important training and support to the elected women representatives towards smooth functioning of the Panchayats. It also looks forward towards the social transformation in rural areas through the involvement of women.

The Chapter on Rural Development with a Feministic Approach: Isssues and Alternatives contributed by Dr. Nishu Bala, has described that in absence of adequate employment opportunities in rural areas, male members of most of the rural families are forced to migrate to the cities. Therefore, female members of the families become the primary bread winner of the family. These women are always seen to be engaged vigorously in familial and farm activities, home-based industrial occupation and contribution, to a great extent, to the family's economy. Therefore, any strategy for rural development must include women as the primary agents. It is with this background that the present paper tends to highlight the role of women in rural development which is often ignored and underestimated.

The Chapter on Micro Finance—An Instrument for Rural Development, jointly contributed by Dr. Y. Ashok Kumar and P. Venugopala Rao has described that the institutional credit markets have never been very friendly with the poverty groups. The amount of credit advanced by the organized financial institutions to the poor has been inadequate. The rate of account the peculiarities surrounding the economic activities undertaken by the poor. As a result, the record to repayment performance has been bad. The exploitative informal credit sources such as the moneylenders, pawn brokers etc., have only worsened the economic well being of the poor. The SHG movements has so far shown that the out- comes have gone beyond thrift, credit and economic well being the movement had served as instrument of social change essentially out of empowerment of women, improvement in literacy levels and children's education, particularly girl education, housing facilities, abolition of child labour, decline in family violence and banning of illicit distilleries in the villages have all been reported in different studies.

The Chapter on Historical Perspective of Panchayati Raj in India—An Overview by Dr. V. Venkateswarlu, argued that land reforms, co-operatives, panchayati raj and community development movements, are supposed to be the four solid pillars on which a prosperous, dynamic and genuinely democratic rural social system is attempted to be built by the government of independent India. Panchayati Raj is also claimed as a real democratic political apparatus which would bring the masses into active political participation and also would establish a genuine political control from below, from the vast majority of the weaker, poorer sections of Rural India. This paper highlighted the historical perspective of Panchayati Raj System in India and also analyzes the structural functional system of Panchayati Raj Institution.

The Chapter on Integrated Decentralized District Planning and the Panchayati Raj Institutions: Theories and Practices contributed by Chandan Kumar Behera, intended to highlight the positive aspects of integrated decentralized district planning process by elaborating the current planning practices and the role of Panchayati Raj Institutions. It also has a focus on the pros and cons of integrated decentralized planning process and ended with indicating some ways forwards.

The Chapter on NREGA—Opportunities and Challenges contributed by Amit Kumar looks at the performance of the NREGS from two perspectives—it examines the opportunities of the programme, as well as the challenges being posed by this schemes. In terms of the efficiency impact, the analysis reveals a clear violation of the formal clauses and the spirit of the NREG Act and thereby undermining the potential of the programme in terms of providing a safety net.

Dr. Sanjoy Roy, in his Chapter Food Insecurity in Rural India—Some Reflections argues that food security could be when all people at all times have access to enough food that should affordable, safe and healthy, culturally acceptable, meets specific dietary needs, obtained in a dignified manner and produced in ways that are environmentally sound. But food security in India raises the twin problems of uncertain food production and unequal food distribution. The impact of unequal food distribution can lead adverse effects on the rural and urban population living below the poverty line. Food insecurity is not only economic problem but also problem of non-humanity approach in India. There availability of the food grains is enough to satisfy their needs. According to the statistical data published by the Food Corporation of India and the government of India foodgrain availability is 229 million tonnes in 2008-09 which is 230 million tonnes in previous year. While it is happening because, foodgrain traders are doing speculation practice and sealing them in high prices than fair prices. Food insecurity is not only natural but also man-made. So, what is now required is a new initiative and strong National Food Security Mission and finally it is a time for a Second Green Revolution in India.

Dr Nagaraj Battu in his paper titled Rural Development, Meaning and Scope has discussed the concept, meaning and scope of rural development.

Mr. Prasanta Bauri in his article Diversification in Agriculture: A Key to Rural Development in the Perspective of Globalizing India highlighted that Indian rural economy has witnessed remarkable changes in the era of globalization. The most striking impact of globalization on Indian crop economy has been in the diversification in agriculture. It is the diversified cropping pattern that is inevitable in the era of globalization as a route to development of crop and as well as rural economy. The paper has tried to focus on the impact of globalization on development of rural economy of India through diversification in agriculture.

The last chapter jointly contributed by Dr. M. Trimurthi Rao and B. Prathima, Research Scholar, Department of Commerce and Business Administration, Acharya Nagarjuna University, Nagarjuna Nagar have described that especially in the era of globalization the income inequalities are increasing between the rich and poor. There was a wide gap between the rich and poor. The process of globalization and liberalization has further marginalized the poor and weaker sections of the society. The paper has highlighted on the existing rural development programmes, changing perspectives of rural development and emerging challenges in the context of globalization and this article also have suggested alternate strategies for the development of rural areas.

Bishnu Mohan Dash
Sanjoy Roy

Contents

List of Contributors

1. Dr. S.P. Aggrawal, Principal, Deshbandhu College (Evening), University of Delhi, Delhi.
2. Dr. Rajiv Nayan, Asst. Professor, Deshbandhu College (Evening), University of Delhi, Delhi.
3. Dr. G. Ram, Professor of Sociology, Assam University, Silchar, Assam.
4. Dr. Y.S. Siddegowda, Professor, Department of Studies and Research in Social Work, University of Mysore, Manasagangotri, Mysore, Karnataka.
5. Dr. K.G. Parashurama, Reader, Department of Studies and Research in Social Work, Sree Dharmasthala Manjunatheshwara College, Ujire, Karnataka.
6. Prof. Mukul Srivastava, Department of Social Work, Institute of Social Sciences, Dr. B.R. Ambedkar University, Agra, U.P.
7. Dr. Chittaranjan Das Adhikary, Sr. Lecturer, Department of Sociology, BHU, Varanasi, U.P.
8. Dr. Manish Dwivedi, Head, Department of Social Work, Nehru Gram Bharati University, Allahabad, U.P.
9. Dr. Anoop Kumar Singh, Assistant Professor (SG), Department of Sociology, DAV P.G. College, Kanpur, U.P.
10. Dr. Brajesh Kumar, Assistant Professor, Department of Commerce, Assam University, Silchar, Assam.
11. Dr. Debashis Sarkar, Reader in Agricultural Economics, Institute of Agriculture and Hony. Deputy Director, Agro-Economic Research Centre, Visva-Bharati, Santiniketan, West Bengal
12. Dr. K. Somasekhar, Asst. Professor, Department of Rural Development, Acharya Nagarjuna University, Nagarjuna Nagar, Guntur, A.P.
13. Dr. G. Venkata Naidu, Associate Prof., Department of Economics, S.K. University, Anantapur, A.P.

14. Trilochan Dash, Head, Department of Political Science, Nongstoin College, North Eastern Hills University, Shillong, Meghalaya.

15. Mr. Gurupada Saren, Assistant Professor in Rural Development, Indira Gandhi National Open University (IGNOU), New Delhi.

16. Dr. Nishu Bala, Lecturer, De4partment of Economics, Baba Farid College, Bathinda, Punjab.

17. Dr. Y. Ashok Kumar, Assistant Professor, Department of Sociology, Social Work, Acharya Nagarjuna University, Nagarjuna Nagar, Guntur (A.P.)

18. P. Venugopala Rao, Research Scholar, Department of Sociology, Social Work, Acharya Nagarjuna University, Nagarjuna Nagar, Guntur, A.P.

19. Dr. V. Venkateswarlu, Assistant Professor & Co-ordinator, Department of Sociology and Social Work, Acharya Nagarjuna University, Nagarjuna Nagar, Guntur, A.P.

20. Chandan Kumar Behera, National UN Volunteer, Chhattisgarh.

21. Amit Kumar, Assistant Professor, Department of Social Work, National University of Jaipur, Jaipur, Rajasthan.

22. Dr. Sanjoy Roy, Associate Professor, School of Social Work, IGNOU, New Delhi.

23. Dr. Nagaraj Battu, Assistant Professor, Department of Human Resource Development, Acharya Nagarjuna University, Nagarjuna Nagar, Guntur, A.P.

24. Prasanta Bauri, M.Phil Scholar in Economics, University of Kalyani, West Bengal.

25. Dr. M. Trimurthi Rao, Assistant Professor, Department of Sociology and Social Work, Acharya Nagarjuna University, Nagarjuna Nagar, Guntur, A.P.

26. B. Prathima, Research Scholar, Department of Commerce and Business Administration, Acharya Nagarjuna University, Nagarjuna Nagar, Guntur, A.P.

CHAPTER

1

Rural Marketing Initiatives in India
Challenges, Opportunities and Strategies

—Dr. S.P. Aggrawal
—Dr. Rajiv Nayan

ABSTRACT

This chapter argues for a new role for rural marketing initiatives in India: Challenges, Opportunities and Strategies that of delivering a better standard of living and quality of life for the rural people. Marketing is the pivot of economic development in rural areas. It is an essential component in income and employment generation in farm and non-farm sectors. Since marketing is one of the pre-requisites for income generation, this article attempts to throw some light both on marketing of rural produce to other areas and improving marketing environment within the rural areas.

Introduction

Rural marketing business environment has evolved and transformed itself at a much faster pace in the recent years. Marketing today has changed the dynamics of the business. As the consumers are getting informative, the business is becoming competitive day-by-day. Marketers are seeking fresher challenges everyday and are looking to increase their realm. The urban consumer has been coddled till now but this market is shrinking prompting the marketer to now explore the rural consumers which promises a huge potential. The market has enough scale to offer and enough desire to consume. In the recent years rural markets have acquired significance and the overall growth of the economy has resulted into substantial increase in the purchasing power of the rural communities. On account of green revolution the rural areas are consuming a large quantity of industrial and urban manufactured products. In the context of a special mark Challenges, Opportunities and Strategies namely rural marketing has emerged.

What is Rural Market?

The Census of India defines rural as any habitation where the population density is less than 400 per sq. km and where at least 75 per cent of the male working population is engaged in agriculture and where the population is less than 10,000 and there is not any municipality or board. The rural market in India is scattered and spread over a wide geographical area. Indian market is divided into urban and rural markets.

Rural Marketing

Rural marketing broadly involves reaching customers, understanding their wants, supply of goods and services and ultimately satisfying consumers leading to more sales. The general impression is that only agricultural inputs like seeds, fertilizers, pesticides, cattle feed and agricultural machinery has a potential for growth in the rural market. However, there is a growing market for consumer goods now. It has been estimated, the rural market is growing at the rate of five-times its urban area.

Potential of Rural Market

Our country is endowed with a degree of ethnic and regional diversity. Around three-fourths of the total population resides in the rural areas and majority of them are dependent upon agriculture for their livelihood. Agriculture contributes about 17.2 per cent to the Gross Domestic Product (GDP) of the country. It also contributes about 13.1 per cent to the total Indian exports. This sector provides employment to 58.4 per cent of the country's workforce and livelihood to more than 650 million people. Despite this fact the condition of these people has not shown any significant improvement. The development of the nation largely depends upon the development of the rural population. Mahatma Gandhi had once said: "India's way is not Europe's. India is not an urban center. India lives in her several hundreds of villages". India is an agro-based economy and the growth of most of the other sectors of economy is driven by rural demand. Urban market is reaching towards the saturation point, thus bringing in and urgent need to focus on rural development. More than 70 per cent of India's population lives in villages and constitutes a big market for industry because of increasing disposal incomes and awareness level. In comparison to just 5,161 towns in India there are 6,38,365 villages in India. Companies are realizing slowly but surely that the key to gain true market leadership lies in tapping the rural potential. However the rural sector in India suffers from different kinds of problems. Some areas are having enough money but their level of awareness and hence consumerism is very low. A look at some facts, which will clear the doubts of skeptics about the potential of rural markets in India:

- About 285 million reside in urban India as compared to 742 million in rural India.
- The number of middle income and high-income household in rural India is expected to grow from 80 million to 111 million by 2007 while urban India is expected to grow from 46 million to 59 million.
- Number of poor household is expected to shrink by half to 28 million in 2006-07 from 61 million in 1997-98, taking rural people from poverty to prosperity.
- Rural marketing involves addressing around 700 million potential consumers, over 40 per cent of the Indian middle-class, and about half the country's disposable income.
- The Indian rural market is almost twice as large as the entire market of USA or Russia.

Indian Traditional Rural Market

Since ancient time Indian villages had the concept of village markets popularly known as the village *Haats*. The *haats* are basically a gathering of the local buyers and sellers. The barter system was quite prevalent and which is still continuing in a number of places even today. *Haats* are basically a weekly event and are central to the village economy. Mind the importance of *haats* in villages. They set up stalls in the villages coinciding with the village *haats* and promote their business. This serves a dual purpose getting the attention of a large number of their target market as well as getting critical insight about the rural consumers' behavior. The village *mandis* and the seasonal *melas* are other important occasions for the marketers to tap.

Special Features of Rural Market

Unlike urban markets rural markets are difficult to predict and possess special characteristics. The featured population is predominantly illiterate, have low income, characterized by irregular income, lack of monthly income and flow of income fluctuating with the monsoon winds. Rural markets face the critical issues of distribution, understanding the rural consumer, communication and poor infrastructure. The marketer has to strengthen the distribution and pricing strategies. The rural consumer expects value for money and owing to his unsteady and meager status of weekly income increasing the household income and improving distribution are the viable strategies that have to be adapted to tap the immense potential of the market. Media reach is a strong reason for the penetration of goods like cosmetics, mobile phones, etc., which are only used by the urban people. Increasing awareness and knowledge on different products and brands accelerate the demand. The rural audience are however critical of glamorous advertisements on TV and depend on the opinion leaders who introduce the product by using it and recommending it. Opinion leaders play a key role in popularizing products and influence in rural market. Nowadays educated youth of rural also influences the rural consumers. Rural consumers are influenced by the life style they watch on television sets. Their less exposure to outside world makes them innocent and fascinated to novelties. The reach of mass television media especially television has influenced the buying behaviour greatly.

Rural Consumers Buying Behavior

People in rural areas are also becoming conscious through media about their buying decisions like their urban counterparts. There has been a significant rise in the brand awareness among the people. As a result they are becoming choosier and demanding than ever before so any company has to properly analyze the psychographics before entering this market. In fact we look at the rural consumers shopping basket, we can see that—of the expenditure on consumer goods in rural household approximately 44 per cent is on food articles such as biscuits, tea, coffee and salt, 20 per cent on toiletries, 13 per cent on washing material, 10 per cent on cosmetics, 4 per cent on Over-The-Counter products and 9 per cent on other consumables.

Brand awareness

Studies indicate that there has been a visible shift in the people's preference for brands. People are upgrading from the use of tooth powders to tooth pastes, and from using traditional mosquito repellants to using mats and coils. Also there is shift from low priced brands to semi-premium brands.

Rural consumers buy lower priced goods

This is one of the most prevalent myths about the rural market. However, what rural consumers are looking for are not cheap goods but they want value for money and if a brand fits into this category they are ready to pay for it. Also when they can afford they experiment with brands.

Rural consumers will buy what we sell to them

The brand loyalty for rural consumers is quite strong in some particular segments and brands like Colgate toothpastes and powders. However if a company becomes complacent and takes the rural consumers for granted it is ultimately going to lose in the market. The companies have to constantly innovate and make their products appealing to the consumers to succeed.

Rural India has common tastes

Some companies have the misconception that the tastes and preferences of the rural consumers are all same for the rural market. In fact it is more varied that the urban consumers. We are not talking about the differences due to geographies. In fact, in North India, the preferences of a Punjabi farmer will be quite different from his counterparts in Bihar or Uttar Pradesh. So the companies have to design strategies to tackle this issue.

Innovative uses of the product

The rural market is quite innovative in the uses of products. Several products are being used successfully for doing jobs what they are not meant for like using washing machines to make "lassi" in Punjab or using Iodex on animals to relieve them of muscular pain. The rural market is an enigma for the marketer and he has to see that the marketing communication is done in the relevant way.

Challenges in Rural Marketing

Though rural markets are a huge attraction to marketers, it is not easy to enter the market and take a sizeable share of the market in the short time due to the following reasons:

Low literacy

There are not enough opportunities for education in rural areas. The literacy level is as low (36%) when compared to all-India average of 52 per cent.

Duplicity in rural market

Most of the products in the rural market are found duplicate.

Seasonal demand

Demand for goods in rural markets depends upon agricultural situation, as agriculture is the main source of income. Agriculture to a large extent depends upon monsoon and therefore the demand or buying capacity is not stable or regular.

Transportation

Transportation is a major problem in rural areas and many rural areas are not connected by rail transport. *Kaccha* roads become unserviceable during the monsoon and interior villages get isolated.

Distribution system in rural area

An effective distribution system requires village-level shopkeeper, mandal/ taluka-level wholesaler or preferred dealer, distributor or stockiest at district level and company-owned depot or consignment distribution at state level. The presence of too many tiers in the distribution system increases the cost of distribution.

Communication problems rural India

Facilities such as telephone, fax and telegram are rather poor in rural areas.

Traditional life rural India

Life in rural areas is still governed by customs and traditions and people do not easily adapt the new practices. For example, even rich and educated class of farmers does not wear jeans or branded shoes.

Cautious in buying

Rural consumers are cautious in buying and decisions are slow and delayed. They like to give a trial and only after being personally satisfied do they buy the product. There is a belief among rural people that experience is more important than formal education and they respect salespersons who can offer practical solutions to their problems. Therefore, it is desirable that sales persons especially those who have been brought up in cities are given a thorough training consisting of both theory and practical aspects of village life. The training will help these sales persons to align themselves with the market realities and settle down smoothly in their jobs. Rural market has a tremendous potential that is yet to be tapped. A small increase in rural income results in an exponential increase in buying power.

People career in rural india

While rural marketing offers a challenging career, rural sales person should require certain qualifications and specialized talent.

Cultural factors

Culture is a system of shared values, beliefs and perceptions that influence the behavior of consumers. There are different groups based on religion, caste, occupation, income, age, education and politics and each group exerts influence on the behavior of people in villages.

Opportunities in Rural Market

The fact that rural India has enormous business potential, is widely accepted across all segments of the industry. It is attributed not merely to the population of 700 million that reside here, other statistics make an equally strong statement. 'Go rural' is the slogan of marketing gurus after analyzing the socio-economic changes in villages. The rural population is nearly three times the urban, so the rural consumers have become the prime target market for consumer durable and non-durable products, food, construction, electrical, electronics, automobiles, banks, insurance companies and other sectors besides hundred per cent of agri-input products such as seeds, fertilizers, pesticides and farm machinery. The Indian rural market today accounts for only about ₹ 8 billion of the total share of ₹ 120 billion thus claiming 6.6 per cent of the total share. So clearly there seems to be a long way ahead. Although a lot is spoken about the immense potential of the unexplored rural market, advertisers and companies find it easier to vie for a share of the already divided urban pie. While rural households contribute to 45 per cent of the total household income of the country and the savings to income percentage in rural at 30 per cent is even higher than urban. Infrastructure is improving rapidly in rural areas. Last six decade only 40 per cent villages have been connected by road and in the next 10 years another 30 per cent would be connected. More than 90 per cent villages are electrified, though only 44 per cent rural homes have electric connections.

Some Social Indicators have Improved in Recent Year

- Number of *Pucca* houses doubled from 22 per cent to 41 per cent and *Kuccha* houses halved (41% to 23%).
- Percentage of BPL families declined from 46 per cent to 27 per cent.
- Rural literacy level improved from 36 per cent to 59 per cent.

There are low penetration rates in rural areas, so there are many marketing opportunities.

Table 1.1 : Marketing opportunities in rural areas

Durables	Urban	Rural	Total (% of Rural HH)
CTV	30.4	4.8	12.1
Refrigerator	33.5	3.5	12.0

FMCGs	Urban	Rural	Total (% of Rural HH)
Shampoo	66.3	35.2	44.2
Toothpaste	82.2	44.9	55.6

Rural Marketers can make effective use of the large available infrastructure.

Table 1.2 : Infrastructures in rural areas

Post Offices	1,38,000
Haats (periodic markets)	42,000
Melas (exhibitions)	25,000
Mandis (agri markets)	7,000
Public Distribution Shops	3,80,000
Bank Branches	32,000

Most of the company target rural market

The Indian rural market has a huge demand base and offers great opportunities to marketers. Two-thirds of Indian consumers live in rural areas and almost half of the national income is generated here. The reasons for heading to the rural areas are fairly clear. The urban consumer durable market for products like colour TVs, washing machines, refrigerators and air conditioners is growing annually at between 7 per cent and 10 per cent. The rural market is zooming ahead at around 25 per cent annually.

Reasons for improvement of business in rural area

- Socio-economic changes (lifestyle, habits and tastes, economic status)
- Literacy level (25 per cent before independence—more than 65 per cent in 2001)
- Infrastructure facilities (roads, electricity, media)
- Increase in income
- Increase in expectations

Future Trends in Rural Marketing

Markets which are not able to face the stiff competition posed by MNCs can restore their profits in the rural sector. The market share of urban market when compared to the rural market is low, hence if Indian industries concentrate on rural markets their sales will increase. If rural markets are brought into the limelight of development, they pave way to prosperity. Prosperity of India lies in the prosperity of every Indian, hence no rural segment should be left untapped.

Fast moving consumer good

Fast Moving Consumer Goods (FMCG) or Consumer Packaged Goods (CPG) is products that are sold quickly at relatively low cost. Examples include non-durable goods such as soft drinks, toiletries, grocery items etc. Though the absolute profit made on FMCG products is relatively small, they generally sell in large quantities, so the cumulative profit on such products can be large. The term FMCG refers to those retail goods that are generally replaced or fully used up over a short period of days, weeks, or months, and within one year. The early success of FMCG, telecom and consumer durables is only a pointer to inherent purchasing power this segment has. Within the rural sector, however there are vast variations in socio-economic profiles. The entire population is spread over 6,30,000 villages across the vast expanse of the country. The income distribution amongst these is highly skewed with some of the villages reaping the rewards of agricultural revolution and enjoying similar standards of living like their urban counterparts, while a bulk of villages are still grappling with the basic issues of electricity and water. These variations are not only at the regional level, but even within the state and the district. The income patterns too are diverse. All the above factors make the execution of rural strategy a daunting task for any product or services provider. To increase the penetration of insurance in this sector, the regulator IRDA, had made it mandatory for insurers to write a growing proportion of its business in the rural market. Most of the early forays of the private life insurance companies in the rural sector have been towards meeting these requirements. At present 53 per cent of all FMCGs and 59 per cent of all consumer durables are being sold in rural India. The biggest FMCG company in India HLL derives more than half of its ₹ 12,000 crore revenues from the rural markets. Though there is a high component of sales in some particular product categories like radios, watches, casette players, the penetration levels are abysmally low, and therefore, offer tremendous potential for growth. The rural market is an enigma for the companies. Due to the lack of deeper insights into the psyche of the rural consumers, companies are hesitant to explore this territory.

Recent Happening in Rural Markets

While the rural market provides tremendous opportunities to the marketers, it is not easy for any company to enter this market and walk away with a sizeable share of the market. In reality, the rural market suffers from a variety of problems including that of distribution and marketing communication. Companies have been trying to tackle these issues in a number of innovative ways. Be it the "e-choupal" initiative of ITC or "Project Shakti" launched by HLL, the aim is to come closer to the rural consumer. To capture the alluring rural market, companies need to formulate strategies, which can deal with issues pertaining to consumer psychographics and appropriate marketing mix.

The company would be able to maintain the supply of stock with the retailers, it would be able to control brand choice, volumes, and in turn, market share. HLL's "Project Shakti" was aimed at creating opportunities to increase rural family incomes, which puts more money in their hands to purchase the range of daily consumption products from soaps to toothpastes.

However, the companies tend to forget that the requirements of the rural market are totally different. The companies need to develop special products and strategies for the rural consumer. If a company wants to force cornflakes in the rural market it is doomed for failure. Using generic advertising to attract the rural consumer is not going to market. Proliferation of large format of Rural Retail Stores which have been successful also in the rural area. Some of the stores are as below:

- DSCL Haryali Stores
- M & M Shubh Labh Stores
- TATA/Rallis Kisan Kendras

- Escorts Rural Stores
- Warnabazaar, Maharashtra (Annual Sale Rs. 40 crore)
- "e-choupal" initiative of ITC
- "Project Shakti" launched by HLL

Table 1.3 : Top 10 Companies in FMCG Sector

S.No.	Companies
1.	ITC (Indian Tobacco Company)
2.	Hindustan Unilever Ltd.
3.	Nestlé India
4.	GCMMF (AMUL)
5.	Dabur India
6.	Asian Paints (India)
7.	Britannia Industries
8.	Cadbury India
9.	Procter & Gamble Hygiene and Health Care
10.	Marico Industries

ITC's e-Choupal Initiative

Calcutta-based tobacco to hotels conglomerate ITC has also been trying to build a platform that others can use. ITC which companies both private and public could market goods and services to Indian farmers. The trust route would hopefully make other companies more willing to sign up with their offerings. ITC's foray into an enhanced distribution network came from the recognition that the existing agri-produce distribution channels were inefficient. The company exports various agricultural products soybean, rice and wheat, to name a few. ITC embarked on an initiative to deploy technology to re-engineer the procurement of soybeans from rural India. ITC's agri-business division Kiosks is called "e-choupals" consisting of a personal computer with Internet access were set up at the villages. He explains that soybean farmers could access this kiosk for information on prices, but had the choice to sell their produce either at the local market or directly to ITC at their hub locations. The e-Choupal infrastructure consists of:

- A kiosk with Internet access in the house of a trained farmer called a *Sanchalak*. This kiosk is within walking distance of target farmers.
- A warehousing hub managed by the former middleman called a *Samyojak*. This is within a tractor-driveable distance of target farmers
- A collaborative network of companies orchestrated by ITC with a pan-India presence.

This is, of course, a simplified structure of ITC and there has been a stream of new initiatives in August 2004, ITC introduced the e-Choupal Sagar a rural retail outlet at the hub. The first was set up at Sehore in Madhya Pradesh in 7,000 sq. ft. mall sells consumer goods as well as agri-products. In a recent move ITC has set up its first urban outlet the other end of the e-Choupal chain to retail fresh fruit and vegetables. The e-Choupal project is already benefiting more than 3.5 million farmers. Over the next decade the e-Choupal network will cover more than 100,000 villages representing one-sixth of rural India and create more than 10 million e-farmers

Hindustan Unilever Ltd—Shakti

Empowering Women Consumers the company's project Shakti (its name means "strength") was born out of this realization, and it has become a case study for business schools and evolved beyond its original goals. The objectives of project Shakti are to create income-generating capabilities for underprivileged rural women by providing a small-scale enterprise opportunity, and to improve rural living standards with greater awareness of health and hygiene. Hindustan Lever's drive into rural India was prompted in part by growing competition. When the Indian economy opened up in early 1990, multinationals such as Procter & Gamble stepped up their activities forcing Hindustan Lever to seek higher revenues and growth by reaching into villages with 1,000 or fewer residents. Launched in 2001, project Shakti was an important part of this strategy. It involved working with rural self-help groups (SHGs) to educate rural women, while also making them part of the company's marketing network.

Strategies Aspects in Rural Market

Rural marketing in India is not much developed there are many hindrances in the area of market, product design and positioning, pricing, distribution and promotion. Companies need to understand rural marketing in a broader manner not only to survive and grow in their business but also a means to the development of the rural economy. One has to have a strategic view of the rural markets so as to know and understand the markets well. In the context of rural marketing one has to understand the manipulation of marketing mix in terms of product usage. Product usage is central to price, distribution, promotion, branding, company image and more important farmer economics, thus any strategy in rural marketing should be given due attention and importance by understanding the product usage, all elements of marketing mix can be better organised and managed. Rural markets and rural marketing involve a number of strategies, which include:

Communicating and Changing Quality Perception

Companies are coming up with new technology and they are properly communicating it to the customer. There is a trade-off between Quality a customer perceives and a company wants to communicate. Thus, this positioning of technology is very crucial. The perception of the Indian about the desired product is changing. Now they know the difference between the products and the utilities derived out of it. As a rural Indian customer always wanted value for money with the changed perception, one can notice difference in current market scenario.

Effective Media Communication

Companies will use media in rural marketing. They can either go for the traditional media or the modern media. The traditional media include *melas*, puppetry and folk theatre etc. The modern media includes TV, radio and e-chaupal.

Communication use of Local Language

The companies have realized the importance of proper communication in local language for promoting their products. They have started selling of quality with proper communication. Their main focus is to change the Indian customer outlook about quality. With their promotion and rural customer started asking for value for money.

Understanding Cultural and Social Values

Companies have recognized that social and cultural values have a very strong hold on the people. Cultural values play major role in deciding what to buy. Moreover, rural people are emotional and sensitive. Thus, to promote their brands, they are exploiting social and cultural values.

Developing Rural-Specific Products

Many companies are developing rural-specific products. Keeping into consideration the requirements, a farm develops these products. Electrolux is working on a made-for India fridge designed to serve basic purposes: chill drinking water, keep cooked food fresh, and to withstand long power cuts.

Giving Indian Words for Brands

Companies use Indian words for brands. Like LG has used India brand name "Sampoorna" for its newly launched TV. The word is a part of the Bengali, Hindi, Marathi and Tamil tongue or use other Indian tonge. In the past one year LG has sold one lakh 20-inch Sampoorna TVs all in towns with a population of around 10,000. By the end of 1999 roughly ₹ 114 crore worth of TV sets sold in the rural markets in a year.

Client and Location Specific Promotion

Client and location specific promotion involves a strategy designed to be suitable to the location and the client. Joint or co-operative promotion strategy involves participation between the marketing agencies and the client. 'Bundling of inputs' denote a marketing strategy, in which several related items are sold to the target client, including arrangements of credit, after-sale service, and so on. Media, both traditional as well as the modern media, is used as a marketing strategy to attract rural customers. Partnership for sustainability involves laying and building a foundation for continuous and long-lasting relationship.

Joint or Cooperative Promotion

Innovative media can be used to reach the rural customers. Radio and television are the conventional media that are reaching the rural audience effectively. But horse cart, bullock cart and wall writing are the other media which can carry the message effectively to the rural customers.

Bundling of Input

Rural marketing is an evolving concept and as a part of any economy has untapped potential, marketers have realized the opportunity recently. Improvement in infrastructure rich promise a bright future for those intending to go rural. Rural consumers are keen on branded goods nowadays, so the market size for products and services seems to have burgeoned. The rural population has shown a trend of wanting to move into a state of gradual urbanization in terms of exposure, habits, lifestyles and lastly, consumption patterns of goods and services. There are dangers on concentrating more on the rural customers. Reducing the product features in order to lower prices is a dangerous game to play.

New Initiative for Rural Jobs

An employment revolution is gathering momentum. In the hinterland many companies in new sectors like telecom, rural BPO and microfinance are creating thousands of jobs in villages and small towns. This could slow down the migration from rural to big cities. Migrants have traditionally found work as labourers, masons or security guards in the cities. For example, 80 per cent of the 5.5 million workforce of security firms hail from villages. Some migrants find better roles with FMCG and consumer durables companies or with the government. At this rate, estimates McKinsey Global Institute, 590 million people will be living in cities by 2030 putting enormous pressure on urban India's physical and social infrastructure. But now for the first time thousands of non-agricultural jobs are being created in villages and small towns giving many like Biroria a new alternative. A host of services-driven companies in emerging sectors MFI, retail, telecom, ITeS, healthcare, infrastructure and logistics are scouting for local talent in small towns or from bordering villages. Companies are building their networks way beyond the top 30 cities.

Need More People for Business Maintaining

The Business of maintaining telecom towers which could employ 2,00,000 people by March 2011 is a good example. There are about 140,000 towers in upcountry locations. About 80 per cent of the 25,000 new towers, to be added this year, will be in rural and remote areas. Their operations and maintenance are managed by specialist firms like Chandigarh based Synergy Telecom which runs 5,000 sites in rural areas. These are ITI diploma holders who join at a monthly salary of 8,000-10,000. Ten such technicians are managed by a supervisor who holds an engineering degree and is paid 15,000-25,000 a month.

Business Process Outsourcing

Rural people in BPOs industry which currently employ 5,000 people could generate 150,000 openings in five years. Microfinance institutions (MFIs) already employ about 50,000. All this is giving India's rural youth new career options, going to the nearest big city is not the only way now. The migration story is now mostly restricted to local movement within the states.

Employment and Recruitment Firms

There have been testing of new models to bridge the challenging last-mile to reach rural talent. Last year Monster.com tied up with ITC to launch *Rozgarduniya* an Internet portal in English and Hindi on the latter's e-choupal's VSAT terminals. It covers 10,000 villages in UP, Maharashtra, Madhya Pradesh and Rajasthan, and has 15,000 registrations till date. To promote the service, job fairs were organised in Hathras, Pilibhit and Fatehnagar (Rajasthan), and 185 job offers have been made. There is a substantial blue-collar workforce in rural areas, but no potent tool to connect them to the main employment market.

Involve NGOs have been around to Help

Firms connect with village talent. But, a new breed of firms is now at hand to help employers' access to rural talent by combining social and commercial objectives in their business models. Among them is Chennai-based v-shesh, which calls itself a 'livelihood exchange'. It places rural youth (including people with disabilities and juveniles) as customer service agents or transaction processing officers in rural BPOs, as loan officers in microfinance institutions and as rural market developers in FMCG and consumer durables companies. There are many people close to employment, but fall by the wayside due to lack of opportunities. "We train them on confidence and basic life skills so that they are employable" said P. Rajasekharan, one of the co-founders of v-shesh, which operates in Madhya Pradesh, UP, Bihar, Orissa, Tamil Nadu and Karnataka.

Government Promote Rural Economy

The rural sector of India is not only observing a massive increase in its per capita income but also in its expenditure and production. To enhance the rural economy of India, the Indian government has increased the monetary incentives allotted for the Mahatma Gandhi National Rural Employment Guarantee Act (MNREGA) to US $8.04 bn in its 2009 Union Budget. Moreover, the government has also allotted US $34.74 bn in its Bharat Nirman Programme for enhancing rural road and rail network. Surprisingly, the rural economy was remain unaffected by the recent global financial meltdown as per the research conducted by Rural Marketing Association of India (RMAI). The research also revealed that the rural economy in India is soon to witness an increase in its earnings which will be largely triggered by the incessant expansion in agriculture for the last four successive years.

Conclusion

There is no doubt that the rural India offers tremendous opportunity for any company to tap. However, companies face many challenges in tackling the rural markets. Some of the important factors being an understanding of the rural customers' needs, a reliable distribution channel, and an effective marketing communication strategy to put their message across to the rural consumer. This calls for a paradigm shift in the thinking of the top management of the companies, which have been reluctant to realize the potential of rural markets. The mantra for success can be further augmented by the Four A Framework—Affordability, Acceptability, Accessibility, and Awareness. These factors will go a long way in providing the company with market value coverage along with a steady source of revenues. The companies which are going to keep in mind the above stated factors are sure to emerge as winners in the rural markets.

REFERENCES

1. Ramanuj Majumdar (2004). *Product Management in India*. PHI Learning. pp. 26-28.
2. *Ravindranath V. Badi and Naranyansa V. Badi, Rural Marketing,* Himalaya Publishing, 2004.
3. K L. K Rao and Ramesh G Taga (2005) *Rural Marketing: A Developmental Approach.*
4. Monish Bali, "The Rural Market Likes It Strong", *The Economic Times*, August 23, 2000.
5. Neeraj Jha, "Gung-ho on Rural Marketing", *The Financial Express*, June 19, 2000.
6. T. P. Gopal Swamy, *Rural Marketing, Environment-Problems and Strategies,* Wheeler Publishing, 1997.
7. The Marketing Mastermind Case Study HLL - *Rural Marketing Initiatives,* ICFAI Press, p. 62, and Feb. 2003.
8. Rural Marketing—A critical Review, *The Hindu, Business Line.*
9. *Businessworld* Marketing Whitebook 2005.
10. *The Economic Times,* 18 November 2010.
11. www.deccanherald.com
12. www.indiantelevision.com
13. www.hill.com
14. www.indiainfoline.com

CHAPTER

2

Panchayats in India
A Historical-Institutional Perspective

—G. Ram

ABSTRACT

There has been a long established tradition of panchas or local elderlies in various types of social collectivities. From the hoary past, the notion of panch parameshwara has signified the existence of panchayats in India. As traditional guards of their respective communities, panchayats have ever been exercising various powers—legislative, administrative and judicial, over the people. Almost defunct under the thrust of the British Empire, these panchayats were resuscitated, later, through statutory efforts under the empire and strengthened in the post-Independence period. After a great debate in the Indian parliament, the panchayats were included in India's Constitution as local governance system in the directive principles of policy for the state which direct the state to make efforts for decentralization of power and for establishment and promotion of the panchayats at all levels of rural self-government. The Balvant Rai Mehta Committee recommended a three-tier system, which was termed Panchayati Raj at the time of its introduction in 1959. This model attained constitutional status through the Constitution (73rd) Amendment Act, 1992. Though the Panchayati Raj Institutions have been in existence for a long time, they could not acquire the status and dignity of viable and responsive people's bodies due to a number of reasons. Therefore, the 73rd Constitution Amendment Act has enshrined in the Constitution certain basic and essential features of Panchayati Raj Institutions to impart certainty, continuity and strength to them, by adding Part IX relating to Panchayats in the Constitution. The panchayats have been studied by applying broadly two approaches, viz., (a) analytical-didactic approach and (b) historical-institutional approach. To understand the evolution of the panchayats in India the historical-institutional approach in its varied forms has been applied here.

The long established tradition of dispute settlement, affair management and functional dispenses through *panchas* or local elderlies, acting by virtue of age and wisdom, in various collectivities such as caste, village, religious group, vocational organization and tribal community has ever since been perpetuating as a distinct feature of Indian society. Coming down from a hoary past, the notion of *panch parameshwara* meaning 'the God speaks through the Five' (Gray 1987: 535) connotes a cognitive set of two attributes of panchayat, i.e., elders' council. Firstly, the very notional term *panch* structurally implies that the panchayat has essentially been a multi-member composition which in practice can and does deviate from the idyllic number of five. Secondly, in a normative sense the term *parameshwara* symbolized the traditional collective wisdom or local customs, handed down to successive generations, which guided the deliberations, decisions and actions of elderlies. As such, panchayat seems to be an evergoing phenomenon of social life. However, at a point of time it appears to be a body of wise elderlies well-versed in their cultural traditions and it is basically different from the institution of arbitratorship in which an individual maintains equi-distance and neutrality towards the parties who agree to appoint someone to decide the matter of dispute.

Studies of panchayats in India have broadly followed two approaches, viz., (*a*) analytical-didactic and (*b*) historical-institutional. From these two approaches a number of variants may be derived, which have been applied to understand a panchayat. These are : (*i*) Historical-institutional approach (Metcalfe 1832; Malviya 1956; Altekar 1958; Mookerji 1958; Grover 1972; Bhat 1974; Zamora 1990; Kumar and Venkataraman 1974; Laxminarayana 1976; Sammiuddin 1976; Sheshadri 1976; Prasad 1980; Sharma 1984; Singh 1987; Zamora 1990), (*ii*) Institutional-legalistic/diagnostic approach (Narain et al. 1970; Meddick 1970; Maheshwari 1971; Dak 1973; Bhatnagar 1978; Hooja 1978; Bhargava 1979; Jain et. al. 1985; Harish 1986; Singh 1986; Singh and Singh 1986; Shah 1986; Mishra 1989), (*iii*) Diagnostic and didactic approach used by those as mentioned in the preceding approach, (*iv*) Reflexive-normative approach (Sharma 1976; Rao and Hazarika 1978; Rao 1980; Singh 1986; Hirway 1989; Bhalla 1989), (*v*) Structural-functional approach (Desai 1969; Narain et al. 1970; Gangrade 1990) and (*vi*) Dynamic class-structural approach (Singh 1987).

Historical-institutional approach studies panchayat institutions in terms of their evolution, changes and significance in various historical periods.

Institutional-legalistic approach describes various features of panchayat institutions in terms of the law under which they are constituted.

Diagnostic-didactic approach looks into causes and solutions of problems faced by panchayat institutions and it is expressed that these institutions ought to exist in India. Diagnostic-didactic orientation predominates over the scientific-analytic orientation and it emanates, firstly, from an exaggerated claim that through ad hoc studies and surveys social sciences can suggest cut and dried formulae for solution of problems of social planning and reconstruction and, secondly, from an essentially historical fact that Mahatma Gandhi attached significance to panchayat and village society, which symbolized a moral commitment and ideology, and it profoundly affects the image of panchayat among Indian elites (Singh 1987: 570).

Reflexive-normative approach critically looks through deliberations and observations into legal-normative patterns of panchayat institutions with a view to suggest a better model for them.

Structural-functional approach views panchayat institutions social systems to analyse actual process of their political structuring and functioning.

Lastly, dynamic class-structural approach primarily discusses economic and political factors drawn from the class structure and its consciousness in rural India along with cultural factors such as caste, dominant caste, casteism, factionalism, etc and, thereby, it introduces methodological richness in the structural-functional approach, i.e., synthesizes the dialectical approach with the functional approach to understand dynamics of social structure (Singh 1987: 571).

Looking to the variety of approaches it is attempted here to understand panchayats in India from various viewpoints covered under historical-institutional perspective.

Historical Evolution

As traditional guards of their respective communities, panchayats have ever been exercising various powers—legislative, administrative and judicial, over the people. Their functioning instilled and strengthened a collective orientation among the members of various communities, which is perceptible in the pan-Indian matrix of three basic structural units; viz., joint family, caste and village. Village panchayats controlled villagers in their daily affairs, protected them from external aggressions and acted as bridge between the larger state and the village-microcosm. Almost defunct under the thrust of the British Empire, these panchayats were resuscitated, later, through statutory efforts under the empire and strengthened in the post-Independence period. Thus, since the pre-historic age the panchayats have undergone adaptations in the process of continuous casting of their relations with the state in course of evolution of Indian civilization. Their historical evolution is discussed below:

Period of Antiquity

Little republic (village) communities, which have been the foundation stone of every empire in India, preserved themselves amidst successive dynasties and revolutions as free, independent and self-sufficient communities (Metcalfe 1832: 33; Majumdar 1970: 556). The Vedas, which keep the earliest record of corporate life in the assemblies and institutions, refered to *samiti* meaning meeting together (Jayaswal 1955: 2), and *Sabha* and *Vidatha* (Altekar 1958: 140). These bodies carried out socio-political activities like communual safety and settlement of disputes. The old inscriptions of the ninth and tenth centuries A.D., also, testify to the existence of highly organized village assembly consisted of, in some places, all adults and, in other places, the select learned and distinguished villagers, enjoying supreme authority in the village affairs and absolute proprietorship of the land and the revenue paid to the government (Majumdar 1969).

In the post-Vedic period these bodies were succeeded by *Pauras* and *Janpadas* (Altekar: *op. cit.*). *Gramni* or *Grampal*—headman or leader, along with the other officials appointed by the villagers, was the lynchpin of the village government and his office, later on, became hereditary whereas the other officials were subordinated to the central authority (Altekar 1958: 226; (Mishra 1980: 30); (Bannerjee 1985: 289-90)). As a *Ratnin*, i.e., one of the jewels in the crown participating personally or through a representative in a coronation ceremony for legitimacy of the king in office, he is known as the *Raja Kirtar* or king maker in the *Shantipath Brahmina*. *Srenis* (guilds) had representation in all popular state bodies and, through the *Ratnin*, they were represented in coronation ceremonies as well. Various religious organizations and numerous castes also had their systems of local self-government. The king usually participated in meetings of *Sabha* and *Samiti* and discussed agrarian life and activities (Jain 1967: 77-78).

As one finds divergent views of authoritative commentators on the meaning and scope of these local bodies termed variously in the original texts such as *Kula, Guna, Jati, Puga, Vrata, Sreni, Sangha, Samudaya, Samuha, Sambhuya, Samutthana, Parishal, Charana* and so on (Malviya 1987: 171-72), the formulation of their comprehensive picture, especially their village level composition and functioning, today, bristles with difficulties. In all, the early Vedic state, essentially a country state, was too small to render any distinction between central and local governments. As the state grew in size, a distinction between their activities necessarily emerged in the course of time (Banerjee: 289).

Period of the Epics

Ghosh and *Gram* officiated by Gosh-Mahattar and Gram-Mahattar respectively were two types of villages in the Valmiki *Ramayana* and the *Mahabharata*. The former, smaller in size, was generally situated near forests where dwelt Gops—the cow herders.

Another highly respected official was *Gramni*, compared with a General-like Rama who killed Ravana. Gramni as well as a record-keeper scribe was appointed by the King. He was accountable to the *Gram Vridhas*—the non-official body of elders chosen in a village assembly. Though he was necessary for both, along with the increasing articulation between the state and the people *Gramni* emerged essentially as a man of the people who was always prepared to protect their interests, to lead the organized volunteers and guardsmen for the defense of village and to realize the state dues and keep their record. The administration of justice was primarily a task of the village level bodies like *Ganas, Kulas,* etc., and the king's court, like that of Rama with a long tradition of predecessors, performed a judicial function of appellate type only. The "Shanti Parva" of *Mahabharata* which mentions of the prompt delivery of criminal justice through learned men of *Ganas* and narrates about the intercourse of Bhisma and Yudhisthara points to the existence and functioning of village level bodies prior to the rise of kingship.

A gradual evolution of the customs and usages leading to confederations gave rise to the institution of kingship commanding their allegiance. Nevertheless the customs and practices called *samayas,* i.e., the resolutions passed in meetings of an assembly of the *Gana* were held with the highest esteem in a king's court which heard appeals against the decisions of those bodies (Malviya: 172-73). Manu has mentioned about the *Gramik* who was responsible for village administration and collection of king's dues. He reported matters to *Dashi*—the official for administration of 10 villages; the *Dashi,* to *Vishanti*—the official for 20 villages; the *Vishanti,* to *Shati*—the official for 100 villages and the *Shati,* to *Sahastra-Gramadhipati*—the official for 1000 villages.

Period of the Canonical Texts

Of the texts dated fifth century B.C., the Buddhist books elaborately refer to the arrangement of villages, towns and forts often mentioned as *Gana, Nigma, Kulas* and *Nagarka* and the Jain texts mention the settlements such as *Ghosha, Kheta, Kharvata, Gram, Palli, Pattana, Samvaha, Uagara, Matamba,* etc.

Buddhist Jatakas sketch the average village as a close dwelling of the families numbering upto 1000 with the *Gram-dwara* (a gate) opening onto the *Gram-kshetra,* i.e., the cultivable area of individual holdings and, lastly, the commonly held village pastures. There was the *Gopalaka* or protector of flocks to look after flocks. The *Bhojak* (village headman) who collected state revenue and organized constructive programmes was in principle selected by villagers following local customs but, in practice, he was hereditary appointee by an essential approval of the villagers. Various occupational bodies headed by a *Pramukh* (Tak 1973: 9) and the religious orders founded by Buddha and Mahavira observing high democratic procedures had been functioning without any interference of the central authority in the period. In the post-Buddhist period, the village headman came to be known as *Jethak* or elder brother who was still respected in the king's court (Mishra 1980: 30).

Period of the Mauryas

Kautilya's Arthashastra which recorded the Mauryan centralized administration (324-236 B.C.) speaks of the villages demarcated by rivers, hills, ditches, tanks, bunds and trees of various descriptions; situated at one or two *krosha* (1 *krosha* = 2 miles) so as to be able to help one another in need and organized under the union of 10 named as *Samgrahana*, of 200 as *Karvatika*, of 400 as *Dronamukha* and of 800 as Mahagrama or administratively *Sthatnuja*—a centre for trade and fairs of the neighbourhood villages. The administrative staff of a village comprised: (*i*) *Adhyaksha*—the headman, (*ii*) *Samkhyaka*—the accountant, (*iii*) *Sthanikas*—the village officials of different grades, (*iv*) *Anikastha*—the veterinary doctor, (*v*) *Jangha Karika*—the village couriers (*vi*) *Chikitsaka*—the village sanitation officer and (*vii*) *Aswa-damak*—the horse trainer to build up a cavalry for needs of war. They were granted landholdings free of rents and taxes, which were inalienable by sale or mortgage (Malviya: 174-75). The village assembly of the *Gram-vridhas* selected by their age, character, wisdom and attainments continued to decide local administrative matters, to act as a court of justice for criminal cases and to look after public property and lands. The headman presiding the assembly was an executive official both for civil and military affairs. The groups like *sanyasis, nuts*, artisans, moneylenders and cultivators had their separate panchayat bodies (Tak: 10). The Gop—officer-in-charge of five to 10 villages—supervised the works of headmen of the villages (Banerjee 1985:294). This system continued through the dark or post-Mauryan period (300-200 B.C.) and under the Imperial Guptas with certain changes of nomenclature. The Imperial Guptas *Grampati* (headman) was assisted by the village assembly consisted of the entire population of war or adult males or the *mahattars*—a select body of elders. The assembly set up a number of committees such as those for acquisition and sale of lands, preservation of common lands and pastures and other aspects of village administration. The village officials comprised headman, accountant, watchman, school-teacher, priest, supervisor of irrigation works and boundary man to be paid from free-hold lands or by giving a share of crop on harvesting (Mishra: 37-38). Brihaspati *Smrti* and Shukracharya's *Nitisara* record that during the King Harsha's rule in the sixth century A.D. and prior to the Turkish and Afghan invasions there were occupational panchayat bodies, besides the village panchayat headed by a headman who reported serious disputes to the unit of 10 villages and, even, to the larger one (Tak: 11, Hooja 1989: 108-9).

Period of the Sultans and Mughals

The Sultans were despotic rulers invested with all legislative, executive, judicial and administrative powers, leaving no space for any representative institutions. Their *laissez-faire* attitude towards the self-governing institutions helped keep alive the tradition of self-government during that period of unstable central government (Quereshi 1942: 12-13).

The Mughal feudalistic system was a highly centralized administration, bringing provinces, districts and villages under the central officials such as *Sardars, Malgujars, Muqaddams* and *Patwaris* (Malviya: 139). It incorporated village as an administrative unit for revenue and police purposes and dealt with it through the *Muqaddam* (headman). The central officials considerably curtailed the judicial powers of panchayats. Yet, they interfered little with the ancient customs and the servants who regulated village affairs in the remaining areas (Tinker 1967: 19). *Mahajan* Panchayat of Merta, composed of *Maheswari* and *Agarwal Vaishyas* in the erstwhile Marwar state in Rajasthan, which, besides other functions, looked after religious affairs such as recitation of *Katha, Vrata, Garudpurana*, etc. for the community members and settled the disputes related to recitation of *Katha* (religious stories) in a *Mahajan* temple. A dispute over the right to recitation between the *Katha-vyas* of the *Dahima* and of the *Parik* was refered to the *Mahajan* Panchayat which was appointed by the two parties to arbitrate. It conducted open proceedings mostly in a temple to hear the contending parties, recorded oral and documentary evidences and decided the matter as to be binding on the two parties. The tradition of panchayats continued even after the King Jasvant Singh I of Jodhpur (capital of the Marwar state) until the Emperor Aurangzeb appointed Muslim officials all over the state (*Rajasthan History Congress Proceedings* 1968: 98-100).

British Period

The British regime in India began at a time when the caste and village panchayats were very effective in various parts of the country. The caste panchayats were also in the forefront to launch some agrarian movements; namely, the *Bijolia* movement of the Dhakar Panchayat in Mewar, the peasant movement of the Kisan Sabha in Shekhawati and of the *Jat Sabha* in the Marwar state and the *Bhil* movement in Mewar against atrocities of the *jagirdars* in Rajasthan (Pande 1974; Surana 1981). In Himachal Pradesh, in view of a lack of regularly constituted panchayats and inaccessibility to law courts of the ruler and other competent officials the contending parties invited two or three *Sianas* or wise men who assembled in a *Santhang* or any other place of convenience, gave a hearing to them and pronounced their verdict which was seldom challenged (*Himachal District Gazetteers*). In Punjab the villagers were divided into *Panas* and each *Pana* into *Thulas*, each, headed separately or in a group by a headman or a large *Pana* by several headmen assisted by a village panchayat constituted by *Thuladars*. The panchayat with its headman looked after a large number of common interests and activities in the village (*Rohtak District Gazetteers*: 249). A highly centralized administration in the early British rule, introduction of the *Zamindari* system of separate property rights along with administrative and judicial functions and autonomy of the government nominees such as headman, *Patwari* and *Lambardar* set in the real decay of old panchayats (Sharma 1962: 21-22, Tak: 12).

With a constant realization of the need for revival of rural local government as a link between the British administration and the villagers, statutory revival efforts stemmed from the ideas of Lord Rippon, the then Viceroy of India, who declared on 18 May 1882 to make it an instrument of political and popular education and outlet for the ambitions and aspirations engendered by western ideas (Alderfer 1964: 71). The most remarkable innovation proposed by Rippon was the network of local rural bodies, emerging as a two-tier system constituted of district board or sub-district board placed at sub-division or tehsil (Tinker: 52). The district boards, composed of officials and elected members, lacked vital spirit of democracy and they could invoke only a lukewarm response from Indians in the village panchayat bodies (Alderfer: 72), killing the Rippon proposal's intentions. The Royal Commission, headed by E.E.H. Hobhouse, set up by British Government in 1909 to enquire into financial and administrative relations among the Government of India, the provincial governments and the subordinate authorities deplored the disappearance of village autonomy in the *Zamindari* system introduced by the British against the *Rayotwari*. For their reconstruction it suggested a separate department of panchayats and, also, the village panchayats, each, consisting of five elected members with the headman as ex-officio chairman endowed with civil and criminal jurisdiction in petty cases and responsibility for minor developmental works under control of the district authorities (Tinker: 64; Sharma: 24-25). Reviewing the working of district and local boards it recommended for an elected majority on all the boards to eliminate the cause of their failure, i.e., unrepresentative character (Singh 1989: 69). After an interregnum of the World War-I Montague, the then Secretary of State for India, on 20 August 1917 promised a gradual development of self-governing institutions with a view to progressive realization of responsible government in India. The resolution of the Government of India of May 1918 contained a proposal for strengthening the local bodies through various measures such as removal of unnecessary controls, provisioning of elected chairman and financial powers and establishment of a department of self-government in every province (Singh and Singh 1986: 85, Mutalib and Khan 1982: 72). Under the Government of India Act of 1919, the provincial governments, along with the Indian ministers, inter alia, were allotted the subject of local self-government and they passed several acts to render it fully a representative character. Following the period of the historic Non-Cooperation movement which encouraged the dispute settlement through informal panchayats and boycott of the government courts there sprang-up numerous panchayats in various parts of the country (Meddick 1970: 19, Bhatnagar 1978: 86). The Government of India Act of 1935 enunciating a parliamentary type fully responsible government and replacing the provincial dyarchy provided the provinces an opportunity for furtherance of democratization, financial powers and developmental functions of the local bodies. But the village panchayats still worked as small *darbars* and petty courts of the British regime (Dey 1961: 9; Maheshwari 1963: 6).

The opportunity for local government appeared short-lived in the wake of intensifying freedom struggle, emerging questions of national and international importance and the governors assuming administrative responsibility on resignation of the popular provincial governments at the outbreak of the World War-II. The indifference to these bodies continued up to 1946 (Narain 1970: 3).

Post-Independence Period

After a great debate in the parliament, the panchayats as local government system were included in the directive principles of policy for the state which direct the state to make efforts for decentralization of power and for establishment and promotion of the panchayats at all levels of rural self-government. A need for review of the structure of the panchayats continuing in different states of Independent India, was felt in the wake of the problems faced by the Community Development Programme. The Balvant Rai Mehta Committee was appointed to study the proposal for setting up of viable units of rural self-government. It recommended for a three-tier system which was enacted into legislative acts by various states under the parliament's authorization. The panchayat system termed as Panchayati Raj working under the model has recently attained constitutional status through the Constitution (seventy third) Amendment Act, 1992.

THE PANCHAYATI RAJ

The Panchayati Raj is basically rooted into the ancient Indian tradition. It finds expression in the Gandhian enunciation of *Ram Rajya*—an ideal construct based on the features of different periods of ancient Indian history, containing the panchayat autonomy as an integral component. His emphasis on national development through autonomous rural organizations, modelled after panchayats prevailing in ancient India, provided conceptual strength to the plea for greater autonomy to rural local bodies (Narain: 1970: 4). Visualizing them as the pivot of polity and future of India, he conceived individual self-sufficiency and absence of exploitation as the basic principles of the democratic decentralization (Jadhav 1984: 108), constituted into a broad-based structure of numerous village panchayats at the bottom, the vibrant and ultimate source of power, and at the apex, a national panchayat, elected by the intermediary district and state panchayats. A village panchayat of five persons—male and female elected annually by the villagers—endowed with legislative, executive and judicial jurisdictions of power was a village government of Gandhiji's conception with a perfect democracy based on individual freedom, i.e., a village republic perfected into the *swaraj* (self-rule) at the bottom (Gandhi 1938: 198, 1942: 238). Thus, reflecting people's aspirations the Panchayati Raj derives itself from Gandhiji's vision of future India of self-reliant villages with political and economic decentralization of powers based on the principle: The greater is the power of the panchayat, the better is for the people (Hirway 1989: 1663). The constitutional assembly while framing Indian Constitution was concerned more with a centralized government for stability, unity and economic progress of the country and it failed to accept Gandhiji's proposal. But only on his insistence, the panchayats could find a place in the Directive Principles of State Policy under Part IV which, though non-judiciable, contain fundamental and binding reference points for the state in the matter of legislation. Article 40 in the Part IV lays down that the state shall take steps to organize village panchayats and endows them with such powers and authority as may be necessary to enable them to function as units of self-government. This part itself reflects a broad philosophy of the Indian constitution.

The Panchayati Raj in India originated as a means for the Community Development Programme (CDP) which itself was seeded into the recommendations of the Grow More Food Enquiry Committee, headed by the late V.T. Krishnamachari. The Committee recommended that food production should form the part of a wider plan for development of village life in its all aspects and that the administrative machinery of Government should be organized and equipped for the efficient discharge of duties imposed on it under the new conception of India as a welfare state (*Report of the Grow More Food Enquiry Committee* 1952: 68-77). Besides the realization of insufficiency of stray and unsystematic efforts for socio-economic development, the inspiration for community development programme emanated from the earlier experiences, also, such as (*i*) the intensive rural development activities carried out at Sevagram and Sarvodaya centres in Bombay state since 1948-49; (*ii*) Firka Development Schemes in Madras initiated by the end of 1946, (*iii*) the experiments to build up community centres for refugees at Nilokheri and other places and (*iv*) specially the Pilot Projects at Etawah and Gorakhpur in Uttar Pradesh (1948) with active assistance of Albert Meyers.

While implementing the decision of the president of Ford Foundation taken in 1951 to improve the conditions of Indian rural masses, 15 pilot projects, more or less on the Etawah line, were undertaken in early 1952. Meanwhile, in January 1952, as per desire of the U.S. Government to finance some programme for India's development the Indo-U.S. Technical Co-operation Agreement—the first scientific and systematic programme of community development in India—was signed (Bhatnagar: 17). Under the agreement the community development programme started on 2 October 1952 in 55 Community Development Projects, each covering three development blocks of 300 villages with the population of about three lacs. It aimed at four-fold objective: (*i*) Transformation of the people's outlook, (*ii*) inculcation of the spirit of self-reliance, (*iii*) generation of the habit of cooperative action through popular bodies and (*iv*) these three objectives leading to new enlightenment, strength and hope (Jain 1985: 17). In view of the people's demand for increase in the number of blocks, on the one hand, and the stress of the Grow More Food Enquiry Committee on improving of the people's socio-economic conditions for success of any programme of agricultural development, on the other, the Government of India implemented the committee's recommendations and introduced one more programme called National Extension Service (NES) on 2 October 1953 in a situation of inability for immediate extension of the comprehensive programme such as the CDP (Bhatnagar: *op. cit.*). Originally CDP aimed to mark an intensive phase of rural development lasting for three years and NES was to become a permanent multi-functional extension agency in a block (Masheshwari 1985: 37) and therefore they were complementary and worked concurrently integrated under the same agency at the centre as well as in the states. CDP was the method and NES—the agency to cover the entire country within a period of the coming 10 years or till 1963. During First Five Year Plan (1951-56), various development activities such as animal husbandry, construction of roads and buildings, health programmes, etc. were launched in the country, divided into blocks, each under a generalist, i.e., Block Development Officer, assisted by a team of extension officers, gram sevaks and gram sevikas, seeking people's participation through village panchayats with a view to limit the role of government up to advice and financial assistance. Expert committees were constituted at the block and the district level (Hussain 1984: 136, Maheshwari 1976: 68).

After the initial momentum of 3-4 years, CDP grew more as government programme in the wake of declining people's participation (Srivastava 1987: 23) due to (*i*) lack of consciousness among the rural masses, (*ii*) too much emphasis on *shramdan* (free-labour), (*iii*) lack of financial resources, (*iv*) wrong approach in the training process, (*v*) absence of proper local leadership, (*vi*) neglect by political parties and (*vii*) lack of proper propaganda (Singh 1971: 18). Therefore, Planning Commission urged National Development Council (NDC) for investigation of the whole issue of rural development by a team of experts (Mukherji 1961: 210-14). Early in 1956 NDC appointed a study team headed by the rural specialist, Balvantray G. Mehta to identify the problems emergent in the rural community development work and, also, to assess the proposal to set up viable units of local self governance in the rural areas, thus, initiating democratic decentralization of authority in favour of villages and groupings of villages, as specified in Article 40 of the Directive Principles of the Indian Constitution (Panchanadikar and Pahchanadikar 1980: XXIII). The team's comprehensive three volume report, submitted in 1957, recommended for a three-tier system of rural local self-government, indirect elections and a genuine transfer of power to the bodies for planning and implementing developmental activities at the levels of village, block and district. The middle tier, i.e., block level body was conceived as the main agency for rural development with vast administrative and financial powers whereas the district body was envisaged only as the advisory-cum-supervisory body. After NDC's approval of the report in January 1958, the parliament enacted the Act and the states also passed Acts to suit the special needs of respective regions.

In August 1958, the scheme was implemented in some areas of Andhra Pradesh on experimental basis but Rajasthan happened to be the foremost state, introducing it once and all with its inauguration by Jawaharlal Nehru on 2 October 1959 at Nagaur. During his inaugural speech Nehru expressed a desire for replacement of the exotic word 'democratic decentralization' by an indigenous one and someone promptly suggested the word 'Panchayati Raj'. While implementing it majority of the states followed three-tier system and the remaining, either two-tier or one-tier system (Jammu and Kashmir) or traditional panchayats (Nagaland and Meghalaya). Andhra Pradesh, Gujarat, Karnataka, Madhya Pradesh, Maharashtra, Punjab, Rajasthan, Tamilnadu, Uttar Pradesh, West Bengal, Arunachal Pradesh and Chandigarh are the states and union territories which adopted the three-tier system.

At present there are three models of Panchayati Raj existing in the country; viz., (*i*) Rajasthan Model with the central role of Panchayat Samiti at the block level, (*ii*) Maharashtra Model with the central role of Zila Parishad at the district level and (*iii*) Gujarat Model in-between Rajasthan and Maharashtra Models (Fadia: 99-110).

As an on-going process of democratic decentralization of powers below the level of the state and to realize rural participation for self-governance and development, Panchayati Raj consists of gradual unfolding of power dimensions, structural adjustments and emerging leadership patterns in the system of the inter-linked panchayats. Iqbal Narain has conceived two objectives of the Panchayati Raj; namely, (*i*) politicalization, i.e., spread of political consciousness among the rural people and (*ii*) invoking people's participation for rural development with a view to strengthen the concept of planning from below (Kumar and Fadia: 100). However, there had been a gradual shift-away from the community or area development towards a sectoral or professional approach. Following disappointment with the community development programme's performance in raising agricultural production, the Government initiated Intensive Area Development Programme in 1960 on the advice of a team sponsored by Ford Foundation on India's Food Crisis. Likewise, in 1960 a group headed by Jaya Prakash Narayan was appointed to study how far and in what manner the CDP and the three-tiered panchayat system could promote economic development and welfare of the weaker sections of community. The group recommended for proper delegation of powers to the Panchayati Raj institutions (Jain: 38).

Obviously, the Panchayati Raj is a process as well as a system of rural local self-government in India, on the one hand, and a consequence of and the means for CDP, on the other. It has evolved through four phases; namely, initial ascendancy, growth and consolidation, phase of decline and phase of resuscitation.

The initial phase was concerned with the establishment of NES (agency) for bringing technical services to the villages by CDP (method) for rural reconstruction during the First Five Year Plan and extended over the bulk of the country during the second plan. The growth and consolidation of the Panchayati Raj institutions took place during the Third Five Year Plan with an emphasis for realization of developmental potential in various sectors. Legislations, defining relations of the Panchayati Raj institutions with the state, coming up in most of the states laid down for the administration of CDP through the Panchayat bodies at intermediary or block level. The zenith of the PR institutions was seen in the mid-sixties when CDP along with representation of the weaker sections covered the entire country (Jain: 39). The mounting food shortage and crop failure in 1966-67 forced the reshuffling of priorities in CDP itself, resulting in an overriding emphasis on agricultural production. In 1966-67 the Ministry of Community Development was reduced to a department which was appended to the Ministry of Food and Agriculture. Nonetheless, the Community Development Department intensified the efforts to gain support at the grass-roots level (Maheshwari 1985:57:59; Jain: 40). By the arrival of seventies the zeal for PR institutions and CDP was on decline.

In 1977 the Ashok Mehta Committee considered the PR system for decentralization of power and people's participation as well as for supporting rural development and strengthening planning process at the micro-level and recommended a two-tier system of Zila Parishad and Gram Panchayat. The former being the focal point of decentralization of power, along with the Mandal Panchayats, instead of Panchayat Samitis of 15,000 to 20,000 population as the intermediary level for linkage between the two. While implementing its recommendations in 1980 the then chief minister R.K. Hegde of Karnataka took steps to introduce a real district government with liberal transfer of powers and resources and effective role of the elected PR office-bearers in the local level planning. Andhra Pradesh, headed by N.T. Rama

Rao, also slightly moved in the direction. During 1980's, the village panchayats in West Bengal were utilized for implementation of land reforms and distributive justice under Tibhaga Movement. In Maharashtra and Gujarat the PR system has been functioning comparatively in a better way. In all these states the PR institutions have provided the weaker sections and intermediary castes with opportunity to rise up on the political ladder (Sharma 1994: 143-44). In 1989 the then Prime Minister Rajiv Gandhi attempted to strengthen the PR institutions by bringing the Constitution (Sixty Fourth) Amendment Act which could not be passed in Rajya Sabha. But with the passing of the Constitution (Seventy Third) Amendment Act, 1992 and inserted as the Part IX of the Constitution, the PR system has attained a constitutional status. The Act made the provisions for regular elections of the PR bodies, conducted by the State Election Commission, in each state and ensured representation of weaker sections such as the Scheduled Castes, Scheduled Tribes, Other Backward Classes and women through reservations of seats in the bodies. Various states have enacted Acts accordingly with variations suitable to their situations and in all but a few states the PR bodies have been constituted over the years.

The Constitution (Seventy Third) Amendment Act, 1992

Though the Panchayati Raj Institutions have been in existence for a long time, they have not been able to acquire the status and dignity of viable and responsive people's bodies due to a number of reasons including absence of regular elections, prolonged supersessions, insufficient representation of weaker sections like Scheduled Castes, Scheduled Tribes and women, inadequate devolution of powers and lack of financial resources. Therefore, the 73rd Constitution Amendment Act has enshrined in the Constitution certain basic and essential features of Panchayati Raj Institutions to impart certainty, continuity and strength to them, by adding Part IX relating to Panchayats in the Constitution. The salient features of the Act are as follows:

1. *Provision for Gram Sabha in a village or group of villages:* A Gram Sabha may exercise such powers and perform such functions at the village level as provided by the Legislature of a State by law.
2. *Constitution of Panchayats at village and other level or levels:* In every State, there are constituted Panchayats at the village, intermediate and district levels. Panchayats at the intermediate level may not be constituted in a State having a population not exceeding twenty lakhs.
3. *Direct elections to all seats in Panchayats at the village and inter-mediate level and to the offices of Chairpersons of the Panchayats:* All the seats in a Panchayat are to be filled by persons chosen by direct election from

territorial constituencies in the Panchayat area. The Chairperson of a Panchayat at the village level is elected in such manner as provided by the Legislature of a State by law and the Chairperson of a Panchayat at the intermediate level or district level is elected by, and from amongst, its elected members.

4. *Reservation of seats for the Scheduled Castes and Scheduled Tribes in proportion to their population for membership of Panchayats and office of Chairpersons in Panchayats at each level:* Seats are reserved for (*a*) the Scheduled Castes and (*b*) the Scheduled Tribes in every Panchayat and the number of seats are reserved for these two groups on the basis of the proportion of their population in the total population in a Panchayat. The reserved seats are allotted by rotation to different constituencies in a Panchayat.

5. *Reservation of not less than one-third of the seats for women:* (*a*) Out of the total number of seats reserved for the Scheduled Castes and the Scheduled Tribes in a Panchayat, not less than one-third of the seats are reserved for women belonging to respective category. (*b*) Not less than one-third (including the number of seats reserved for women belonging to the Scheduled Castes and the Scheduled Tribes) of the total number of seats to be filled by direct election in every Panchayat is reserved for women and such seats are allotted by rotation to different constituencies in a Panchayat. The same proportion of reservation is available to the Scheduled Castes, Scheduled Tribes and women for the office of Chairperson in the Panchayats.

6. *Fixing tenure of 5 years for Panchayats and holding elections within a period of 6 months in the event of supersession of any Panchayat:* Every Panchayat continues for five years from the date appointed for its first meeting. An election to constitute a Panchayat is completed before the expiry of its duration or, in case of dissolution under law, before the expiration of a period of six months from the date of its dissolution.

7. *Devolution by the State Legislature of powers and responsibilities upon the Panchayats:* The Act endows the Panchayats with such powers and authority as to enable them to function as institutions of self-government with respect to (*a*) the preparation of plans for economic development and social justice and (*b*) the implementation of matters listed in the Eleventh Schedule (Article 243G); namely, (*i*) Agriculture, including agricultural extension, (*ii*) Land improvement, implementation of land reforms, land consolidation and soil conservation,

(*iii*) Minor irrigation, water management and watershed development, (*iv*) Animal husbandry, dairying and poultry, (*v*) Fisheries, (*vi*) Social forestry and farm forestry, (*vii*) Minor forest produce, (*viii*) Small scale industries, including food processing industries, (*ix*) Khadi, village and cottage industries, (*x*) Rural housing, (*xi*) Drinking water, (*xii*) Fuel and fodder, (*xiii*) Roads, culverts, bridges, ferries, waterways and other means of communication, (*xiv*) Rural electrification, including distribution of electricity, (*xv*) Non-conventional energy sources, (*xvi*) Poverty alleviation programme, (*xvii*) Education, including primary and secondary schools, (*xviii*) Technical training and vocational education, (*xix*) Adult and non-formal education, (xx) Libraries, (*li*) Cultural activities, (*lii*) Markets and fairs, (*liii*) Health and sanitation, including hospitals, primary health centres and dispensaries, (*liv*) Family welfare, (*lv*) Women and child development, (*lvi*) Social welfare, including welfare of the handicapped and mentally retarded, (*lvii*) Welfare of the weaker sections, and in particular, of the Scheduled Castes and the Scheduled Tribes, (lviii) Public distribution system and (*lx*) Maintenance of community assets.

8. Sound finance of the Panchayats by securing authorisation from State Legislatures for grants-in-aid to the Panchayats from the Consolidated Fund of the State and assignment to, or appropriation by, the Panchayats of the revenues of designated taxes, duties, tolls and fees: The Legislature of a State may, by law, (*a*) authorise a Panchayat to levy, collect and appropriate such taxes, duties, tolls and fees in accordance with such procedure and subject to such limits; (*b*) assign to a Panchayat such taxes, duties, tolls and fees levied and collected by the State Government for such purposes and subject to such conditions and limits; (*c*) provide for making such grants-in-aid to the Panchayats from the Consolidated Fund of the State; and (*d*) provide for Constitution of such Funds for crediting all moneys received, respectively, by or on behalf of the Panchayats and also for the withdrawal of such moneys therefrom, as may be specified in the law.

   The *Governor of a State*, at the expiration of every fifth year of Panchayats, constitutes a Finance Commission to review the financial position of the Panchayats and to make recommendations to the Governor for (*i*) the distribution between the State and the Panchayats of the net proceeds of the taxes, duties, tolls and fees leviable by the State; (*ii*) the determination of the taxes, duties, tolls and fees which may be assigned to, or appropriated by, the Panchayat; (*iii*) the grants-in-aid to the Panchayats from the Consolidated Fund of the State; (*iv*) the measures needed to improve the financial position of the Panchayats and (*v*) any other matter referred to the Finance Commission by the Governor in the interests of sound finance of the Panchayats.

9. *Auditing of accounts of the Panchayats* : The Legislature of a State, by law, makes provisions with respect to the maintenance of accounts by the Panchayats and the auditing of such accounts.
10. *State Election Commission:* The superintendence, direction and control of the preparation of electoral rolls for, and the conduct of, all elections to the Panchayats is vested in a State Election Commission consisting of a State Election Commissioner to be appointed by the Governor.

Conclusion

In India the panchayats have a long tradition. Therefore, under the democratic set up of Independent India they were given adequate importance for democratization of rural society and empowerment of the masses. Yet, Panchayati Raj bodies of Independent India could not work efficiently and effectively due to various reasons. Therefore, Indian parliament enacted the Constitution (Seventy Third) Amendment Act, 1992. The 73rd Amendment Act is a revolutionary step towards decentralization of power and democratiza-tion in rural India as it empowered the weaker sections such as Scheduled Castes, Scheduled Tribes and women and also ensured their uninterrupted working through constitutional measures. After its implementation, participation of these sections is found mandatorily ensured and this has increased their participation at all levels of panchayats. Yet, illiteracy, poverty and ignorance among these sections have inhibited their real participation in the various bodies. Even now, either proxies of representatives from the weaker sections exercise powers and carry out functions on behalf of them in the bodies or the representatives from the weaker sections remain physically present in the meetings of the bodies but practically they have to depend on directions from the dominant sections. Real empowerment of the rural people is possible only after elimination of poverty, illiteracy, ignorance and gender difference. Hopefully the Government of India's policy of inclusive growth will reduce the inequalities and remove socio-cultural hurdles from the path of rural development and thereby improved social conditions will pave the way for rural people's empowerment and effective self governance.

REFERENCES

1. Alderfer, Harold F., 1964, *Local Government in Developing Countries*, London: McGraw-Hill Book Company.
2. Altekar, A.S., 1958, *State and Government in Ancient India*, Delhi: Motilal Banarsidas.
3. Banerjee, P., 1985, *Public Administration in Ancient India*, New Delhi: Uppal Publishing House.
4. Bhalla, Deepak, 1989, "Panchayati Raj—An Appraisal", *Kurukshetra*, Vol. XXXVII, No. 6.
5. Bhargava, B.S., 1979, *Panchayati Raj System and Political Parties*, New Delhi: Ashish Publishing House.
6. Bhatnagar, S., 1978, *Rural Local Government in India*, New Delhi: Light and Life Publications.
7. Bhatt, K.S., 1994, *Panchayati Raj Administration in Maharashtra*, Bombay: Popular Prakashan.
8. Desai, A.R. (Ed.), 1969, *Rural Sociology in India*, Bombay: Popular Prakashan.
9. Dey, S.K., 1961, *Panchayati Raj: A Synthesis*, Bombay: Asia Publishing House.
10. Fadia, B.L. n.d. *Rajasthan mein Grameen Vikas ke liye Panchatati Raj* (Hindi). Udaipur: HCMRIPA.
11. Gangrade, K.D., 1990, "Revamping Panchayati Raj Institution", *Yojna*, Vol. XXXIV, Nos. 14 & 15.
12. Gray, Hugh, 1987, "The Problem" in A.R. Desai (Ed.), *Rural Sociology in India*, Bombay: Popular Prakashan.
13. Grover, V.P., et al., 1972, *Panchayati Raj Administration in Rajasthan*, Jaipur: Laxmi Narayan Aggarwal.
14. Harish, R., 1986, "Panchayats: Are they a Field for Experiments?" *Kurukshetra*, Vol. XXXIV, No. 6.
15. Hussain, S.S., 1984, "Indian Polity and Its Federal Principle: An Analytic Evaluation" in Rajput, R.S. and Meghe, D.R. (Eds.), *Panchayati Raj in India*, New Delhi: Deep and Deep Publications.
16. Hirway, Indira, 1989, "Panchayati Raj at Cross Roads", *EPW*, Vol. XXIV, No. 29.
17. Government of India, 1952, *Report of the Grow More Food Enquiry Committee-1951-52*, New Delhi.
18. Hooja, B., 1989, "On Village Planning", *Shodhak*, Vol. XVIII Nos. 53 and 54.
19. Jadhav, V.D., 1984, "Impediments in the Proper Functioning of the Village Panchayats" in Rajput, R.S. and Meghe, D.R. (Eds.), *Panchayati Raj in India*, New Delhi: Deep and Deep Publications.
20. Jain, L. C., et al., 1985, *Grass without Roots: Rural Government under Government Auspices*, New Delhi: Sage Publicaion.
21. Jayaswal, K. P., 1955, *Hindu Polity: A Constitutional History of India in Hindu Times*, Bangalore Printing and Publication.

22. Kumar, S. and Venkataraman, K., 1974, *State-Panchayati Raj Relations: A Case Study of Supervision and Control in Tamilnadu,* Bombay: Asia Publishing House.
23. Lakshminarayan, H. D., 1976, *India's Villages at Cross Roads,* New Delhi: National Publishing House.
24. Maheshwari, B., 1963, *Studies in Panchayati Raj,* Delhi: Metropolitan Book Co. Pvt. Ltd.
25. Maheshwari, S. R., 1976, *Local Government in India,* New Delhi: Orient Longman.
26. Maheshwari, S. R., 1985, *Rural Development in India,* New Delhi: Sage Publication.
27. Majumdar, R.C., et al., 1969, *Corporate Life in Ancient India,* Calcutta.
28. Malaviya, H. D., 1987, *Village Panchayats in India,* New Delhi: All India Congress Committee.
29. Meddick, Henry, 1970, *Panchayati Raj in India,* Longman Group Ltd.
30. Metcalfe, Sir Charles, 1832, "Select Committee of House of Commons", Appendix 84, Vol. III, quoted in Jathar, R.V., *Evolution of Panchayati Raj in India,* Dharwar Institute of Economic Growth.
31. Mishra, S.N., 1989, *New Horizons in Rural Development Administration,* New Delhi: IIPA.
32. Mishra, S.N., 1980, *Politics and Society in Rural India,* Delhi: Inter-India Publications.
33. Mookerji, Radkha Kumud, 1958, *Local Government in Ancient India,* Delhi: Motilal Banarsidas.
34. Mukherji, B., 1961, *Community Development in India,* Bombay: Orient Longman.
35. Muttalib, M.A. and Khan, A. A., 1982, *Theory of Local Government,* New Delhi: Sterling Publishers Pvt Ltd.
36. Narain, Iqbal, et al., 1970, *Panchayati Raj Administration—Old Controls and New Challenges,* New Delhi: Indian Institute of Public Administration.
37. Panchanadikar, K. C. and Panchanadikar, J., 1980, *Democratic Structure and Socialization in Rural India,* Bombay: Popular Prakashan.
38. Pande, Ram, 1974, *Agrarian Movements in Rajasthan,* Delhi: University Publishers.
39. Prasad, S., 1980, *Panchayats and Development,* New Delhi: Ashish Publishing House.
40. Quereshi, J. H., 1942, "The Administration of the Sultanate of Delhi", quoted in Khanna, R.L., *Panchayati Raj in India,* Chandigarh: The English Book Shop.
41. Rao, D.V.R., 1980, *Panchayats and Rural Development,* New Delhi: Ashish Publishing House.
42. Rao, V.V. and Hazarika, N., 1978, "Democratic Decentralization: Theory and Practice", *Indian Journal of Public Administration,* Vol. XXIV, No. 3.
43. Sammiuddin, A., 1976, *A Critique of Panchayati Raj with Special Reference to Uttar Pradesh,* Agra: Sahitya Bhavan.
44. Shah, B.L., 1986, "Panchayati Raj: Its Functioning and Difficulties", *Kurukshetra,* Vol. XXXIV, No. 6.

45. Sharma, R., 1974, *Village Panchayats in Rajasthan*, Jaipur: Aalekh Publisher.

46. Sharma, Shakuntla, 1994, *Grass Root Politics and Panchayati Raj*, New Delhi: Deep and Deep Publication.

47. Sharma, S. K., 1976, *Panchayati Raj In India*, New Delhi: Trimurti Publications.

48. Sharma, V.S., 1962, *Panchayati Raj*, Hoshiarpur: Vidya Mandir Book Sellers and Publishers.

49. Sheshadri, K., 1976, *Political Linkages and Rural Development: A Comparative Study* of the Political Process and Interaction between Different Levels of Government in two Indian States (Andhra and Gujarat). New Delhi: National Publishing House.

50. Singh, C. M., 1988, *Dynamics of Rural Development Administration*, New Delhi: Spick and Span Publishers.

51. Singh, Sahib and Singh, Swinder, 1986, *Local Government in India*, Jalandhar: New Academic Publishing Co.

52. Singh, S. K., 1971, "Panchayati Raj: A View Point", *Kurukshetra*, Vol. XII, No.19.

53. Singh, S. R., 1986, "Revitalization of Panchayats", *Kurukshetra*, Vol. XXXIV, No. 6.

54. Singh, Yogendra, 1987, "The Changing Power Structure of Village Community: A Case Study of Six Villages in Eastern U.P.", in Desai, A.R. (Ed.), *Rural Sociology in India*, Bombay: Popular Parkashan.

55. Srivastava, K.V., 1987, Continuity and Change in Panchayati Raj, *Kurukshetra*, Vol. XXXVI, No. 3.

56. Surana, Pushpendra, 1981, *Social Movements and Social Structure*, Delhi: Manohar.

57. Tak, B.L., 1973, *Sociological Dimensions of Gram Raj*, Gaziabad: Vimal Prakashan.

58. Tinker, Hugh, 1967, *The Foundations of Local Self-Government in India, Pakistan and Burma*, Bombay: Lalvani Publishing House.

59. Zamora, Mario D., 1990, *The Panchayat Tradition: A North Indian Village Council in Transition 1947-62*, New Delhi: Reliance Publishing House.

CHAPTER

3

Role of NGOs in Marketing Self-Employment

A Case Study of Rural Development and Self-Employment Training Institute

—Dr. Y.S. Siddegowda
—Dr. K.G. Parashurama

ABSTRACT

The problem of unemployment is rapidly assuming dangerous proportions in many countries as their economies and educational systems are unable to accommodate unemploymed youths. In many developing countries even low levels of economic growth are not predicted, and thus limit their labor absorptive capacity. Indeed shrinkage of their economies, and related livelihood opportunities are expected. Economists advise that the current system will not meet the supply of labor available. Thus, youth unemployment is an urgent global issue that has repercussions in demographic, social, economic, health, and environmental spheres. These impacts will be felt at the individual, familial, national and global levels if not addressed, and this is a prescription for disaster.

This clearly indicates the need for promoting self-employment entrepreneurial ventures among the unemployed. Of late, Government and Non-Government agencies have taken certain initiatives and implementing many schemes to promote self-employment programmes and micro enterprises activites. However, the efforts seem to be inadequate against the gigantic unemployment problem.

It is under these circumstances that Rural Development and Self-Employment Training Institutes (RUDSETI) came into being and making concerted efforts to promote entrepreneurship especially among rural youths. RUDSET institute is an institutional framework to promote Rural Development. Its objective is to facilitate self-employment through developing self-confidence among the youth, build up capital in rural India through better utilisation of resources and transfer of appropriate technology. The institute is jointly sponsored by Sri Dharmasthala Manjunatheshwara Educational Trust, Syndicate Bank and Canara Bank.

This paper attempts to conceiually analyse the problems of unemployment and the importance of self-employment. Also highlight the role of NGO's in marketing self-employment. And also presents a case study of one NGO RUDSETI in marketing self-employment programme.

The problem of unemployment is rapidly assuming dangerous proportions in many countries as their economies and educational systems are unable to accommodate unemployed youths. In many developing countries even low levels of economic growth are not predicted, and thus limit their labor absorptive capacity. Indeed shrinkage of their economies, and related livelihood opportunities are expected. Economists advise that the current system will not meet the supply of labor available. Thus, youth unemployment is an urgent global issue that has repercussions in demographic, social, economic, health, and environmental spheres. These impacts will be felt at the individual, familial, national and global levels if not addressed, and this is a prescription for disaster.

But youth unemployment has other national and global impacts, notably, increased violence, crime and political instability. Desperation can drive many people into living outside the law both to survive and as a means of expressing dissatisfaction at the apparent neglect of their very existence. Many of the most unstable countries are also those with very high youth unemployment rates.

At one point of time unemployment was not a problem in India. All small and big people were able to pursue their own vocations. These vocations were pursued from generations to generations and more efficiency was acquired in their jobs as time went by. But today, the sons of the farmers, the potters, the blacksmiths, the goldsmiths, etc. pass graduate and post-graduate examinations. They aspire to become doctors, engineers, administrators, lawyers, chartered accountants and company secretaries. If they cannot become any of these, they cannot forget to become at least clerks because they ashamed to take up their ancestral professions. Such people belong neither here nor there. They slack touch with their traditional vocations and also not positioned to get government jobs. In these circumstances, what can be expected if not mounting unemployment?

India's educated youths are facing some serious issues like educated unemployment and underemployment. Currently, in India, we have fairly low inflation but unemployment is high. In particular, educated unemployment is very high. It is around 20 per cent among graduates. One suspects that political instability in the country, lack of entrepreneurship, lack of quality education and quality students, for instance is the result of excessive unemployment

The problem of unemployment means the problem of providing work to those who are willing to work. A large number of educated and uneducated people, who are capable of work and are also willing to do it, roam here and there without any job. So the problem has assumed an acute form.

There is a large number of people who are either partly employed or wholly unemployed. The lives of such people, as well as of their families, are extremely miserable.

It is a well known fact that ours is a thickly populated country. The population is increasing by leaps and bounds. But jobs and gainful avenues cannot be created in the same proportion. So, naturally, a large section of the people is left unemployed. Moreover, our education system is also responsible for this problem. The problem of educated unemployment is peculiar to India. India is only country in the world where even highly educated persons fail to get employment. Every year thousands and thousands of graduates pass out of schools and colleges. They are unfit for any work, except office work. All of them cannot be absorbed in services. This increases employment.

The problem of unemployment is mainly an economic one. It is essential, therefore, that the economic policy of the country be overhauled. In our country, labor is available in abundance. We should provide avenues for employment for them through cottage and small-scale industries.

More stress should be laid on technical and vocational education. The present bookish education which produces clerks alone should be restricted. When people get technical and vocational education, they will not hanker after services on completing their education, they will come out well prepared to stand on their own legs. The problem will be half-solved, if this suggestion is implemented.

Our joint-family system is gradually breaking down. This may be a good change from certain points of view, but from the point of view of unemployment it is harmful. When we live jointly, some family members get employed in family professions. One who gets a job, supports others who may not be equally fortunate. We should not be hasty in breaking down this system.

Our country cannot advance economically, politically, or socially, unless this problem is solved. Many a social evil is spread through the unemployed. Frustration, drug-addiction, even suicides are, by and large, the evil results of unemployment. Unrest and disorder increase in society. It is, therefore, the duty of the government to make every possible effort to solve this problem. However, we may stress again that the problem cannot be solved till the population explosion is not checked. The two are closely inter-linked, and the people must be made to realize this through and adequate process of social education.

The unemployment, and much more so, the underemployment of graduates, are devastating phenomena in the lives of graduates. However, the incidence of underemployment among the graduates is much higher. Maximum students in this country are from middle class. Parents spend lakhs of rupees on them in a view that he will get a job after completing his graduation. But when the student fails to get a job, his mental position deterorate and gets depressed.

The problem of unemployment is a world-wide reality. The developed countries like the U.S., England, France, Germany, Italy, etc. also suffer from this problem, but it is more pronounced in India. With the passage of time it has become worse. It has become a threat to India's economic well-being and social development. It is one of the major causes of our poverty, backwardness, crimes and frustration among the people. India is the second largest country after China in terms of populations and man-power. But because of large scale unemployment there is no suitable employment for them. They are forced to remain idle.

There are millions of young men and women waiting and waiting for job opportunities. This chronic problem of unemployment is not confirmed to any particular class, segment or society. It is all pervading. There is massive unemployment among educated, well-trained and skilled people, and it is also there among semi-skilled and unskilled laborers, small and marginal farmers and workers. Then there is underemployment. The jobs being created have miserably failed to keep pace with the ever increasing number of job-seekers. It is a problem which presents a great challenge to leaders, thinkers, planners, economists, industrialists and educationists.

If provided with an enabling environment and opportunities, youth in both developed and developing countries can be key agents for social change, economic development and technological innovation. Youth bring with them boundless energy, imagination, creativity, ideals, and a limitless vision for their future and the societies in which they live. If not utilized, they are a wasted resource. Thus, it is imperative that youth are harnessed as part of society. This can be achieved through providing sustainable and decent employment and livelihoods opportunities and self-employment for them.

All these clearly indicate the need for promoting self-employment entrepreneurial ventures among the unemployed youth and women. Of late, Government and Non-Government agencies have taken certain initiatives and implementing many schemes to promote micro enterprises. However, the efforts seem to be inadequate against the gigantic unemployment problem.

It is under these circumstances that Rural Development and Self-Employment Training Institutes (RUDSETI) came into being and making concerted efforts to promote entrepreneurship especially among rural youths. RUDSET institute is an institutional framework to promote Rural Development. Its objective is to facilitate self-employment through developing self-confidence among the youth, build up capital in rural India through better utilisation of resources and transfer of appropriate technology. The Institute is jointly sponsored by Sri Dharmasthala Manjunatheshwara Educational Trust, Syndicate Bank and Canara Bank.

RUDSETI's MODEL IN PROMOTING SELF EMPLOYMENT

What is Marketing Self Employment?

Marketing Self Employment is the process of creating awareness about self-employment opportunities and training in the unemployed person to be self employed in his interested field.

Genesis of RUDSETI

Syndicate Bank and Canara Bank, the two progressive banks took the initiative in mitigating the unemployment problem under the leadership of Padmabhushana Dr. D. Veerendra Heggade, a great visionary and a religious head of a famous pilgrim centre at Dharmasthala in Karnataka. The collective thinking gave concrete shape in providing an institutional framework in the form of RUDSETI in 1982 at Ujire, a small village in Dakshina Kannada district of Karnataka.

Encouraged by the success of Ujire experiment, RUDSETI has now established 23 units in India.

Training Programmes

1. The Institute conducts more than 50 training programmes for the first generation entrepreneurs. These programmes are of short duration, ranging from 1 to 8 weeks under four broad categories viz;
   (*i*) Agricultural Entrepreneurship Development Programmes like—dairy, poultry, sustainable agriculture, bee keeping etc.
   (*ii*) Product EDP's like—dress designing, aagarabathi making etc.
   (*iii*) Process EDP's like—servicing/repairs of electrical/electronic equipment, pumpset repairs, photography etc.
   (*iv*) General ED programmes for establishing and managing general business enterprises.

2. RUDSET Institutes conduct Entrepreneurship Awareness Programmes to sensitise the youth towards self-employment as an alternative career in collaboration with colleges, volunteer organisations, banks, etc.
3. Apart from training programmes for the first generation entrepreneurs, RUDSET Institutes are conducting skill upgradation/ growth training programmes for established entrepreneurs. RUDSET Institutes have also organised special training programmes for Jail inmates enabling them to lead productive life after their release.
4. RUDSET Institutes also provides training to bank officials, in rural development activities to facilitate identification of potential rural entrepreneurs and credit appraisal. RUDSETI conducted 'Personality Development Programmes' for the elected representatives and government officials to enhance the delivery mechanism of welfare schemes of the government.
5. Village level workers of several voluntary organisations/commercial organisations, working for rural development, social animators and Self-Help Group organisers, were also trained by RUDSET Institutes to act as change agents.

Performance

In its endeavor to develop entrepreneurship among the unemployed youth and women during the last 26 years of its existence through its 23 centers across the country, the Institute's has been given in table 3.1.

While conducting women training batches, RUDSET Institute emphasises to cross their threshold barrier blocks, which helps in women empowerment.

Amongst the total trained candidates 70 per cent have established their self-employment projects in their villages or towns. This is a record performance when compared to other organizations in the country where the maximum settlement rate reported is less than 50 per cent.

RUDSET Institutes have so far trained 46,665 beneficiaries selected under Prime Minister's Rozgar Yojana (PMRY) of the Central Government for which EDP training is mandatory. Though some of the beneficiaries came with the sole purpose of obtaining the training certificate which is a precondition to avail bank finance and subsidy, the training inputs and atmosphere at RUDSETI made them to realise the importance of training in their self-employment ventures and also transformed their mindset.

Table 3.1 : Performance at a glance (as on 31.10.2010)

Particulars		Cumulative
Self Employment	Batches	7553
	Candidates	247259
Wage Employment	Batches	33
	Candidates	904
Skill/Growth programmes	Batches	269
	Candidates	5451
Rural Development Programmes	Batches	969
	Candidates	47447
HRD/Sensitisation Programmes	Batches	469
	Candidates	15782
Settlement	With Bank	82813
	Own Fund	85512
	Wage Employment	6476
	Total	174801
Women (Out of Total)	Trained	90431
	Settled	62959
SC/STs (Out of Total)	Trained	56133
	Settled	28276
Awareness Camps	Number	7022
	Participants	499338

Organisational set-up

RUDSET Institute is registered under the Societies Registration Act, 1860. The supreme policy-making body of the Institute is the Board of Governors which consists of the Chief Executives of sponsor organisations. The policies are implemented and monitored by a Governing Council aided by the Central Secretariat headed by an Executive Director—an officer deputed by the sponsor banks. Dr. D. Veerendra Heggade, a great visionary and a religious head is the President of the Board of Governors as well as Governing Council.

Each unit of RUDSETI has a Local Advisory Committee (LAC) with representatives of sponsor organizations, government officials and eminent personalities. It periodically reviews and assists the progress of RUDSETI.

An officer on deputation, with experience in development banking either from Syndicate Bank or Canara Bank manages each RUDSETI units.

Each Institute has a definite area of operation covering 2 to 4 districts. Each Institute is administered and training programmes are co-ordinated by professional bankers with vast experience in rural banking, entrepreneurship training and thus are well qualified to conduct entrepreneurship training programmes.

Post-Training Follow-up

The cutting edge of RUDSETI training is the post-training follow-up to sustain the motivation level and overcome teething problems of new entrepreneurs. It co-ordinates with other agencies influencing the setting up of self-employment ventures viz. banks, government departments, etc. Banks have supported in a big way by financing the trainees to establish their ventures. Business counselling and project consultancy services are provided on an ongoing basis, besides networking for business development.

Recognition

Recognising the unique and result-oriented efforts of RUDSET Institute in the field of social service, the following have been achieved.

1. *FICCI* has conferred its prestigious award for "Outstanding Achievement in Rural Development" during 1998-99.
2. Govt. of Karnataka has awarded "Kannada Rajyotsava Award" on 1st November '06 under Social Service category at Bangalore.
3. CITI Bank "Best Entrepreneur Award" for the year 2007-08 to Sri K.C. Amin, Brahmavar RUDSETI, Trained Entrepreneur and for the year 2008-09 to Smt. Doretta Cristabella, Bangalore RUDSETI, Trained Entrepreneur.
4. Among RUDSETI trained women candidates, 5 entrepreneurs have won "National Award for Best Rural Women Entrepreneurs" instituted by IMM- NABARD. Premier development agencies like SIDBI, NABARD, VISHWA of Govt. of Karnataka, KSWDC etc. have accepted the training modules of RUDSETI as model training and Govt. of India, Ministry of SSI recognized and advised all states to establish RUDSETI.
5. Recognizing the success of RUDSETI approach of youth empowerment, Government of Karnataka in its budgetary proposal for 2002-03, has envisaged implementing RUDSETI model widely in the state. Acknowledging the impact of dedicated training of RUDSETI, Ministry of SSI, Govt. of India recommended to every

state governments to establish RUDSETI model Institutes to promote micro enterprises.

6. The Ministry of Rural Development. Govt. of India, New Delhi sanctioned a grant assistance of Rs. 6.56 crores for infrastructure facilities in eight centers of RUDSETI one each in the state of Rajasthan, Madhya Pradesh, Andhra Pradesh, Orissa, Kerala, Karnataka and two in Uttar Pradesh.

Philosophy of RUDSETI

The entrepreneurization of rural youth has to take place by stimulating their psyche followed by bringing technology, training and credit within their reach, thereby developing self-confidence.

In the context of employment generation the three terms i.e. income generation, self-employment and entrepreneurship are often cited. In rural areas one has to work in all the three categories since they are interdependent.

Entrepreneurship development can take place in short duration intervention. It does not begin from 'Zero' level. Generally young people have gained some experience in life. This experience serves as a launching pad for accelerated learning. It is therefore possible to train young people in a short period of 1 to 4 weeks to enhance and enlarge behavioural dimensions such as increased awareness, understanding, knowledge, skill and formation of positive attitude.

The training can be effective if it is residential. Campus approach helps the participants to shape their attitude and personality. The duration of learning is stretched beyond structured hours in this approach.

RUDSETI Approach in Developing Entrepreneurs

1. A carefully designed selection process to identify and select only interested and potential youths taking into account their interest and aptitude.
2. Suitably designed programme schedules keeping in view the absorption level and future requirements of the candidate.
3. Use of experiential learning, group discussion, and field level experience and participation methods to impart training.
4. Use of market survey, interface with entrepreneurs and other techniques to acquaint trainee with field level situation.
5. Provision for technical training wherever needed.
6. Close and systematic follow-up and monitoring system after the training so as to provide post-training counselling, support and liaison services.

Keeping in view the fact that most of the unemployed youths are from poor/middle class rural families, who are already burdened financially, entire training is provided 'free of cost including free boarding and lodging'.

Capacity of the Organisation

Infrastructure: Each Institute has well-developed campus consisting of the administrative office, classrooms, work-shed, dormitories to trainees and guest houses to guest faculties and mess facilities. Library and recreational facilities are also available. The Institutes are equipped with audio-visual aids like OHP, slide projector, book projector, TV, Video and to the latest multimedia etc.

In Karnataka, all the 7 units have acquired owned campus with the financial assistance of Rs. 1.90 crores from the Department of Industries & Commerce and Rs. 184.3 lakhs from the Department of Rural Development & Panchayat Raj, Government of Karnataka. At Madurai also, own campus is constructed with the financial assistance from RDPR and the sponsoring organisations of RUDSETI.

The construction of building from the funds made available from the Ministry of Rural Development, Govt. of India, New Delhi at Anantapur, Jaipur and Agra have been completed and inaugurated.

Resource Persons: Director of the Institute, an officer deputed from sponsor banks, possess rich experience in development banking, rural development and administration. These officers supported by in-house faculty are handling behavioural inputs, managerial inputs, banking, launching formalities etc. All these officers are exposed to professional training in Entrepreneurship Development and Management in reputed organisations. Besides this, every Institute has a panel of qualified and experienced resource persons drawn from technical, entrepreneurial, professional, social and other fields.

The expert practitioners in the respective field, who provide their services out of social concern, impart skill training. Most of these experts are RUDSETI trained entrepreneurs.

Course Modules: Training modules of RUDSETI are so designed that the Entrepreneurship Development is achieved through Human Resource Development.

The course modules structured out of practical experience, research and experiment facilitate development of the necessary skills in a systematic manner in a short period. The training modules of EDP/Skill development programmes of RUDSETI have been accepted as standard modules by the funding agencies like SIDBI, NABARD, Department of Industries and

Commerce, KSWDC etc. RUDSETI reviews these course modules on an ongoing basis and revise and update them.

Training Methodology: The widely acclaimed effectiveness of RUDSET Institute's training is attributed to the unique training methodology adopted. Through structured psychological exercises, the participants are stimulated to shed inhibitions and develop interest in learning. Besides lecture sessions, behaviour simulation games, exercises, field visits, hands on experience, interaction with role models, interface with supporting system, group discussions, role play, case study etc. are effectively used in the training. Training sessions are conducted in vernacular languages.

Committed staff and training atmosphere: Under the guidance of visionary leadership, the committed workforce of the Institute has successfully created and maintained a conducive atmosphere, for learning. Cordial trainer-trainee relationship, discipline, guidance for personality development and socialisation with fellow trainees offers excellent scope for effective learning.

Sensitised supporting system: Through excellent liaison with various Govt. departments, developmental agencies, banks and networking with other NGO's, RUDSET Institute has been able to provide support to the trained entrepreneurs for establishing their ventures.

Past experience: Under the stewardship of visionary leader Padmabhushana Dr. D. Veerendra Heggade and aided by total support from the sponsors, RUDSET Institute has successfully executed challenging assignments and conducted innovative experiments in Rural Development.

Special Assignment Undertaken by RUDSETI

EDP for leather artisans of Athani: RUDSETI in collaboration with ASCENT had experimented EDP for leather artisans of Athani, Belgaum district by bringing together husband and wife for the empowerment programme. Apart from the common inputs, information on group management, technical as well as design skills and management of enterprise were given through a team of management experts. Inputs on SHG concept, common fund management, credit linkage and conflict resolution helped the women in knowing the SHG concept clearly and ways of applying it in their settings. So far RUDSET Institute has conducted eight such programmes.

Capacity Building of NGO's – Training to NGO field staff under SWASHAKTI Project: "SWASHAKTI" a World Bank funded project of Government of India is implemented through Karnataka State Women Development Corporation (KSWDC) in four districts of Karnataka viz. Kolar, Chitradurga, Bellary and Tumkur. Building self-reliance and self-confidence in women so as to have greater access as well as control over economic and social resources and the political processes are the objectives of the project.

It is envisaged to achieve the objectives by organising the women under self-help groups under the guidance and training of NGO field staff. To achieve the objectives, different orientation programmes and trainings are planned at various levels for different agencies involved in the implementation of the project. RUDSETI conducted the following training programmes for 160 community workers of Chitradurga, Kolar, Tumkur and Bellary districts:

Phase I: "Management of savings and credit, records and registers of SHGs"

Phase II: "Bank linkages with SHGs, Government schemes, Panchayat Raj institutions and role of women in Panchayat Raj"

Apart from the specified technical inputs, RUDSET Institute's additional inputs on Group Dynamics, Human Relations, Leadership, Effective Communication, interaction with SHG's and interface with Bank officials added value to the programmes.

Swarna Jayanthi Gram Swarozgar Yojana (SGSY): Swarna Jayanthi Gram Swarozgar Yojana (SGSY) is an ambitious scheme of Govt. of India for the poverty alleviation through Self-Employment. The scheme envisages inter alia careful selection of Swarozgaries out of BPL list, organising them into Self-Help Groups, training them with skills and managerial inputs to enable them to carry out viable income generating activities besides providing credit support.

RUDSETIs imparted training to the Government and Bank functionaries involved in SGSY, facilitators/social animators in promotion, forming an administration of self-help groups. They also assisted the Zila Panchayat/ DRDAs in identification and selection of key activities, activity clusters and preparation of project profiles.

EDP for International Participants: A special EDP was conducted in English and Telugu at RUDSETI, Anantapur in which community development professionals from Brazil, Mexico, Kenya, South Africa and Philippines participated. These youth are being developed as business as well as social entrepreneurs under the ambitious youth empowerment project. The training was sponsored by World Corps India, Chennai, a voluntary organization, having its H.Q. at Seattle, USA, committed to mobilizing young adults worldwide to become effective business entrepreneurs, community leaders and global citizens. The international participants impressed by the programme and expressed their desire to replicate RUDSETI model in their countries. This EDP was specially designed for identified youth from Kuppam Assembly constituency represented by Sri. Chandrababu Naidu, Hon'ble Chief Minister of Andhra Pradesh.

Human Resources Development Training: RUDSETI has conducted exclusive customized Human Resource Development programme to senior officers and academicians. Director of vocational education, Government of Karnataka desired to rejuvenate the vocational education by adapting the element of motivation in vocational courses offered at plus 2 level in the colleges of Karnataka. A suitable three-day HRD programme was designed and conducted at six RUDSET Institutes in Karnataka to the Deputy Directors, the district in-charges of vocational education in Karnataka and Principals of vocational education colleges. The programme proved effective in enabling them to understand various elements of HRD and equip them with motivational skills. The programme was well received and created a visible impact. HRD training programmes are also conducted on regular basis to officers of Grameena Banks and sponsor banks.

Trainers' Training Programme in Entrepreneurship Development: RUDSETI has also conducted trainers training Programmes in entrepreneurship development in vernacular languages (Hindi, English and Kannada) at various RUDSET Institutes from time to time for the benefit of co-ordinators of NGOs.

Intrapreneurship Development Programme: Intrapreneurship Development Programmes for the workers of SSIs were also conducted successfully to enhance the motivation and managerial skills of employees, besides stimulating their creative abilities.

RUDSETI-KAWAD Livelihood Project: Karnataka Watershed Development Society (KAWAD), a registered society sponsored by Department of International Development (DFID), Government of United Kingdom and Government of Karnataka has undertaken watershed activities with a goal to minimize the rural poverty in a sustainable manner in three districts of Karnataka viz. Bijapur, Chitradurga and Bellary. Recognizing the quality training model and dedicated efforts of RUDSETI, KAWAD has collaborated with RUDSETI for promoting micro enterprises in non-land based activities. RUDSETI has trained 627 persons in Entrepreneurship Development Programme, of which, more than 400 stakeholders of the project have initiated self-employment ventures.

Training for Facilitators in Entrepreneurship Development Process: RUDSET Institute has entered into an MOU with KAWAD for providing comprehensive training and handholding services to around 500 landless stakeholders in Doddahalla Watershed Development Project in Bijapur district for promoting micro enterprises. Capacity building of partner NGOs of watershed projects in the districts of Bijapur, Chitradurga and Bellary in Karnataka is one such service. RUDSETI conducted a training programme for NGO facilitators in Entrepreneurship Development process in this regard.

Rudseti-Sujala Project: The Watershed Development Department of Government of Karnataka has launched a watershed programme called 'SUJALA' with the objective of providing livelihood support. SUJALA project intends to increase the income of vulnerable families by promoting income generation activities and micro-enterprises. In order to empower the vulnerable families to take up income generation activities or to set up micro-enterprises it was felt necessary to avail services of professional specialist agencies working on entrepreneurial development sector.

RUDSETI has been identified as one of the specialist agencies with responsibilities such as providing guidance to field functionaries of FNGOs and LNGOs through Training of Trainers and further guidance for pre-EDP and post-EDP follow-up and the implementation of IGA/ME and marketing linkages, conducting entrepreneurship development training programmes (EDP) to the SHG members selected by the project, providing guidance to the trained entrepreneurial members and help to prepare business proposals, providing necessary information of agencies for organizing the skill training programmes and need-based exposure visits for the selected entrepreneurial trainees etc.

RUDSETI has provided EDP training to more than 3000 stakeholders of SUJALA Watershed Project in Chitradurga district, Karnataka. The Institute has also imparted Training of Trainers (ToT) to the facilitators of Field Non-Governmental Organizations under the project. In addition to this, the institute has imparted training in 14 batches to 72 beneficiaries.

Consultancy Services: RUDSETI has been providing consultancy and handholding services to various organizations to set up Entrepreneurship Development Institutes.

Results of Self-employment Programme

Direct Benefits

10.1.1 At the estimated settlement rate of 70 per cent, RUDSETI trained unemployed youth would be starting their own entrepreneurial ventures and will be self-employed by second year and 350 established entrepreneurs will add 25 per cent more profit to their business.

10.1.2 Increased income to the concerned families and increase in savings and capital formation.

10.1.3 Enhancement in the overall productivity particularly in the rural sector.

10.1.4 Promotion of service sector, particularly in rural and semi-urban areas.

Indirect Benefits

10.2.1 Establishment of units by new entrepreneurs will have tremendous demonstrative effect on the neighbourhood population leading to better appreciation of entrepreneurial values, positive self image and social transformation.

10.2.2 It acts as a check on migration from rural to urban areas.

10.2.3 Increased awareness among rural people particularly women to go for self-reliant and sustainable economic activity.

10.2.4 Decreased pressure on Govt. to provide alternate employment to these trainees who would otherwise is found in the job seekers market.

REFERENCES

1. *Annual Report RUDSETI*, 2009-10.
2. Drucker, Peter, 1993, *Managing the Non-Profit Organization*, Delhi: Macmillan.
3. Fernandes, W., 1989, *Voluntary Action & Government Control*, New Delhi: Indian Social Institute.
4. Gangrade, K.D., 1988, Social Welfare & Social Development, New Delhi: Northern Book Center.
5. Garain, S., 1998, Organization Effectiveness of N.G.O's, Jaipur: University Book House.
6. Griffin, *Management*, New Delhi: A.I.T.B.S. Publishers & Dstribution.
7. Grunig , J.F. & Hunt, T., 1984, *Managing Public Relation*, New York: Hott, Rinehart & Winston.
8. Handy, C., 1990, *Understanding Voluntary Organizations*, London: Penguin Books.
9. Jackson, J., 1989, *Evaluation for Voluntary Organizations*, Delhi Information & News Network.
10. Korten, David C., 1993, *Getting to the 21st Century: Voluntary Action & the Global Agenda*, New Delhi: Oxford IBH Publishing Pvt. Ltd.
11. Mabey, C. & Sealama, G., 1995, *Strategic Human Resource Management*, Oxford: Blackbell.
12. Misra, S.K. & Puri, V.K., *Economic Environment of Business*, Himalaya Publishing House.
13. Mukherjee, Mukherjee, S., 1989, *Guidebook for Strengthening Voluntary Organizations*, Ghaziabad, Kendra.
14. Mukherjee, M., 1993, *Participatory Rural Appraisal; Methodology & Applications*, New Delhi: Concept Publishers.
15. Powell, Gaery, 1988, *Women & Men in Management*, Beverley Hills, California: Sage Publications

16. PRIA, 2001, *Strategic Planning for Village Development Organizations Workshops*: Manual for Facilitation, New Delhi: Society for Participatory Research in Asia.

17. PRIA, 2000, *Legal Framework for Non-profit Institutions in India*, New Delhi: PRIA.

18. PRIA, 1999, *Management of Voluntary Organizations*, New Delhi: Society for Participatory Research in India.

19. PRIA, 1991, *Non-Government Organizations in India: A Critical Study*, New Delhi: Society for Participatory Research in Asia.

20. Raman, B.S., *Introduction to Accountancy*, Mangalore: United Publisher Ltd.

21. Rao, T.V., *Human Resource Development—Experiences, Interventions & Strategies*: Sage Publications India Pvt. Ltd.

22. Singh, B.P. & Singh, A.K., *Essentials of Management*, Excel Books.

23. Stephen, P. Robbins, *Organization Theory, Structure, Design & Application*, Prentice Hall of India Pvt. Ltd.

24. Stephen, P. Robbins, *Organizational Behaviour.*

25. Vishwanat, 1993, *NGOs & Women Development in Rural South India: A Comparative Analysis*, New Delhi: Visthar.

26. Warham Joyce, 1975, *Introduction to Administration for Social Workers*, London: Routledge & Kegan Paul.

27. Weiner, M, *Human Service Management*, Illinois: The Dorsey Press.

CHAPTER

4

Essential Techniques for Social Work Practice in the Fields of Community Development

—Prof. Mukul Srivastava

ABSTRACT

Community practice techniques have been neglected by social work educators and authors, reflecting a lack of fit with real world practice needs. To sharpen the debate, the different Social Work Professionals identify five techniques that are helpful, if not essential for community practice: (1) Force Field Analysis; (2) Program Evaluation Review Technique; (3) Nominal Group Technique; (4) Delphi; and (5) Q-Sort. He views that the analysis of these could spark a dialogue leading ultimately to a universally accepted set of community practice techniques in social work curricula. Social work educators who interact with practitioners will confirm what practitioners demand from educators or what students demand from their practicum guide: to place greater emphasis on teaching what social workers do to affect change. The real world of practice demands competencies in what social workers actually do, rather than how much theory they know. Competent community practice necessitates a repertoire of skills and techniques to effect change along a continuum of system from individuals through family, groups, organizations, to community. However, classroom textbooks and journal articles are dominated by discussion of theories, value dilemmas, and case studies, creating a disconnect between what educators, students and practitioners want and need, and what they get.

Introduction

Community practice techniques have been neglected by social work educators and authors, reflecting a lack of fit with real world practice needs. Community practice is defined as including community organizing, community development, and social planning. To sharpen the debate, the different Social Work Professionals identify five techniques that are helpful, if not essential for community practice: (1) Force Field Analysis; (2) Program Evaluation Review Technique; (3) Nominal Group Technique; (4) Delphi; and (5) Q-Sort. It is anticipated that the analysis of these could spark a dialogue leading ultimately to a universally accepted set of community practice techniques in social work curricula. Social work educators who interact with practitioners will confirm what practitioners demand from educators or what students demand from their practicum guide: to place greater emphasis on teaching what social workers do to affect change. The real world of practice demands competencies in what social workers actually do, rather than how much theory they know. Competent community practice necessitates a repertoire of skills and techniques to effect change along a continuum of system from individuals through family, groups, organizations, to community. However, classroom textbooks and journal articles are dominated by discussion of theories, value dilemmas, and case studies, creating a disconnect between what educators, students and practitioners want and need, and what they get.

In community practice, the lack of fit is very evident and warrants serious examination. To address this need, at least in part, the professionals have identified five techniques or tools for practitioners that are most helpful, if not essential, for community practice. The lack of attention by professionals and researchers of community-oriented literature in the professional journals to techniques of community practice is noteworthy. After an extensive review of professional social work journals with a macro focus, one must conclude that during the past decade attention to community practice techniques has been overlooked. A review of Social Service Review, Child Welfare, Journal of Social Work Education, Journal of Community Practice, and the Journal of Baccalaureate Social Work from 1995 to present indicates a complete absence of articles devoted to identifying and discussing techniques for community practice. A review of macro practice course syllabi of social work indicates that there is little mention of community practice techniques, and some programs do not reference them at all.

Deptt. of Social Work, Institute of Social Sciences, Dr. B. R. Ambedkar University, Agra

With few notable exceptions, the attention to community practice techniques in textbooks is almost as bleak. Hardcastle, Wenocur, and Powers (1997), present both theory and skills with some techniques, whereas Sheafor, Horejsi, and Hoejsi's (1988) undergraduate text does an excellent job of presenting and explaining how to use (community) practice techniques. Beyond this, the landscape changes rapidly. Classic community practice texts like Rubin and Rubin (2001) and Delgado's (2000) urban oriented text have no techniques. The premier book on community practice by Rivera and Erlich (1995) with people of colour has also no mention of techniques, and, surprisingly, neither does the manual by Babo, Kendall, and Max (1991), found any such references.

Defining Terms

For the purpose of this article, a technique is viewed as a "circumscribed, goal-oriented behavior performed in a practice situation by the social worker. It is a planned action deliberately taken by the practitioner" (Sheafor, Horejsi, & Horejsi; 1988). The application of a simple technique could be very brief, whereas more complex techniques may require several hours (Sheafor, Horejsi, & Horejsi, 1988). Community (social work) practice, as used in this article reflects the three models of community intervention identified in Rothman's historic typology (Rothman, Erlich, & Tropman, 2001). Initially referred to as locality development, social planning, and social action, the professionals/practitioners prefer the more contemporary terminology of community development, social planning, and community organizing (Hardcastle, Wenocur & Powers, 1997).

Techniques and its Usages

Techniques are used to assist in the implementation of intervention models. Without techniques, implementation of any theory or model is awkward, at best, and wholly impossible, at worst. Techniques are where theory is translated in to practice. The utilization of tools and techniques are the beginning of a practice continuum, leading to a greater and greater degree of competence. Is that not what we mean when we think of or describe a practitioner, one whose skills and techniques are honed to a high degree? Techniques are specific, repeatable, demonstrable, and measurable actions to be applied in appropriate contexts. Practitioners either know a technique and know how to apply it or they don't. One has either developed a level of competence in utilizing the specific technique, or one has not. Either the practitioner has learned the necessary techniques and how to effectively implement them in practice, or they have not. Theory is essential, but is not enough. One must be able to operationalize the theory and operationalizing at theory requires a technique or, better yet, a set of techniques. A broad, vaguely defined piece of knowledge cannot be measured, displayed, or applied without employing a technique. Techniques must be learned, and professional education is the process to learn the basic core techniques.

While there is general agreement of a set of techniques for micro practice (individual and small group), it becomes difficult, if not impossible, to find the same agreement on an operational concept of a set of community social work techniques. This is, in part, due to the lack of a fundamental dialogue among academic members of the community on a desired set of techniques. Clearly, identifying applicable techniques for a world where real practice occurs in a fundamental part of social work education. Techniques are used to implement theory and to intervene and produce change in situations that range in difficulty from simple to complex. The more techniques a practitioner has to draw upon, the greater the options available to address a growing variety of client's situations. Therefore, the level of competence of a practitioner would, in part, depend upon the number of techniques known and used appropriately in a wide variety of situations.

Identifying Essential Community Practice Techniques

Hardcastle, Wenocur, and Power (1997) define community practice as the application of practice skills to alter the behavior patterns of community groups, organizations, and institutions or people's relationship and interactions with these entities. Further, community practice, as part of macro-practice, includes the techniques associated with community organization and development, social planning and social action, and social administration (Hardcastle, Wenocur, and Powers, 1997). Whereas community organization and community development work with parts of a community, such as a neighborhood or a group of people, social planners address the needs of people through agencies and delivery systems to best meet the larger scale community functions and responsibilities. Common to the three parts of community practice (organizing, development, and planning) is the desire of community practitioners to assist the community to function as efficiently and as responsively as possible to its member constituents. With such a common purpose and a common core of knowledge, it equally follows there should be a common, or core, technique base. In other words, if community practitioners essentially do the same task, then they should have the same techniques. Community practice begins with finding out what people want as individuals, determining which of those desires are shared and then helping them find collective ways of achieving it. The foundation and common purpose of community organizing is based upon relationships and self-interest. The same could be said for all community practice.

According to Rothman, Erlich, and Tropman (2001), there are two basic elements of community practice requiring a corresponding technique base: problem solving and understanding, and using influence. If they are correct, then the identification of essential techniques for problem solving and understanding, and using influence is appropriate and necessary. The trick is link essential elements of community practice with essential techniques for community practice. The following five essential or fundamental techniques in the conduct of community practice are identified and suggested:

- *Force Field Analysis (FFA),* for assisting in problem solving and understanding planned change.

- *Program Evaluation Review Technique (PERT),* for scheduling activities to assure successful and timely completion of a community or planning project (or in foreseeing and preventing problems).
- *Nominal Group Technique (NGT),* for facilitating structured group decision-making, assuring full and equal access participation by all members.
- *Delphi,* for forecasting/future planning or to obtain a reliable consensus of opinion.
- *Q-Sort,* for assisting small or large groups to identify and prioritize common concerns.

These practice techniques reflect essential techniques that correspond to the essential elements or tasks useful in all phases of community practice encompassing organizing, planning, and development (Table 4.1). These techniques have been chosen in the context of the practitioners, educators, researchers and service agencies recent attempts to incorporate a set of essential techniques in their own professional domain. In this context it is almost impossible to find any empirical research identifying essential techniques for community practice after an exhaustive review of the literature. As a result, the techniques proposed came directly out of discussions with practitioners working as planners, developers, and organizers who cited these techniques as being most relevant to their fields of practice. These identified proposed techniques are the outcomes of several focus groups with multiple one-on-one interviews and a series of professional meetings with agency practicum supervisors in consultation with the School of Social Wok field practicum office.

Table 4.1 : Proposed Community Techniques

Community Techniques	Elements of Practice		Community Intervention Approaches	Purpose of Techniques
	Problem solving	Influence	Planning/Organizing/ Development	
F.F.A.		×	×	Analyzing for change
P.E.R.T.	×		×	SchedulingTechnology
N.G.T.	×		×	Medium-large group Decision making
Delphi		×	×	Forecasting/future planning
Q-Sort	×	×	×	Prioritizing & focusing issues

• *FORCE FIELD ANALYSIS*

Force field analysis (FFA), developed by Lewin (1969), assists in solving problems and planning change. Social workers in community practice utilize FFA to identify and assess forces affecting a decision regarding a social problem or issue. This technique organizes data concerning the forces that could impact the outcome of change efforts and enables social workers to identify the forces that may foster or impede a particular change. A plan of action can be developed based upon that analysis. A Force Field Inventory may be constructed, which could suggest the individuals, groups, and coalitions relevant to the issue. The group then identifies driving and restraining forces most likely to effect the change effort. The strength of each force is assessed and ranked. The amenability to change of each force is ranked as high, low, or uncertain. Both are recorded on the Force Field Inventory. A strategy for change is then devised based on the inventory. The advantages and the limitations of this technique may be summarized as follows :

Advantages

- Can be used with small or large groups
- Easy to grasp and simple to use
- Requires good facilitation skills
- Open format encourages creativity
- An assessment tool that shapes a plan of action

Limitations

- Tendency to focus on forces against change at expense of forces for change (i.e., tends to elicit negatives).
- "Forces" usually described in generalities and requires more facilitation for specificity.
- Lack of structure allows discussion to be dominated by a minority.

• *PROGRAM EVALUATION REVIEW TECHNIQUE*

The Program Evaluation Review Technique (PERT), is used extensively in social planning as a scheduling tool. PERT charting, standard fare in all social planning texts, was given prominence by Armand Lauffer's (1978) landmark text and is identified as a technique for social workers in everyday practice. PERT provides a visual representation of a project, assisting in a clear understanding of the organization of the time, resources, events, and activities necessary for the project's completion. In short, PERT is a flow or time chart allowing for the monitoring of activities and anticipation of problems so changes or improvements can be made as the project progresses. The first task is to define the goal. Once a goal is defined, a sequence of tasks or activities is depicted in the order they must be accomplished. A specific time frame is assigned, estimating how long each task will take and, ultimately the time it will take to reach the primary goal. PERT charts utilize timelines with specific deadlines to achieve each task so it is incumbent upon the group through the facilitator to set a realistic goal and corresponding time frames in which to achieve the desired result. The chart also identifies the people or groups responsible for each part and any resources to be obtained or provided. The advantages and the limitations of this technique may be summarized as follows:

Advantages

- Outcome is very precise for sequencing and time requirement of events
- PERT chart itself assists in monitoring and oversight
- Reduces vagueness and ensures accountability

Limitations

- Initially can appear too complex
- Requires major time allocation
- Typically viewed as a "professionals only" tool, although it can be used by citizens with equal success
- Requires sophisticated facilitation skills
- Skills in task analysis helpful

• NOMINAL GROUP TECHNIQUE

The nominal group technique (NGT), first reported by Delbecq, Van de Ven, and Gustafson (1975), is used within a structured group and is focused upon group decision-making regarding a central topic through the identification and generation of multiple ideas by individual group members. Participation by all group members is the desired goal, and each member is given an equal voice, minimizing the potential for a select few to dominate the group. The group gathers in one location, and the leader presents the issue and asks members to work silently and reflectively to identify ideas. The group is subdivided into small groups of five to seven members. After a "round robin" of presentation and clarification of ideas, the small group selects two to three best ideas. The "round robin" presentation approach allows questioning only to clarify an individual's ideas but never to challenge them. Each group merges with another group, and the process is repeated until eventually one large group is formed and the best ideas emerge from the multilevel process.

The group then ranks the ideas, and a group decision is made based upon the statistical result of the aggregated individual ideas. A facilitator is required to guide the group and allow members to generate multiple ideas focused on solving the question or concern presented. NGT provides a forum for people to generate ideas in a face-to-face format, but these ideas are initially developed independent of other members. The advantages and the limitations of this technique may be summarized as follows:

Advantages

- Process assures full and equal participation of all persons (very inclusive)
- Requires a moderate level of facilitation by the leader
- Process almost assures a successful outcome
- Can be used with groups of any size from 15-20 plus
- Excellent process and facilitator can encourage critical thinking
- Encourages facilitating innovations (i.e., voting by stickers instead of hands)

Disadvantages

- Can feel too restrictive to some people
- Best if several people facilitate
- Requires some preplanning

• *DELPHI*

The Delphi, named after the Greek priestess from Delphos who forecast future events, is a technique to harness expert opinion for critical decision-making (Faherty, 1997). Planners currently consider the Delphi an effective forecasting tool. The Delphi Technique is one alternative to face-to-face meetings where reaching a consensus is more important than having people vote by majority rule just to have a decision. Although completing the steps of the Delphi takes a longer period of time than holding a one or two-shot "majority wins" meeting, the likelihood of greater and faster implementation far outweigh the additional time needed to reach a decision (Stahl & Stahl, 1991). Idea generation by a panel of experts who are individual, independent, isolated and anonymous occurs by a series of questions posed in writing. In order to generate even more creativity, a summary of the responses from the first round are given back during the subsequent rounds, and additional responses are elicited. The answers, or summary statements, move toward agreement or consensus (Brooks, 1979). Typically, three rounds are sufficient to reach the desired level of consensus. The Delphi may be used in the practice with certain given strengths and functional limitations:

Advantages

- Excellent to generate creative and free association of ideas.
- Low cost and efficient process to synthesize quantitative data.
- "Expert" input can be by mail or e-mail and requires no oral facilitation skills.
- Does not rely on a single expert, a one-shot group, average, or a round-table discussion.

Limitations

- Participation can drop off.
- Rather lengthy process and not to be used if quick results are desired.
- The quality of the results entirely dependent upon the high caliber of the "experts".

Q-SORT

Q-Sort, originally from psychological research, is a technique that is employed in community practice to assist groups (small or large) to sort through options and develop priorities. Q-Sort allows a meeting facilitator to reduce dozens of suggestions or issues to three to five items by group priority. The group identifies multiple issues through brainstorming. The group then weights or sorts each item depending upon its importance. The leader records the issues in two columns: most important and least important. The group takes the items in the "most" column and sorts again into most important and least important categories. Typically, a group needs to do the sorting exercise a minimum of three times to achieve the desired outcome. Q-Sort assures an open decision-making process. All data sheets should be retained from the initial random listing of items as well as each Sort, for if the outcome is questioned, the facilitator can review the process and how the outcome was achieved. A facilitator can typically conduct a Q-Sort with a large group using three sorts in an hour. In about an hour and a half, a facilitator can brainstorm ideas, conduct a complete Q-Sort process, and identify the group's priorities for the agenda at the next meeting. Unlike the nominal group technique, which assures equal participation of everyone, the Q-Sort is more responsive to verbal participants. The advantages and the limitations of this technique may be summarized as follows:

Advantages

- Process almost assures satisfactory outcome.
- Can be used with any size group.
- Audience participation is usually high since all ideas are at least initially valued.
- Simple process to facilitate consensus.

Disadvantages

- Process can be dominated by a few persons.
- Requires excellent facilitation skills.
- Best if two facilitators used.

The following example illustrates the use and effectiveness of a technique for best practice in community social work.

INCORPORATING COMMUNITY PRACTICE TECHNIQUES IN SOCIAL WORK CURRICULA

The teaching of essential community practice techniques must be preceded by a general agreement amongst practitioners and faculty as to what, if any, techniques can be considered core. Faculty members teaching the spectrum of courses of different levels need to be able to define and describe core techniques and, further, to demonstrate competence in the techniques. Without this, we are faced with a situation whereby core knowledge is not understood by faculty who are educating social workers to engage in advanced social work practice. We are faced with a situation in which social workers are not being prepared to effect change along the continuum of systems through community. Bisno and Cox (1997) assess the current state of social work education and conclude that the demand on social work education to include an ever-increasing array of subjects is becoming unrealistic and the result of this demand is superficiality of preparation and training. The professionals acknowledge the demand dilemma and, at the same time recognize the need for greater emphasis on technique development. Practitioners come out with a wide theoretical base but lack a specific skills and techniques base, directly applicable to their chosen field of practice. In an exhaustive literature review, the authors discovered a dearth of articles studying community practice techniques, with the exception of a few commentaries and exploratory articles calling attention to this issue among social work educators (Ahearn, Bolan, & Burke, 1975; Bisno & Cox, 1997; Franklin, 1994; Sanfort, 2000; Thyer, 1994). But the issue is not whether or not we teach techniques in the social work curriculum, for we do. The issue is whether we will teach techniques for community practice and, specifically, whether we can agree on the essential community practice techniques that practitioners should be taught. Is there or is there not a very basic need for standard or base techniques in community practice? If there is, then essential community practice techniques must be integrated in the curriculum.

The lack of specific community practice content in curricula arises from a vaguely depersonalized concept of community and the idea that one does not engage a community in fact-to-face interactions. On the contrary, community practice is all about working with individuals and groups and often in very intimate settings. Community practitioners need excellent relationship-building capabilities. Community practice techniques are tools for the practitioner to connect with individuals in groups to effect a positive outcome. If we conceptualize community as abroad, nonspecific entity, then it is understandable that educators would not be committed to teach specific practice techniques. If, as suggested earlier, community practice texts seldom (and sometimes never) identify techniques for community practice, one need only look at how the term community and community practice has been conceptualized. If one thinks of building community as a vague concept, then it follows that practice technique would not be part of the discussion and, in fact, community-specific knowledge would also be vague. If, however, one conceives of building community as a process with specific goals and objectives, then one should teach specific techniques in order to carry out the goals and objectives. The implications for social work curricula are clear. How community is conceptualized and what a practitioner does should lead educators to teach a very specific set of community practice techniques for planning, organizing, and community development. Central to these arguments is the proposal that all social work curricula should have both foundations in community theory contents and advanced community technique modules based upon a set of essential community practice techniques.

Ethical mandates (NASW, 1999) require the continued development of techniques and provide the impetus for social work practitioners to increase professional knowledge, skills, and techniques in their field of practice. This issue is reflected in the NASW Professional Standards that guide professional competence. While a range of professional standards are included such as clinical social work, case management, and personnel practices (NASW, 2001), the NASW Professional Standards do not include standards for community practice. This may be a call for a dialogue. Creating a standard for community practice within the NASW Professional Standards would be a step toward correcting this deficit. The techniques proposed by the authors represent those suggested practitioners who are planners, developers, and organizers. Empirical studies need to be conducted to move beyond the conceptual framework proposed by the authors. Further technique identification needs to occur through research on what community practitioners do, linked to what technique(s) they employ or implement. Finally, the field of community practice needs to resolve definitional issues. Agreement must be reached on what is a skill, or a technique, or a tool. Students of community practice look to the journals and textbooks for consistency, yet it is not there.

This textual analysis may be considered a first step toward sharpening our terms and becoming more precise about what comprises competency at the community practice level. We have to make attempt to expand the dialogue initiated by a handful of social work educators by first identifying and operationalizing five essential techniques that can be universally applied by social workers in any community practice setting. Rather than viewing technique identification as a reductionist task, the assignment, should social work education step up to the plate, is to expand a base that we are only now beginning to identify. The conceptual framework offered should enable social work educators to move to constructive dialogues about adopting a commonly accepted set of community practice techniques and how these can be incorporated into social work curricula.

REFERENCES

1. Ahearn, F. L., Bolan. R.S., Burke, E. (1975), "A social action approach for planning education in social work", *Journal of Education for Social Work,* 11 (3), 5-11.
2. Bisno, H. & Cox, F. (1997), "Social work education: Catching up with the present and the future." *Journal of Social Work Education,* 33 (2), 372-387.
3. Bobo, K., Kendall, J., & Max, S. (1991), *Organizing for social change: A manual for activists in the 1990s,* Westwood, WA: Seven Locks Press.
4. Brooks, K. W. (1979), "Delphi technique: expanding applications". *North Central Association Quarterly,* 53 (3), 377-385.
5. Delbecq, A. L., Van de Ven, A. H., & Gustafson, D. H. (1975), *Group techniques for program planning: A guide to nominal group and Delphi processes,* Glenview, IL: Scott, Foresman, & Co.
6. Delgado, M. (2000), *Community social work practice in urban context,* New York, NY: Oxford University Press.
7. Faherty, V.E. (1997), "Using forecasting models to plan for social work education in the century". *Journal of Social Work Education,* 33(2), pp. 403-411.
8. Franklin, C. (1994), "Must social workers continually yield current practice methods to the evolving empirically supported knowledge base? Yes!" in W.W. Hudson & P.S. Nurius (Eds.), *Controversial issues in social work research* (pp. 271-282). Boston. MA: Allyn & Bacon.
9. Hardcastle, D.A., Wenocur, S., & Power, P. R. (1997), *Community practice: Theories and techniques for social workers,* New York: Oxford University Press.

10. Heyel, C. (1982), "PERT Program Evaluation and Review Technique", in C. Heyel (Ed.), *The encyclopedia of management (*3rd ed., pp. 868-871), New York: Van Nostrand Reinhold Co.
11. Lauffer, A. (1978), *Social planning at the community level,* Englewood Cliffs, NJ: Prentice Hall, Inc.
12. Lauffer, A. (1981), "Recognizing community organization: notes on changes in practice and needed changes in the graduate school curriculum", *Social Development Issues,* 5(2-3), 166-179.
13. Lewin, K. (1969), "Quasi-stationary social equilibria and the problem of permanent changes", in W. G. Bennis, K. D. Benne, & R. Chin (Eds.), *The planning of change* (2nd ed., New York: Rinehart & Winston.
14. National Association of Social Workers (1999), *NASW Code of Ethics* (Revised), Washington, DC: Author. Copy available: *www.naswdc.org/code/ethics.htm*
15. National Association of Social Workers (2001), *NASW Professional Standards and Clinical Indicators,* Washington, DC: Author Copy available: *www.naswde.org/practice/standads.htm.*
16. Rivera, F.A., & Erlich, J. (1995), *Community organizing in a diverse society* (2nd ed.). Boston, MA: Allyn & Bacon.
17. Rothman, J., Erlich, J.L., & Tropman, J.E. (2001), *Strategies of community intervention: Marco Practice* (6th ed.), Itasca, IL: F. E. Peacock Publishers.
18. Rubin, H. J., & Rubin, I. S. (2001), *Community organizing and development* (3rd ed.), Boston, MA: Allyn & Bacon.
19. Sanfort, J. R. (2000), "*Invited Commentary: Developing new techniques for community practice in an era of policy devolution", Journal of Social Work Education,* 36(2), 183-185.
20. Sheafor, B. W., Horejsi, C. R., & Hoejsi, G. (1988), *Techniques and guidelines for social work practice* (4th ed.), Boston, MA: Allyn & Bacon.
21. Stahl, N. N., & Stahl, R. J. (1991), "We can agree after all! Achieving consensus for a critical thinking component of a gifted program using the Delphi Technique", *Roeper Review, 14*(2), 79-89.
22. Thyer, B. A. (1994), "Are theories for practice necessary? No!" *Journal of Social Work education,* 30(2), 148-151.

CHAPTER

5

Self-Help for Chronic Poor

*An Assessment of Micro-Finance as a Policy Choice**

—Dr. Chittaranjan Das Adhikary

ABSTRACT

One of the major challenges which keep us ceased is the large scale poverty that we inherited since the time of independence. The development efforts started immediately after World War II did affect our approach to the poverty question. This paper begins with critically examining the evolution of our approach towards poverty alleviation over the years through trickle down to **'Garibi Hatao'** *and beyond. Then it seeks to expose the gaps in our poverty measurement and the inadequacy of income poverty or calorie intake to capture all dimensions of the poor. In conclusion it argues that we need a shift in the poverty paradigm and consider the merit of microfinance as an alternative.*

Incredible India continues to grow. Latest triumph being the end of nuclear apartheid which is said to have profound consequence for the poor. In his Union Budget, 2008-09, Finance Minister, P. Chidambaram was upbeat on all sectoral development indices (the last time we were so) combining for an above eight per cent GDP growth. A recent United Nations annual report on millennium development goals also echoes similar lines. Riding on the better indicators like health and primary education, India has achieved an over 27 per cent decline in poverty and is well on track to meet the millennium development goals set for 2015 (*ToI*, Sept. 12). World Development Report 2000 estimates that a fifth of the world's people live on less than $ 1 a day,

* This is a revised version of the paper presented in a seminar on 'Eradicating Chronic Poverty: Policy Issues and Challenges', CPRC, IIPA & CSSS, Jawaharlal Nehru University, New Delhi, 2008.

and 44 per cent of them are in South Asia. Our own Planning Commission estimate gives also an impressive figure of development and poverty reduction. It shows that during the period between 1973-74 and 1999-2000, the incidence of poverty declined continuously from 54.9 per cent to supposedly 26 per cent. Poverty has been declining with increased economic growth and prosperity. According to 61st round National Sample Survey report 21.8 per cent (as given in Table 5.1) people are below poverty line in 2004-05.

Table 5.1: Poverty Ratio by Mixed Recall Period Method (Per cent)

Category	1999-2000	2004-05
Rural	27.1	21.8
Urban	23.6	21.7
All India	26.1	21.8

Source: Economic Survey, 2007-08.

All this have been possible because of a consistent focus on development and poverty since India became independent. At the time of independence the new government inherited a very poor economy with the bulk of people governed by anachronistic customs and earning a meager income by traditional techniques of production. Therefore attaining political independence, one of the important tasks on the agenda of national government has been the pursuit of economic growth as a deliberate objective. So initially, till the end of Fourth Plan period in particular, the overriding concern was economic growth and agricultural self sufficiency. Implicit in this economic growth was the concept of 'trickle down' (Hirschman, 1958). Trickle down approach advocates polarization as strategy of development and trickle down as strategy of distribution. Polarisation of development entails creating centres of economic activities using high technology on a pilot basis. This growth poles generates wealth. The wealth so generated gradually trickles down to the poor as increased income through the mechanism of market and commercial activities. However the emphasis on growth that assumes trickle down failed to reach the poor. The growth poles created by government led only to localized development. Major section of our population remained excluded from the development process. Probably it is the failure of economic growth to eradicate poverty (as high as 55% in 1973-74) which led to the change in approach to development expressed through *'Garibi Hatao'* slogan. Poverty comes to engulf the policy space especially after Fifth Plan by targeting the poor through different poverty alleviation programmes. It became a fashion with every new government coming to power, to declare new development schemes or merge and restructure some of the existing schemes. As in Tenth Plan period, a host of schemes pertaining to Self employment (e.g. IRDP, TRYSEM, DWCRA, Swarnajayanti Gram Swarozgar Yojana from 1st April 1999 etc.), Wage employment (NREP, RLEGP, JRY and JGSY from 1999, SGRY from Sept. 2001 etc.), Rural Housing Schemes, Social Security Schemes (NOAPS, NMBS, NFBS), Land Reform measures are now being implemented. Based on the strength of these schemes, the approach paper to the Tenth Plan expects a 15 per cent decline in poverty in 2011-12 in comparison to 1999-2000 (Tenth Five Year Plan, 2002-07).

WHO ARE THE POOR

The euphoria over growth fuelled by economic liberalization in the '90s camouflage larger issue of distributing the development benefits. Has the benefits of impressive growth reached the bottom of our society? There are two issues involved here. Has it reached the intended people, i.e. poor? And who are the people included and defined as 'poor'? The draft tenth five year plan was itself candid to tell us that most of the land reform measures have failed. It is now being replaced by 'liberalisation of land laws in order to promote large scale corporate farming' (Tenth Plan, *op. cit.*). The coverage of social assistance programmes is limited by financial constraints. The fund utilization by the field staff, namely DRDA, under SGSY is depressed by sluggish social mobilisation and group formation. Poverty reduction continues to be a challenge. Nearly one-fifth of our population are reeling under absolute poverty. 71.65 per cent are in six states of Bihar, Uttar Pradesh, West Bengal, Maharashtra, Madhya Pradesh and Orissa and 75 per cent are in rural areas (Mehta & Saha, 2001) (Table 5.2).

Table 5.2

State	% of India's Poor in 1999-2000	% of Population in 2001
Uttar Pradesh*	20.36	17
Bihar*	16.36	10.69
Madhya Pradesh*	11.47	7.91
Maharashtra	8.76	9.42
West Bengal	8.20	7.81
Orissa	6.50	3.57

Source: CPRC Working Paper 7.

Let us come to the next question of who are the poor? There is a general agreement that poverty is one of the greatest social evils in our country today. However there is wide difference of opinion on the definition of poor. It is said that poverty and beauty are easy to perceive but difficult to describe. The whole gamut of anti-poverty programmes in India is based on a normative understanding of absolute poverty christened as poverty line. The question of defining poverty was first raised by Indian Labour Conference in 1957. Based on this a working group was set up in 1962 by Planning Commission to deliberate on the question of quantifying poverty in terms of a minimum requirement (food and non-food) of individuals for healthy living. The money value of the minimum requirement was set as per capita consumption expenditure of Rs. 100 at 1960-61 prices for a family of 5 persons and was termed as poverty line. This definition was revamped based on the recommendations of the "Report of the Task Force on Projections of Minimum Needs and Effective Consumption Demand", 1979 and later modified on the basis of the recommendations of the "Report of the Expert Group on Estimation of Proportion and Number of Poor", 1993. Both the Task Force and the Expert Group were set up by the Planning Commission, Government of India. Based on the age-sex specific calorie requirement recommended by 'Nutrition Expert Group' (1968), the task force defined the poverty line as per capita consumption expenditure level, which meets the average per capita daily calorie requirement of 2400 kcal per capita per day in rural areas and 2100 kcal per capita per day in urban areas along with a minimum of non-food expenditure. This calorie requirement norm was converted to its monetary equivalent using 28th round NSS consumption expenditure survey at a per capita monthly expenditure of Rs. 59.15 in rural areas and Rs. 73.51 per month at 1977-78 prices. The 1993 Expert Group constituted by the Planning Commission to redefine the poverty line, made two contributions in recommending, among other things, state specific poverty lines against a national poverty line separately for rural and urban areas and use of state specific Consumer Price Index for agricultural labourers for estimating and updating rural poverty line and Consumer Price Index for industrial workers for estimating and updating urban poverty line. The expert group also recommended for a fixed consumption basket consisting of food, fuel and light, housing and footwear and miscellaneous for survey of consumption expenditure. Government of India has since 1997 used this expert group methodology for estimating poverty (Sharma, 2004). The basic approach to defining the poor is to know his level of consumption expenditure, as income data is hard to arrive at, that can ensure required calorie intake, through uniform or mixed recall period in different rounds of national sample surveys the findings of which are anchored to state price indices. Since 1962 a poor has come to be defined by his inability to get a national minimum of food (including food not fit for consumption but with some calorie value) or corresponding consumption expenditure level.

Poverty estimates based on certain level of consumption expenditure, a proxy for income, has been questioned more often recently for more than one reason. It relies on a vary narrow base to separate the poor from the non-poor, a passport to public provisioning. Poverty line, as it has become famous, gives only a measure of absolute poverty in terms of bare minimum standard of life. It gives no idea of relative distribution of income. High consumption expenditure tells very little about somebody's source of income. Income earned through immoral ways is not accounted for. Thus a prostitute who is engaged in this highly paid but morally degrading profession is not entitled, by virtue of her size of income, to benefits from public provisioning efforts. Another problem which is inherent in fixing a poverty line is that it does not reflect the depth of poverty. As such estimates do not take into account the distance from the poverty line at which a poor is located. All the poor do not make for a homogeneous group. There are people at different levels of poverty, the severe and chronically poor for example, who have different priorities and demands different development strategy. Estimates of poverty based on income are misleading for the simple reason that income is itself a derived variable which depends on ownership and exchange. But no less importantly, it is also the case that many essential commodities are not bought and sold in the market in the usual way, and conventional estimates of real income may not give us a good idea of the command over a number of inputs which can play a crucial role in the removal of poverty, such as educational services, health care, clean water, or protection from infectious epidemics. Income is a rather dubious indicator of the opportunity of being well nourished and having nutrition related capabilities (Sen and Dreze, 1989). Coming to the calorie intake norms which take the form of relating income deficiency to dietary deficiency has been severely criticized. Critics have emphasized the importance of interpersonal variation as well as adaptive adjustments influencing the relationship between food intake and nutritional status. There is no reference to protein deficiency which is also a cause in malnutrition especially among children. Scholars have argued that it is impossible to have a single estimation of minimum calorie requirement for it depends on socio-cultural norms and personal habits that can be adjusted depending on circumstances (Sukhtame, 1977; Minahs, 1974. Dietary habits are also subject to distortion by marketing propaganda resulting in new preferences and spending on food and non-food items are dependent on market situation (Mehta & Venkataraman, 2000; Pattanaik, 2006).

All this add up to describe the inadequacy of income poverty or the calorie norm to capture the different dimensions of poverty. Poverty manifests itself in land relations, ill health, discrimination, ignorance, violence and so many things (Robb, 1999; Narayan et al., 2000). We should include these dimensions in our estimation of poverty. There is a need to take a multi-dimension index approach like HDI or HPI in measuring poverty. Poverty has to be seen as a severe failure of basic capabilities that are important to a persons well being. If a person does not have the capability of avoiding preventable mortality, unnecessary morbidity or escapable under-nourishment, then it would certainly be agreed that the person is deprived in a significant way. Deprivation is best seen in terms of the failure of certain basic functioning rather than in terms of variables such as income or calorie intake which should be seen as means and not as ends in themselves.

SELF-HELP FOR THE CHRONIC POOR

The official discourse on poverty might still be anchored to the idea of a poverty line. Poverty studies are surely inching towards a paradigm shift with its emphasis on multiple dimensions of deprivations suffered by the poor. This has also necessitated a shift in the approach to fighting poverty. Self Help has become a popular slogan in the development literature as a response to the shift in anti-poverty approach. Some of the government anti-poverty programmes has turned towards 'social mobilisation in groups' in a big way. Recently a Microfinance (Regulation and Development) Bill has been passed in 2007. It rests on the premise that poor either have land or labour or both. Self-help will step in with small capital to help them escape poverty.

Self-help Groups are informal associations of up to twenty women who meet regularly, usually once a month, to save small amounts typically Rs. 10 to Rs. 50 a month. While they are formed with the encouragement of NGOs and other SHPAS, they are expected to select their own members, are therefore sometimes called affinity groups. After saving regularly for a minimum of six months and using the funds to lend small amounts to each other for interest, which is ploughed back into group funds, and satisfactorily maintaining prescribed records and accounts, they become eligible to be linked by the local bank branch under a NABARD sponsored programme called the SHG Bank Linkage Programme (SLBP). Lending to groups, whatever they are called, entails joint and several liability, which is more moral than legally enforceable, and is exercised through peer group pressure and the fear of being denied future loans. Village women take the oath, they are administered when becoming members, extremely seriously. Thus the peer group pressure among the members along with the mutual trust they share, is being used as social collateral in repaying the loans. From the banks point of view, it leads to fulfilment of social goals (like reaching out the poor) and achieving operational efficiency by externalizing part of their transaction cost, as some of the banking responsibilities regarding loan appraisal, follow up, recovering etc. (Dasgupta, 2001). From the SHG members viewpoint, they now have access to credit, hitherto not available, without paperwork, collateral, identity certificate or even traveling anywhere. The very concept of microfinance is based on the assumption that poor have the ability to escape poverty if they are given access to credit at their doorstep. Micro-finance by making available small loans, enable the poor to take up income generating activities and improve living standards. Thus it will lead to creation of employment, income generation, poverty alleviation, empowerment and inclusion of the unbanked poor in the development process.

Many Indian studies (Nenduraman et al., 2001; Das, 2003; Singh, 2001; Mishra & Hossain, 2001; Nair, 2995; Wanchoo, 2007; NABARD, 1997) have reported positive impact of micro-credit programmes. All these studies point to the fact micro-finance initiatives help poor households in meeting their basic needs and protecting them from risk, promote entrepreneurship, bring gender equality and empowerment to rural women, and the longer the association with self-help groups, the clearer the positive influence of micro-finance. Another important aspect is that of decrease in dependence on moneylenders, to the extent of 15 per cent for self-help group members. Studies found that 51 per cent members closed their debit with moneylenders with SHG loan. Though majority of SHG loans are for meeting consumption needs, there is evidence of SHG loans being increasingly used for Health, education and housing. In Tamilnadu it was found that nearly 14 per cent loan had been used for housing purpose. In Andhra Pradesh, it was found that nearly 6 per cent members used their loan for children's education. In Tamilnadu nearly 74 per cent SHG members have invested their loans in creating various assets like land, livestock, and household durables after joining SHGs. On the contrary, there are also studies which have found that the economic impact of SHGs is limited and it rather enables the members to cope with situations rather than deal with them. The economic orientation is more protectional than promotional.

It is argued that women are more likely to be left out of access to credit. Even cooperatives refuse women membership if their husband happens to be a member. Micro-credit programmes are therefore predominantly targeted at women (90% SHGs are women SHGs). It is assumed, giving small loans to women through micro-credit, will lead to enhancement of their capacities as economic agents, meet their basic needs and empower them. Studies have also concluded that members of women SHGs emerge as more confident, financially more secure, more in control of their lives and are in a stronger position vis-à-vis their family members. The personal abilities, ownership of assets, development of skills, ability to decide about self and political participation are likely to improve if the women members continue to participate for a longer period.

A large study conducted by (EDA and APMAS, 2006) EDA Rural Systems and Andhra Pradesh Mahila Abhivridhi Society titled 'Self Help groups in

India—A study of lights and Shades' touches upon the development impact of micro-finance. The study combined a survey research method with a search for stories and found that 66 per cent SHGs are single caste SHGs and 55 per cent of all group members are from SC and ST category. With regard to empowerment and political participation, the study found an increase in political engagement and an encouraging trend of community participation. Another study, titled 'Do self groups provide value for money?' emphasized equity and democratic content of SHGs and found that empowerment benefits, in terms of increase in income, is found among 25 per cent of members. Another study (APMAS, 2005) sheds lights on the dynamics of ageing and provides descriptive information on various dimensions of micro-finance pertaining to cost of securing linkage, timely loan and other procedural problems faced by the group and the bankers (Adhikary, 2006; Ghate, 2007; Sujatha, 2007).

My own field survey in Jamalpur block of Mirzapur district, Uttar Pradesh corroborates many of the findings about self-help activites. Data from the field diary of investigators studying 10 SHGs, funded by nationalised banks under SGSY scheme from the block, suggest that the groups are female groups. There is evidence of entrepreneurial buoyancy among the poor SHG members. Income data are not very clear. The confidence level of the members has gone up. SHG movement is more popular among women despite Mirzapur being one of the most backward and conservative district.

Sceptics point that self-help groups operate on principles of risk and cost minimization and profit maximisation. Many contend that it does not reach the poorest of the poor as they are unable to save from their limited resources and they are also not the preferred clients of micro-credit programmes as they have nothing to return due to their poor entrepreneurial skill. No one would team up with them. The apprehensions seem misplaced given the compatibility that severely poor and self-help share.

- Severely poor are more frequently from those groups who are engaged in insecure work environment, caught in adverse exchange relations and work as casual labourers in the unorganised sector. Their condition of being untouchables for doing business is more a cliché than real. No one want to team up with them not because that they are poor but because they have low social and political capital. Being unorganised they need organisation in the most. Self-help builds up their social capital base by organising them into affinity groups. Social capital is a cause as well as consequence of self-help.
- The gender dimensions in chronic poverty are also taken care of as majority of the SHGs are women groups. Normally a woman in chronic poverty is more likely suffer deprivations longer than man because

of her gender. Her gender itself turns out to be strength in self-help activities. Self-help operations are built upon economic prudence of all women group members.

- Self-help needs to be promoted more among the poorest of the poor because they are, in all likelihood, the one to remain excluded from institutional finance. The self-help operations and the financial institutions need to reorient the emerging micro-finance market to the advantage of these chronic poor.
- It has been found that severely poor have more survival/ consumption needs as opposed to long-term needs for asset creation and accumulation. Self-help experience attests to the fact that credit use from self-help groups is skewed in favour of consumption like meeting marriage expenses, seeing off a lean agricultural season or coping with exogenous shocks. There is no contradiction in self-help for the poor.
- Chronic poor gets training and skills through SHGs. Being illiterate and unaware self-help participation improves his skill, strengthen their capacity to deal with development dealers, escape indebtedness and bring about all round development.
- Chronic poverty also has a structural dimension. Some caste and/or minority groups especially SCs, STs, OBCs, linguistic minority groups etc. are consistently severely poor. Caste and other identities that causes disability for the chronic poor becomes organising principle of self-help groups and these social resources are used to maintain and expand social capital base.
- One of the principal causes of chronic poverty remains landlessness. Land redistribution has been stuck in the blame game and least likely to succeed. Income transfer directly to the poorest of the poor is hard to come by because of financial constraints and lack of political commitment. Banks have operational constraints in reaching the bottom. The poor and the chronic poor in particular stand to gain from self-help prescription in this situation. It will enable him to productively use his labour with the micro money available from the SHG and scale up his protection against multi-dimensional deprivations.

In conclusion it can be said that measurement of poverty and measures to remove poverty both warrants a re-examination. A broad-based understanding of poverty enable us to appreciate the relevance of self-help for the poor and chronic poor.

REFERENCES

1. *The Times of India*, Friday, September 12, 2008.
2. *Economic Survey, 2007-08*, Ministry of Finance, Government of India, available at http://indiabudget.nic.in.
3. Hirschman, A O (1958), *The Strategy of Economic Development*, Yale University Press, New Haven.
4. *Draft Tenth Five Year Plan*, 2002-07, Planning Commission, Government of India.
5. Mehta A. and Saha A. (2001), *Chronic Poverty in India—an overview study*, Chronic Poverty Research Centre working paper 7, New Delhi.
6. Sharma S. (2004), *Poverty Estimates in India—Some Key Issues*, ERD Working Paper 51, Economics and Research Department, Asian Development Bank, Philippines, available at *http://www.adb.org/Documents/ERD/Working_Papers/wp051.pdf.*
7. Sen A. and Dreze J. (1989), *Hunger and Public Action*, Clarendon, Oxford.
8. Sukhtame, P.V. (1977), "Incidence of Under nutrition", *Indian Journal of Agricultural Economics,* July-September.
9. Minahs B. S. (1974), *Planning and the Poor*, S Chand, New Delhi.
10. Mehta J. and Venkataraman (2000), "Poverty Statistics—Bermicide's Feast", *Economic and Political Weekly,* Vol. 35, July 1.
11. Pattanaik U. (2006), *Poverty and Neo-liberalism in India*, Bahadur Kale Memorial Lecture delivered at Gokhale Insitute of Politics and Economics, Pune, February, 03.
12. Robb, C. (1999), *Can the Poor Influence Poverty? Participatory Poverty Assessments in the Developing World,* The World Bank, Directions in Development Series, Washington D.C.
13. Narayan D., Chambers R., Shah M., and Petesch P. (2000), *Voices of the Poor: Crying Out for Change*, Oxford University Press, New York.
14. Dasgupta R. (2001), "Working and impact of rural Self-Help Groups and other forms of micro-financing", *Indian Journal of Agricultural Economics*, Vol. 56, No. 3, July-September.
15. Nedumaran S., Palanisamy K. and Swaminathan K.P. (2001), "Performance and impact of SHGs in Tamilnadu", *Indian Journal of Agricultural Economics*, Vol. 56, No. 3.
16. Das, S. (2003), "Self Help Groups and Micro credit—Synergic Integration", *Kurukshetra*, Vol. 50, No. 10, pp. 25-27.
17. Singh D.K. (2001), "Impact of Self-help groups on the economy of marginalised farmers of Kanpur Dehat district of Uttar Pradesh, *"Journal of Agricultural Economics*, July 1.
18. Mishra S. N. & Hossain M. M. (2001), "A Study on the working and impact of Dharmadevi Mahila Mandal"—A rural Self-help group in Kalahandi District of Orissa, *Journal of Agricultural Economics*, July 1.

19. Nair A. (2005), *Sustainabillity of Self-help groups in India: Would Federating Help?*, World Bank Policy Research Working Paper 3516.

20. Annual Reports, NABARD, 1997 available at *http://www.nabard.org/fileupload/Annual Reports Display.aspx.*

21. Rajat Wanchoo, 2007, *Microfinance in India—The changing face of micro-credit schemes,* MPRA Paper No. 3675, July 2007 available at *http://mpra.ub.uni-muenchen.de/3675/1/MPRA_paper_3675.pdf.*

22. Adhikary C. D. (2006), "Banking with the Poor: A Case study of Self-Help Groups in Orissa" in Sahoo et al (Ed.), *Trends in Sociology- Education, Development and Diaspora*, Abhijit Publication, New Delhi.

23. Ghate P. (2007), *Indian Microfinance—The Challenges of Rapid Growth*, Sage, New Delhi.

24. Sujatha B. (2007), *Financial Inclusion—Concepts and Strategies*, ICFAI University Press, Hyderabad.

CHAPTER

6

Rural Development Planning
Theoretical Reflections

—Dr. Manish Dwivedi

ABSTRACT

The present study is a critical review/appraisal of strategy, and based on it programmes for rural development as reflected in post-independence India's planning and development experience. The plan document and the related official surveys and report. The present author has consulted a few other relevant studies for the purpose of developing the critique. The appraisal is in the nature of a theoretical and methodological critique of the strategy and programmes of rural development. This follows from the basic premise that a strategy essentially presupposes a "theory". The inter-relationship between theory, strategy and programmatic action/ implementation through complex, imply an integral relationship. A critical appraisal of a policy programme and implementation in isolation or de-linked from the strategy and its contextual dependence on theory, is not only not likely to be illuminating but oftentimes misleading. The basic methodological approach of the critique in the present study here, is to lay bare the "Internal" links between theory, strategy and programmatic action.

The appraisal is in the nature of a theoretical and methodological critique of the strategy and programmes of rural development. This follows from the basis premise that a strategy essentially presupposes a "theory". The inter-relationship between Theory, Strategy and Programmatic action / implementation through complex, imply an integral relationship. A critical appraisal of a policy programme and implementation in isolation or delinked from the strategy and its contextual dependence on theory, is not only not likely to be illuminating but oftentimes misleading. The basic methodological approach of the critique in the present study hence, is to lay bare the 'internal' links between theory, strategy and programmatic action.

What is attempted, however, is not so much a philosophic, methodological critique, but to indicatively point out the theoretical basis of a strategy, but focus essentially on the strategy-policy programme linkage.

In the context of development debate in India, especially with reference to the Five Year Plans, and their performance, the present study, somewhat schematically identifies three strategies or perspectives of development:

(a) Based on growth

(b) Combining growth with poverty removal

(c) Reconciling growth with distributive justice,

These strategies are inter-related. The shift from one to the other no way implied less emphasis on growth, but the issue of poverty and inequality became for too serious and embarrassing. The "formal" commitment to "socialism" and "welfareism" necessitated a shift in emphasis.

(a) The strategy of development implicit in the First Five Year Plan is based on growth, the first Plan did not have an overt strategy, it can be shown that the theory of growth implicit in the Plan is aversion of "Harrod Demar type of post-Keynesian growth model......." The Plan recommended: ".......this country should set itself to double the per capita national income within the space of about a generation"

(b) A shift in perspective of development, from growth to combining growth with poverty removal, was signalled in the early sixties, by now a famous document prepared by the Perspective Derision of the Planning Commission in 1962.

That we were poor was known, but the degree and intensity of poverty in statistical terms that the Note revealed was something that struck at the complacency of development planners. Growth was not enough, how can we conceive of development in terms of increase in GNP, with so much of poverty around? We must combine growth with antipoverty measures.

But, how do we do it? Do we resort to strategies for redistribution of income? The document says, No. What is the way out? We rely on growth. The strategy of growth was justified on the hypothesis:

> "... the income of the poorest segments as a result in more or less the same proportion as a total income in any county. The attainment of a specified level of minimum income within a given period then becomes purely a function of the rate of development."

The Note thus rules out any change in property relation, or any major structural change. The strategy for raising the levels of living of the poor relied in programmatic terms on stepping up investment and redistributing consumer expenditure.

The 1962 Note is supposed to have provided a new perspective of development: to guarantee a minimum level of living to all citizens by a set target date. But the Note "was quietly shelved", the new perspective strategy reappeared again under the meteoric *"garibi hatao"* is one of the basic documents in the formulation of the Fifth Five Year Plan 1972.

(c) Development strategy based on combining growth with poverty removal enunciated by the 1962 Note, already implied the principle of reconciling growth with distributive justice. But the later acquired currency in Indian Politics and Planning only in the early seventies.

The immediate impetus and provocation for the acceptance of the "new" thinking of the World Bank from one of its officials, Mahboob-Ul-Huq, Senior Advisor to the Economics Department of the Bank, and formerly Chief Economist of the Pakistan Planning Commission. What "disturbed" the World Bank Expert was the paradox as he perceived it, of fairly respectable growth rates in the poor countries of the world in 1960s with continuing mass poverty. In India, too the new idiom gained currency. The antipoverty thrust of the development planning of the early sixties forgotten for a decade was restored. This is expressed in the document "Towards an Approach to the Firth Plan". Henceforth, we began to talk of reconciling growth with distributive justice. The question was raised: Can they reconciled? The Approach document said: "... the Indian economy has reached a stage where larger availability of resources make it possible to launch a direct attack on unemployment and poverty, and also assure adequate growth." Social justice implied reduction of inequalities. Inequality was understood in terms of inequality of income, while underdevelopment was understood in terms of inadequate growth, rather than a consequence of social inequality.

To sum up: the development strategy based on the principle of reconciling growth with distributive justice, which critically influences development planning, policy and programmes since the Firth Five year Plan, period, is one that assumes that distributive can be secured without altering property relations. Development here is conceived essentially in terms of warfare reformism.

What is the theoretical basis of the strategy/perspective of development in each case? This is an extremely complex and vast issue. An indication as to the sort of direction in terms of which the answer may be sought, may however be indicated here.

What is the theoretical basis of the strategy/perspective in each case? It is provided by the tradition of the Anglo-American economics of the supply and demand theories, the Keynesian and the neo-classical economics and institutionalism. Derived from this broad tradition, is the development of economics, growth models, etc. These theories are not neutral: they represent the ideology of competitive and advanced capitalism. As ideology, the value the theories seek to rationalize and operationalise are profit maximization and accumulation of capital through privatisation. One objective of the early marginalist tradition was negative: an alternative economic theory that would "take care" of the theories of Ricardo and Marx: to explain away the conflicting interests between the wage earners and the capitalists rationalize profits on the plea of reward for the "abstinence" on the part of the capitalists and to do away altogether with the notion of exploitation through the doctrine of "the symmetrical role of capitalists and wage earners in production by depicting the services of both as analogous in being essential prerequisites for production to proceed." Finally, poverty, unemployment and inflation, were either explained away, or it was argued, that they could be dealt with, without altering the existing structure of property relations.

Any appraisal of the perspectives of development and the related strategy, need to reckon with the ideological biases of the theory—we need to go to the roods, to grasp and appraise, as to where the trouble lay in so far as the development strategies have failed.

It has been said often by the Indian economists and the planners that the western models (growth models, development theories etc.) do not suit our conditions—conditions of underdevelopment. Thus, Mahalanobis said in 1961 that,

> "the accepted economic theory in the capitalist countries does not help the idea of economic planning. Unfortunately, no economic theory is at present available to guide our thinking on this matter. Therefore, it seems urgently necessary to start serials and systematic studies to build up a general conceptual framework to handle questions of economic development, and particularly to formulate a programme of action to assist the underdeveloped countries."

But nevertheless, did we not continue to depend on the wisdom of the Anglo-American experience? It would not be simplistic to say, that, we might have made modifications here and there, complained about Keynesianism which do not apply to un-underdeveloped economy such as ours.

What development strategy inspired our planning, and its performance has never been and cannot be a technical, analytical issue, but one crucially dependent on power. Who decides what soot of development is envisaged? Who influences decision making in these matters?

A clue to an answer to this question may be sought through an illustration. This is with reference to the First Five Year Plan. It is not for anything, that the late G.D. Birla, whole-heartedly approved the philosophy of development embodies in the plan:

> "The most important economic event for this country which took place last year in India's Five Year Plan. I welcome the plan because it is a document which gives a concrete shape to the earnestness of the government to grapple with the problem of Indian poverty... I am glad the government have confined their task to the undertaking of a few economic programmes of basic and public character... Excepting the branches of economic activity, agriculture, irrigation and transport, reserved by the Government for its own work, it has left the entire field of economic enterprise to private effort. And this is a right thing they have done... The days of criticism should now come to an end. Mutual recriminations should now be replaced by mutual understanding and mutual cooperation ... Those who talk of lack of capital in India seen to be insufficiently aware how modern financial technique coupled with financial discipline can work wonders."

The ideology bias built into the economic philosophy of Anglo-American tradition is that of promotion and cultivation of capitalism. Surely, capitalists and monopolists in this country endorse the expression of this trend in our plans. They influence the making of the plans in terms of objectives that would promote the cause of capitalist development itself. The exports, the technicians and the academic expert planners do, what they are "required" to do!

Thus, the theory, methodology and strategy of development we are experimenting in the post-independence India, is experimenting in the capitalist development, notwithstanding the rhetoric of "socialism" and "Socialistic Pattern" suited to the need of the country.

The Report of the National Commission of Agriculture brings this out, though implicitly:

> "From the beginning of the planning era, welfare of the society through improvement in living standards of the people has been the main objectives of development. Successive five year plans have emphasized development policies in this respect. During the First Five Year Plan, the Community Development Programme was taken up on the basic premise that the overall development of rural India could be brought about only with the effective participation and, to the extent possible, the initiative of the people backed by technical and other services necessary for securing the best from such recognized that the benefits of economic development must 'accrue more and more to the relatively less privileged classes of the society. The Third Plan also emphasized the need for a sizeable increase in national income so as to raise the levels of living in the country and reduce inequalities in income and wealth. In all these plans, the accent

was on overall growth, the programmes were not specifically designed for the removal of poverty. Due to a greater awareness of the very low levels of consumption of the poor there was recognition in the Fourth Plan, of income distribution. Separate schemes were initiated for the development of backward areas and the weaker sections. In the Fifth Plan removal of poverty has become a primary consideration for formulating programmes."

In respect of planning strategy and programme, Indian approach to rural development has been influenced by the United Nations, the World Bank (IBRD), and International Labour Organization. Hence, the UN perspectives on rural development might be relevant to delineate. From the point of view of political economy, the UN connection, and its influence, might be useful to trace. It might be stated, that quite a good may rural development prefects in India are funded especially by the World Bank.

What is attempted in this essay is a quick critical survey of some of the rural development programmes in post-independence India with reference to the aims (growth or growth with distributional or equity objectives), the biases of the programme and assessment. This appraisal includes identifying content-wise policy formulations at the level of the World Bank and its role, policy formulations as reflected in official documents identifying the political economic reasons/compulsions that led to the initiatives, and a conceptual and methodological critique of the assumptions—explicit or implicit—underlying development objectives in the specific context of the programme. The programme selected for appraisal are: Grow More Food Campaign, Community Development, IADP, Minimum Needs Programme, Employment, IRDP, Land Reforms, and the use of the New Agrarian Technology (HYV).

A brief critical review of the official policy in respect of institutional support to rural development is attempted. These include: content analysis to policy implications in respect of Panchayati Raj, Co-operative Movement and People's Participation.

Implicit in the critical appraisal of the rural development programmes, is the issue of power/production relations. The development planning needs to be viewed in the totality of overall politico-economic process.

An attempt is made to contextualise the issue of power relations in terms of what the social scientists themselves are saying. The politics of rural development sketched in this study attempts to indicate the sort of concerns reflected in a few recent critical studies. The foreign advisers to the Indian government have played a central role in the shopping of the strategy of development that is giving a unified pattern to the dynamics of Indian agriculture in all its aspects. They have exerted a considerable influence in shopping India's agricultural policy ever since the first days of economic planning in India.

"Of course, no strategy could have been accepted actually, if it had not been supported by powerful domestic interest. The strategy has received increasing support from the rich farmers as well as by industrial entrepreneurs, the interests of both of whom are served by the strategy. Who are these foreign advisors? The role of foreign agencies including the United Nations bodies like the IBRD, FAO, ILO and the World Bank may also now be concretized and elaborated."

The first and perhaps a major step in rural development was taken by India, when it announced the launching of the Community Development Programme. From the beginning, it was "... related to and supported in part by most of the other projects under Indo-American Technical Co-operation Programme" which laid down the following conditions: The fertilizers acquired and distributed in accordance with the "Project for Acquisition and Distribution of Fertilizers" Similarly the iron and steel needed for farm implements and tools would be acquired and distributed in accordance with the "Project for the Acquistion and Distribution of Iron and Steel for Agricultural Purpose." The tube-wells to be constructed in the project areas would be allocated from the "Project for Ground Water Irrigation". The training of village local workers as project supervisors would be carried out under the "Village Workers Training Programme".

There was almost no sphere of activity under the Community Development Programme, which was not dependent on American assistance. The terms of the Indo-American Technical Co-operation Agreement reveals its character:

"... the Director appointed by the USA and his staff shall be required as part of the diplomatic mission of the Government of the USA and shall share fully in the privileges and immunities including immunity from suits in the courts of India..."

Thus the first of our major rural development programme was funded, directed Gandhian economist J.C. Kumarappa was forthright we are now to be led by the American, he implied that neoculturalism was now to rule us:

"The Indo-US Technical Co-operation Agreement signed by our Prime Minister and the US Ambassador, is unworthy of any self respecting independent country as it confers diplomatic immunity to private citizens working in our county. This helps to create foreign pockets in our land. While the USA contributes only two annas in the rupee, it is given a controlling voice in the affairs of Community Projects.

"The whole scheme reflects an amazing lack of confidence on the part of the Prime Minister in the ability of his colleagues that he should bow so low to invite foreigners to rebuild our countryside...

"The scheme seems to bypass the fundamental rural question, land reform. Hence, its is futile...

"There is a danger falling prey to the American bloc. So those of us who are committed to non-violence cannot be associated with the scheme.

"Generally my fear is this is the thin end of the era of American Financial Imperialism striving to fill in the vacuum crested by an inefficient administration in the wake of departure of British Political imperialism..."

The trends in rural development policy and programme as formulated by the World Bank (IBRD) (also FAO, ILO) for illustrative purposes may now be indicate:

While in the early 1950s and 1960s, the main theme of development efforts was the transfer of western type technology focused on providing infrastructure for Agricultural production, by the mid-1960s interest shifted gradually to agricultural development as such.

A World Bank paper under Rural Development series says:

"In the early years of Bank Operations, the focus was on providing adequate infrastructure for increasing agricultural production. In the early 1960s the approach to agricultural development was widened to include the provision of rural credit and on farm inputs. Problems of tenure were seen to have an indirect bearing on production, mainly because they influenced on farm investment decisions and determined the efficiency of resource use, especially irrigation water."

The orientation then shifted to the new agricultural technology inaugurating the era of "green revolution". Around 1965, the international opinion was forecasting economic catastrophe in the third world. The new technology has effected a breakthrough. The varieties of wheat and rice which were developed at that time, were looked upon as "the solution to the problems of malnutrition". They quickly became famous throughout the world, "A vast technological transfer was organized to Southern and South East Asia."

Agricultural productivity increased as result of the use of new technology, but so also was poverty. Various studies by United Nations Research Institute for Social Development (UNRISD) and by the International Labour Organization (ILO) documented conditions of worsening distribution of income and the declining real income of rural poor. A characteristic of all the countries under study was the highly skewed distribution of landownership.

An agricultural sector paper of 1972 said:

"In developing countries, land presents a much higher proportion of total wealth... And in egalitarian patterns of landownership are a major sources of income inequality. Furthermore, the owners of land usually possess political and economic power which can be exercised in ways that harms the interests of the bulk of rural poor."

The Nairobi speech by the President of the World Bank, McNamara in

1977, now signalled a shift in policy on rural development. The policy was one of "poverty removal", surely this was to be at the expense of growth.

The "discovery" was made that past development efforts had not trickled down to the rural poor, the poor need to be reached directly for delivery of benefits.

The "poverty line" came into prominence, and so emerged the concept of providing minimum needs for alleviation of poverty. The strategy led to the formulation of directed distribution programmes for providing minimum food, housing, health care, etc.

In 1975, the International Bank of Rural Development announced its concept of rural development as a strategy to improve the lot of the rural poor. What has followed in India and elsewhere in the concerned third world is perhaps a mere reiteration of this view, hence as a "basis" formulation we quote IBRD's views at some length.

"The central concept of rural development presented by sustained increases in the productivity and incomes of low-income rural workers and households." Understanding rural development conceptualization, the related strategy and based on it the praxis-considerations, both economic and political which are intrinsically related are indispensable. It is the prejudice of the neo-classical tradition that considers the "political" as externalities to the economic system. The issue of power and its use is explained away by assuming that, "ownership patterns" of resources do not affect the use of the services of resources. Secondly, in what is considered to be the norm in liberal theory, the use of resources is also not governed by power.

REFERENCES

1. Bagchi, Amiya Kumar, *The Political Economy of Under-development*, Combridge University Press, 1982.
2. Bradhan, Pranab, "Greem Revolution And Agricultural Laborers", EPW, Vol. (Nos.29-31) Bombay, July 1970, pp. 1230-1246.
3. Bardhan, Pranab, "On the Minimum Level of Living and the Rural Poor: Further Note", *Indian Economic Review*, Vol. (No. 1) 1970.
4. Bose, A. N. "Regional Planning for the Era of Transition from Poverty", *Indian Journal of Regional Science*, Vol. VI, No. 2, 1974.
5. Dandekar, V.M. and Rath, N. "Poverty in India" *EPW*, Vol. VI (Nos. 1 & 2), 1971.
6. Friedman, Milton, *Capitalism and Freedom*, University of Chicago Press (Phoenix Edition), 1963.
7. Joshi, P.C., *Land Reforms in India*, Institute of Economic Growth, Delhi, 1975.
8. Kurien, D.T., *Poverty, Planning and Social Transformation*, Allied, 1978.
9. McNamara, R.S., *Address to the Board of Governors*, World Bank, Nairobi, 1977.
10. Myrdal, Gunnar, "Growth of Social Justice" in the spirit of India, Vol. II Smt. Indira Gandhi Abhinandan Granth, 1975.

CHAPTER

7

Towards Reform of Land Acquisition Framework in India

—Dr. Anoop Kumar Singh

ABSTRACT

In India's recent history of infrastructure growth, there are many instances in which projects have faced delays and interruptions owing to disputes over land acquisition. Examples of Nandigram and Singur in West Bengal, the Reliance Special Economic Zone (SEZ) in Raigad, Maharashtra and the Bhushan Steel Plant in Jharkhand ,Yamuna and Ganga Expressways in U.P. are recent examples in this regard. One key factor that contributes to these problems is the absence of effective communication between promoters and affected communities, resulting from little or no community involvement in the acquisition process. Very often, promoters provides only promises to community involvement by holding a few inconsequential community consultations – just to prove that the community of project affected persons (PAPs) has been taken on-board. This leads to mistrust among PAPs, which is reinforced when the promoters fail to honour their commitments relating to rehabilitation and resettlement. In addition to the basic land acquisition law special enactments related to land acquisition exist in many states, which separately empower the relevant authorities to acquire land for designated purposes. An examination of the implication of these legislations indicates a possible scope for rationalisation of the multiple legislations. Social Impact Assessment (SIA) and Environmental Impact Assessment (EIA) are key component for establishing and sustainability of any project.

Introduction

India's geographical area is about 329 million hectares with an average population density of 325 persons per square kilometer (Census, 2001). However, with population growth, per capita land availability declined from 0.89 ha in 1951 to 0.3 ha by 2001, and per capita agriculture land declined from 0.48 ha in 1951 to 0.14 ha by 2001. With a projected population of 1581 million by 2050 (Visaria and Visaria, 1996). With rise in population density and demand for new development projects, land acquisition proposals for private or public use are likely to witness on increasingly stronger and wider resistance than before, because not only more land is being demanded, but also more people have to be displaced for the same size land.

Land, where supply is limited by its very nature, has been subject to rising and competing demands over the years. The economy and society have not been able to cope with relative increasing scarcity of land because of two interrelated reasons: First, a large part of land mass is held by households who earn their livelihood from land. This means that if incremental demand were to be met, invariably some household will have to give up land. Second, generally speaking, the bulk of the people dependent on land (through agriculture and related activities) do not have the skills to survive without land; nor are there enough job opportunities to absorb unskilled labour. So the transition to an industrial on service economy from an agrarian economy is not easy for most people. This is in fact, one of the main reason why there is growing social discontent relating to land acquisition. Add to that poor compensation and undervalued market price of land and therein lies the recipe of many a dispute by the affected population, thereby impacting land acquisition.

Uncertainties, risks and delays resulting from protest and resistance on the part of people displaced due to land acquisition have become one of the most important bottlenecks for investment, especially in the infrastructure sector, as evidenced by the recent spate of protests in Bengal, Orissa, Kerala, UP and Maharashtra. Land acquisition and rehabilitation have been assures around which much population mobilization and protest against the state have taken place in India and continue to do so.

These protests reflect not only equity concerns (of project affected people) but also ecological concerns) several environmental protests that have had a mass following had their roots in the problems of land acquisition that sought to change the concept of land use. Popular concerns for both equity and ecology stemming from land acquisition and the consequent delays, cost over runs, and risks have increasingly impacted the viability of several projects (Morris and Pandey, 2009).

There have been a tendency in recent year by most project promoters to acquire land by using eminent domain powers of the state, rather than market negotiations. Typically, people whose lands and habitation are acquired by the state without their consent deeply aggrieved and their protest, while ineffective, have regulated in much social loss and evoked the sympathy of the civil society, which now views all development projects with suspicion. Such anti-development attitudes have taken deep roots. Development today is seen as being anti-poor in a direct, easily recognized sort of way.

Land acquisitions, whether for state sponsored development or for private business projects have always faced opposition. The reasons for opposition have become more broad-based over the years. Our analysis of land acquisition has identified three distinct reasons for opposition, namely environmental concerns, social well-being concerns and benefit sharing concerns.

Political Economy of Land Acquisition

The genesis of land acquisition in India lies in the Bengal Regulation Act (I) of 1824, inacted to promote British commercial interest in the country. This was replaced by the Act (I) of 1850, by which the provision for land acquisition was extended to Calcultta Town, so that land needed for public works could be obtained without any legal problems. By 1857, various acts consolidated as Act IV was applicable to the whole of British India. Finally, the Land Acquisition Act of March 1894 replaced all previous laws relating to land acquisition.

The concerns of the colonial legislation were quite evident. The state had to be enabled to acquire land swiftly while minimizing compensation payment, seen as a drain on the state exchequer. The imperial instance was evident in one simple fact: public purpose, was neither defined nor elaborated by the law: It was sufficient for the state to declare it to be so.

The end of colonial rule in 1947 and the Republican Constitution of India 1950 did not bring about any significant change in land acquisition law. The Constitution of India, by Art 372, allowed all colonal law to remain in force unless they were explicitly repeated.

Reconstructing India (1956–1980)

India in the 1950, was primarily an agricultural economy whose new political leadership was, at the time, proactively grappling with the landlessness and acute poverty. Abolition of *zamindari* system and the land reform measures that followed led to the redistribution of surplus land from the *zamindars* to landless, in various degrees, at the behest of the respective state governments. In the socio-cultural milieu, it was not difficult for the Nehru govt. to get away with token compensation to a handful of rich *zamindars* for land acquired for development purpose.

This was, however, not easily done when land was sought from the small farmer. The national government had, at that time, adopted a policy of heavy industrialization largely under the domain of the public sector, with private companies and multinationals functioning under strong governmental control through intimidating licensing systems. There was an enormous increase in infrastructure development and industrial activities by the state as compared to the colonial period. Numerous large dams, power plants, mines, and steel plants came up on land acquired using the 1894 law; thus causing massive displacement of small farmers, agricultural labour, landless village workers, artisans and forest dwellers. The issue become complicated when decisions had to be taken on paying the price for the land acquired. Public sector and the government projects were not the only purposes for which land was forcibly acquired by the state. Rather, state acquired land for private companies too on the pretext of public purpose in the interest of states.

According to Polit and Bhattacharjee (2008), the government from 1960, through to the 1980's played the role of a 'venture capitalist'. The fact of matter was that, the government needed land and just took it, not only by venture of the Land Acquisition Act, but also a host of other acts and laws. The tracts of land acquired were huge. It was not always for building industries such as the Durgapur steel plant or for infrastructure projects, such as Damodar valley corporation, often it was for building township such as Bhubaneshwar, Durgapur, Gandhi Nagar, and Chandigarh all of which certainly entailed large-scale displacement.

Post-Liberalization Era

In the post-liberalization era means after 1990's private investment was invited with open arms into a plethora of activities that were historically dominated by the public sector such as generation of power, and setting up of SEZ, (Special Economic Zones) to boost forex earnings.

The government now started acquiring large tracts of land on behalf of private companies categorizing nearly every excise for private activity as 'public purpose' in order to invoke the Land Acquisition Act of 1894.

Popular protests have, in the recent past, been frequently politicized by complex interplay of vested interests. The latest instances of this can be seen in the series of events that ultimately led to the netneat of Tata Motors from Singur in W. Bengal. Similarly Salem withdraw from Nandigram and POSCO from Orissa. Being foreign companies, they had no choice but to let the government as intermediaries, and as always, the Act was misused. So it is inevitable to know entire elaboration of the Land Acquisition Act of 1894.

THE LAND ACQUISITION ACT, 1894

Displacement and State Power

The Land Acquisition Act (LAA) 1894 is a law that has survived generations, seen three centuries, and thrived when India was a colony, and later, through independence. It has been influenced by years of land reforms when the state performed, even it partially, the radical task of land redistribution and vesting land in the tiller, having wrested it from the landlords. The legitimacy that this exercise in land reforms gave to the power of the state of expand its power of eminent domain has had an impact on the way the law has developed. The LAA 1894 is an expression of the doctrine of eminent domain, which invests power in the state to take over private land for public purpose.

The LAA 1894, when pared to its essentials, sets out a procedure for state take over of land owned, held, or used by 'person interested' which includes these exercising easement rights [Section 3 (b)].

The process of taking over land may be initiated when 'it appears to the government that land in any locality is needed or likely to be needed for any public purpose. The process outlined in the LAA 1894 includes:

1. A preliminary notification indicating the intention to take the land [section 4(1)];
2. A 30 days period from the date of the preliminary notification when any person interested may about (in writing) to the acquisition of the land or of any land in locality (Section 5A).
3. Giving the person objecting an opportunity to be heard (Section 5A(2).
4. A decision taken by the government, after receiving reports from the collector who is the person with the authority to receive, and hear, objections; and the decision of the government on the objections, shall be final.
5. A declaration that the 'land is required for a public purpose' this must be announced by publication in the official gazette, and in two daily newspapers and by public notice in the locality.

There are few spaces for challenging the acquisition itself. What is left in this procedure that bridges the space between continuing interest in the land sought to be acquired, and the acquisition. Acquisition sunders all rights and interests and leaves a 'person interested' with no further legal rights or interest in the land.

Next step, after the declaration of the requirement of the land for a public purpose, involves marking, measuring, and setting out the plans as a prelude to taking over the land (Section 8). The process of determining compensation follows and, when the award of compensation is made, the collector who is acquiring authority is empowered to take possession of the land, which shall thereupon vest absolutely in the government free from all (Section 16).

The procedural friction is also laid aside in what the LAA 1894 terms 'cases of urgency' (Section 17).

Public Purpose

There is a presumption of morality and a notion of the greater good attaching to 'public purpose' that has acquired exaggerated validity. It is projected as displacing private on individual interests, which are lesser interests and may need to be sacrificed for the common good. Over the decades, what may constitute public purpose permitting coercive acquisition has become immune to challenge. This has meant that competing version of what constitutes 'public purpose' the probability of impoverishment, the dislodging of livelihoods, and the breakdown of cultural contiguities and continuities have, for instance, not been relevant elements in judicial challenge to the meaning of public purpose. The consequences of compulsory acquisition and dispossession are not the concern of the LAA 1894. Mass displacement which affects those pursuing a range of other occupations and professions, and yet others who constitute the community is not the constituency of the LAA 1894.

Public purpose does not include acquisition of land for the companies. The complicity of the state in effecting displacement to facilitate a company's project is built into the law. The process of acquisition under the LAA 1894 is not to be 'put in force in order to acquire land for any company, the provision reads' unless with the previous consent of the government (Section 39) before according consent, the government is required to enquire whether:

(*i*) Such acquisition is needed for the construction of some building or work for a company which is engaged or in taking steps for engaging itself in any work which is for a public purpose.

(*ii*) The such acquisition is needed for the construction of some work, and that such work is likely to prove useful to the public [Section 40(1)].

Compensation

Compensation tones down the coercion implicit in the taking over of land under the LAA 1894, and represents what transpires under it as a transaction. It is also the only aspect of the process of taking over that can be taken to count, and this allows for impression of justifiability. The statue does not provide any help in acknowledging mass displacement or in working out policies of rehabilitation.

Compensation, as set out in the statute, is confirmation to monetary compensation. Resistance to project displacement has given rise to promises and policies. The court draws distinction between 'Compassionate appointment' and the provision of jobs in circumstances such as these created by compulsory acquisition carries the weight of contradiction. It is not that count adjudges the equality of opportunity in public employment to be an invariable rule.

'Interest of justice' and protection from 'destitution, one evidently reasons that can assist in carving out the exception. Land acquisition in the process of executing projects tate a burdens of experience that includes impoverishment, uncompensated losses, problems in creating or finding livelihood options, and social dislocation. It is, then, not immediately clear how the count can deny the status of the 'exception to the rule' to cases where land is acquired under the LAA 1894.

Computing Compensation

The LAA 1894 lists the matters to be considered (Section 23), and neglected (Section 24), in determining compensation. Essentially, it is the market value of the land at the date of publication of preliminary notification, when it is first notified that the land may be needed for a public purpose, that constitutes compensation. This has become contested as being a formula that is bound to impoverish the person from whom land is acquired, especially where mass displacement occurs. It is harder still on a marginal or subsistence farmer who cannot expect to replace the land lost with the compensation amount so paid. The distortion that mass displacement introduces into the land market has raised demands that the difference between the market value and the replacement value should be borne by the project, and ought not to fall the dispossessed.

This has not resulted in any amendment to the LAA 1894. There is, however, a variant that has found its way into rehabilitation policies. In the Draft Rehabilitation Policy circulated in 2005, for instance, Clause 9 of the guiding principles reads; 'while determining compensation, replacement value at the operative market rates must invariably be the basic principle'. In other policies a variant, represented by the principle of land for land, has been written in, even if the anticipation of non-availability of land may, on occasion, deter the policy maker, and the option of a cash equivalent may be built into the policy. The 2003 policy, for instance, in Clause 6.4 provides for up to a maximum of hectare of irrigated land on two hectares of unirrigated land or cultivable waste land where the project affected family loses to entire land to acquisition.

If implemented, the policy of providing land to the displaced may prove to be an equitable remedy. It would also ensure that land dependent communities do not have their livelihoods taken away from them, except where they are a determining part of the decision-making process to change their way of life.

The life and times of the LAA 1894 reveals that, over the years, it has judged the state uncomfortably close to being in possession of absolute power in relation to land, and consequently over the lives and livelihoods of people dependent on land. The evolution in practice of the doctrine of eminent domain, and the absence of forum to challenge the understanding of what constitutes public purpose. The LAA 1894 is a significant element in effecting mass displacement. Yet mass displacement is not acknowledgement in the law; nor do the displaced attract the laws concern.

The LAA 1894 has not shown any flexibility in assessing, determining and re-imagining compensation. Those losing land to acquisition have begun to moot alternatives, such as shareholding in the company that takes over use of the land leasing rather than losing land to acquisition, so that their interest in the land continues, returning it to one from whom it is acquired if the public purpose is either abandoned or altered. Makes of law and policy have, however, maintained a steady silence and refused to engage in the many possibilities that are emerging (Cernea, 2007).

LAND ACQUISITION (AMENDED) ACT 2007

Proposed Land Acquisition Bill, 2007 presents wide amendments in the LAA 1894. The bill redefines 'public purpose' as land acquired for strategic defence purposes, infrastructure, and contiguity purposes or for any project useful to public purposes. According to bill, if an individual want to initiate any project for public purpose and 70 per cent of land will be acquired by state. Here individual denotes any organization, structure authority, whether in corporate or not.

But the clause for a company has been omitted throughout the principal act. The provision of Social Impact Assessment (SIA) is inducted in the bill for projects involving physical displacement of 400 or more families in plain areas or 200 or more families in tribal or hilly areas. Desert Development Programmes (DDP) blocks or areas are mentioned in schedule V or schedule VI to the Constitution. The compensation will be determine on the basis of targeted use of land and existing market value. It is also specified in the bill that in timely disposal of compensation disputes civil courts will not intervene and proposes to set up dedicated dispute settlement authorities in each state and at the central level. If the acquired land is suppose to be sold again then 80 per cent of capital gain will be provided to original landowner and his or her successor.

INTEGRATIVE FRAMEWORK OF LAND ACQUISITION

Much has been written on the legal, normative and sustainable development for ensuring that host communities have the opportunity to provide their Free, Prior and Informed Consent (FPIC) to give land to a project. Integration of sustainable development concerns into land acquisition proposals may be difficult but not impossible. While existing framework, as specified by regulation, give the companies legal permits to operate, the promoters may not gain the much needed social license to start new projects. For this to happen, the first and foremost prerequisite is the willingness of promoters to go beyond the current legal and regulatory frameworks that control land acquisition. Companies have to look at new framework that expand the scope of existing environmental and Social Impact Assessment (SIA) frameworks. We present below an integrative framework that internalizes environmental, social and equitable benefit sharing into land acquisition.

Internalizing Environmental Concerns into Land Acquisition

The existing framework look at project specific impacts separately on air environment, water environment, biodiversity etc.

However, the highly integrative and interactive nature of these sub-systems as part of a composite ecological system and the flow of benefits it provides for human and business well-being, have now received global recognition (Millennium Ecosystem Assessment, 2005).

In our integrative framework, instead of EIA (Environment Impact Assessment), project promoters should look at impacts of land acquisition proposals on the flow of ecosystem services. By adopting 'a' not net loss of ecosystem service flows as a principle, promoters can simultaneously internalize both social being and business well being concerns in to their proposals.

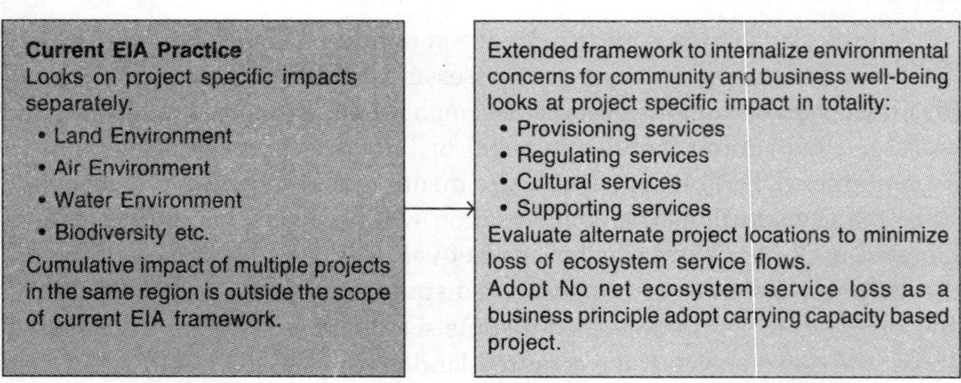

Fig. 7.1: Environmental sustainability framework.

Source: The World Resource Institute (WRI, 2008).

Internalizing Social Well-Being Concerns into Land Acquisition

The scope of Social Impact Assessment (SIA) in India is typically limited to minimizing the impacts on livelihoods. Here I am proposing broader framework that aims at maximizing social well being of affected communities. It is proposed that social well-being concerns in land acquisition proposals are extended to provide sustainable livelihood options and comprehensively cover all affected stakeholders viz: landless, jobless, homeless and destitute. The contribution of each infrastructure project to the social well-being of the local communities should be monitored and evaluated by Millennium Development Goals (MDG) as benchmarking. It is envisaged that the new framework, when aligned with project proposals in the true spirit, will reduce conflict between project promoters and communities.

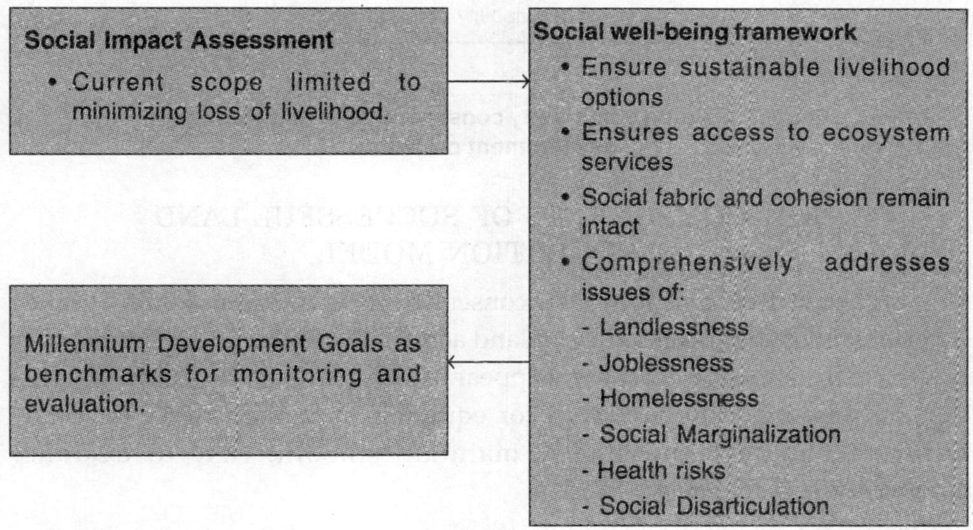

Fig. 7.2: Social well-being framework.

It has been observed that sustainable development concerns are the basic premise on which the local communities oppose land acquisition for infrastructure projects. The Fig. 7.3 presented proposals that by internalizing environmental, social and equitable benefit sharing concerns into infrastructure project proposals, promoters can not only gain community cooperation but also consent for land acquisition and operation.

As gaining community consent also paves the path for smooth implementation of projects and eventually to their sustainability and commercial viability.

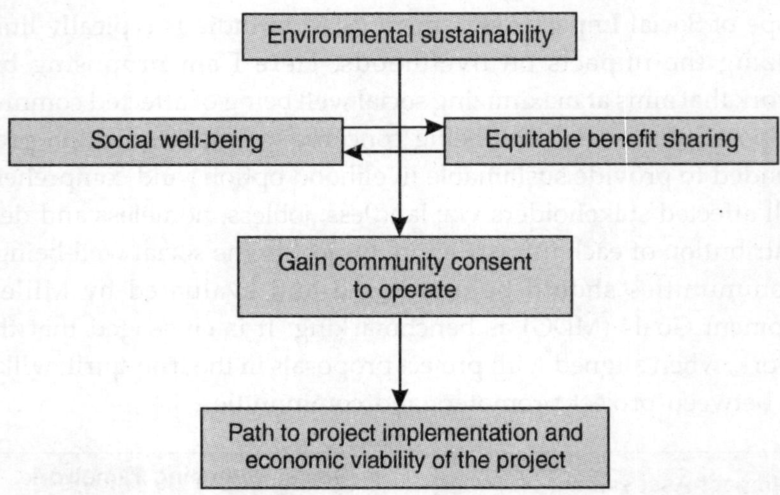

Fig. 7.3: Gaining community consent for land acquisition for development projects.

KEY COMPONENTS OF SUCCESSFUL LAND ACQUISITION MODEL

Gaining prior, free, and informed consent from local communities is a key determinant of success or failure of land acquisition for business. The chances of success in gaining social consent appear to increase when project proponents demand loss of fertile land, opt for equitable sharing, directly negotiate with stakeholders and finally maintain smooth, easy to decipher communication channels.

Figure 7.4 shows the process pattern of a successful strategy. In the first stage, following a few rounds of discussion on the proposal, the private business enters into a formal memorandum of agreement (MOA) with the appropriate state government.

In the second stage business directly entered into dialogue with stakeholders. The involvement of middlemen and other parties (including NGOs) is kept to the essential minimum. Care is also taken not to communicate any false signals through the media or other sources to the locals. A few concessions and a conciliatory stance from both the parties result in the project going to stage three wherein all clearance are obtained. This lays foundation for stage four. Figure 7.5 gives an example of a successful land acquisition model adopted by O.P. Jindal group.

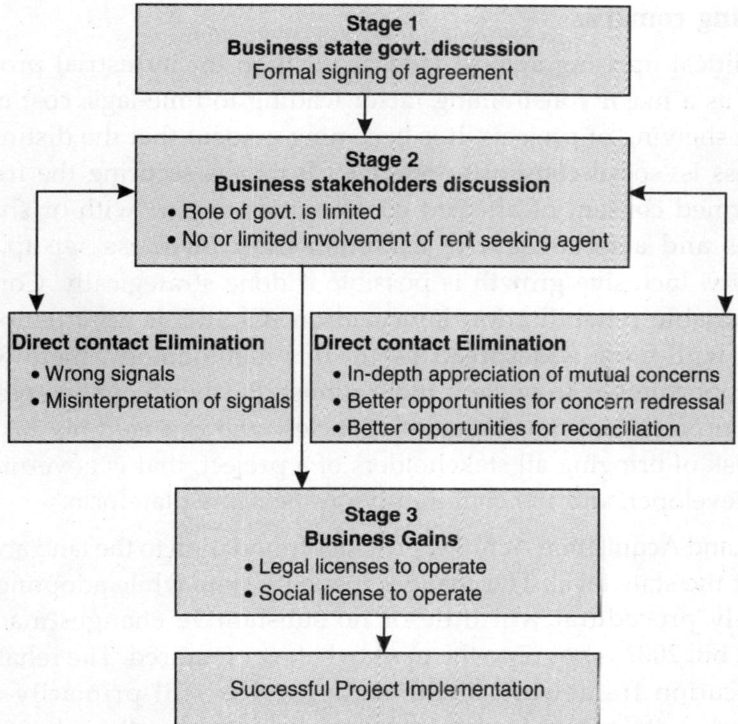

Fig. 7.4: Successful land acquisition pattern.

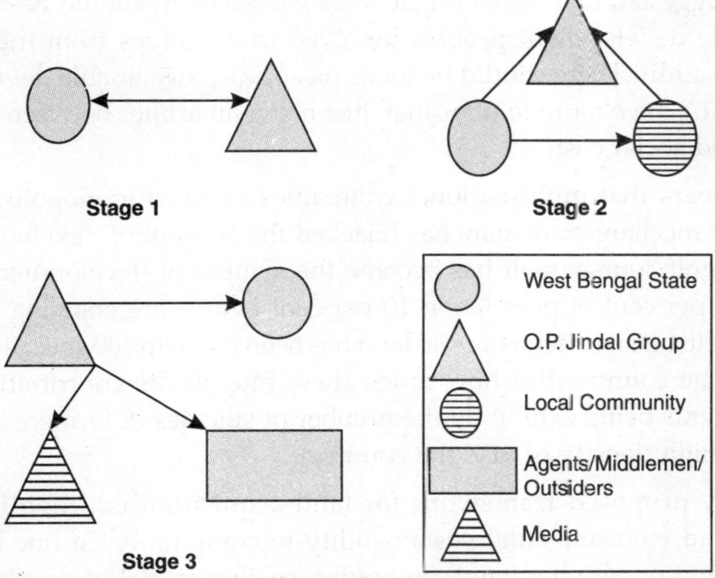

Fig. 7.5: JSW Bengal Steel Project: A Successful Land Acquisition Model.

Source: India Infrastructure Report - 2009

Concluding remarks

Socio-political uprising against land acquisition for industrial projects has emerged as a major constraining factor leading to time-lags, cost overruns, and even shelving of projects. It is becoming evident that the distinguishing for success is 'social consent to operate'. It means securing the free, prior, and informed consent of affected communities to part with or share their resources and also consent to establish their business set-up in their community. Inclusive growth is possible if done strategically. Community led sustainable rehabilitation intervention (CLSRI) is an attempt in this direction with more widespread use of this methodology, there would be greater opportunities to make it more robust. Further there emerges a clear need for professional development agencies who can credibly take on the critical task of bringing all stakeholders of a project, that is government, the private developer, and the community on the same plateform.

The Land Acquisition Act 1894 provides foundation to the land acquisition regime at the state level. The changes made by state while adopting the law are largely procedural will little or no substantive changes made. Even amended bill 2007 is not upto the mark whatever required. The rehabilitation and relocation framework at the state level is still primarily a policy frame-work, with only a few states having adopted legally enforceable R & R laws.

It is suggested that Social Impact Assessment (SIA) should be an integral part of the development process involved in all stages from inception to follow-up audit. There should be focus on socially sustainable development. SIA and EIA have more to offer than just being an arbiter between economic benefit and social cost.

It appears that multi-national companies (MNCs) monopolized media and entire mechanism of state has hijacked the concept of development. Hi-tech city, golf course, mall has become the symbol of development. On the cost of 90 per cent of population 10 per cent people are enjoying luxurious life. Hitherto one lac hectare fertile land has been given to 300 special economic zones in the country. But how much these models are contributing in the developments being exhibit by the number of suicides of farmers in Andhra Pradesh (high density of SEZ the country).

Finally proposed framework for land acquisition is providing socio-cultural and environmental sustainability to community on one hand and development on another hand, otherwise existing model of development is forcing the food security, the manpower of country in danger.

REFERENCES

1. Census (2001), *Census of India*, G.O.I., New Delhi.
2. Millennium Ecosystem Assessment (2005), *Ecosystem and human well-being synthesis,* Island Press, Washington, DC.
3. The World Resource Institute (2008), *The Corporate Ecosystem Services Review,* Visions, Washington, DC.
4. Visaria, L and Visaria, P (1996), *Prospective population growth and policy options for India, 1991-2001*, The Population Council, New York.
5. Morris, Sebastion, Pandey, Ajay (2009), "Land Market in India. Distortions and Issues" in N. Mohanty, Rura Farkar, Ajay Pandey (ed). *India Infrastructure Report, 2009; Land – A Critical resource for infrastructure,* Oxford University Press, New Delhi.
6. Cornea, Michael, (2007) 'Financing for Development Benefit Sharing Mechanism in Population Resettlement, *Economic and Political Weekly* 42(2), 24-30 March.
7. Social Development Report, (2008), *Development and Displacement Council for Social Development,* Oxford University Press, New Delhi.

Chapter

8

Present Value Paradigm and Rural Development

—Dr. Brajesh Kumar

ABSTRACT

Rural development is a multi-dimensional problem and in the same manner needs comprehensive treatment using knowledge from across the subjects touching different aspects of the rural life in general and sociology, economics and politics in particular. As a phenomenon, rural development is the end-result of interactions between various physical, technological, economic, social, cultural and institutional factors. As a strategy, it is designed to improve the economic and social well-being of a specific group of people—the rural poor. The question of development has thus been examined from different angles by the scholars and thinkers in the respective field of investigation. Therefore, development is multidisciplinary examination of finding ways and means of material and spiritual upliftment in development. Keeping in mind the proposition stated, it is pertinent to see the same challenge in some newer way and this is the objective of the present study. In this paper the problem has been examined from demand-side management of the rural development within the domain of socio-psychological complexities of rural life determining the characteristics of socio-political demand for development in the countryside where the same has been investigated from supply-side angle of the problem in majority of the studies in this regard. The paper finds that the Rural Development lies in our ability to induce thought in the mind of the people, faith in the heart that their efforts will yield for them in time and reality. Fear of losing their rights and welfare, if they fail to remain vigilant and united, also play a vital role for enhancing work culture and productivity of human resources in rural India.

Rural Development: Challenges and Characteristics

Rural development in general is used to denote the actions and initiatives taken to improve the standard of living in non-urban neighbourhoods, countryside, and remote villages. These communities can be exemplified with a low ratio of inhabitants to open space. Agricultural activities may be prominent in this case whereas economic activities would relate to the primary sector, production of foodstuffs and raw materials is inherently viewed as a positive thing; it is seen as something that brings together groups of individuals with automatic positive implications and outcomes. Policy rhetoric frequently uses popular terms such as involvement, participation and power sharing to describe rural development activities. However, the reality of experience on the ground does not necessarily concur with these ideals. It is not always clear who ultimately benefits from rural development: the state, the community or rural development practitioners (McAreavey, 2008).

There are no universally accepted approaches to rural development. It is a choice influenced by time, space and culture. The term rural development connotes overall development of rural areas to improve the quality of life of rural people. In this sense, it is a comprehensive and multi-dimensional concept, and encompasses the development of agriculture and allied activities, village and cottage industries and crafts, socio-economic infrastructure, community services and facilities and, above all, human resources in rural areas. As a phenomenon, rural development is the end-result of interactions between various physical, technological, economic, social, cultural and institutional factors. As a strategy, it is designed to improve the economic and social well-being of a specific group of people—the rural poor. As a discipline, it is multi-disciplinary in nature, representing an intersection of agriculture, social, behavioural, engineering and management sciences (Katar Singh, 1999). In the Indian context rural development assumes greater significance as 72.22 per cent (according to the 2001 census) of its population still live in rural areas. Most of the people living in rural areas draw their livelihood from agriculture and allied sectors (60.41% of total workforce), and poverty mostly persists here (27.1% in 1999-2000). At the time of independence around 83 per cent of the Indian population were living in rural areas. Accordingly, from the very beginning, our planned strategy emphasized rural development and will continue to do so in future. Strategically, the focus of our planning was to improve the economic and social conditions of the underprivileged sections of rural society. Thus, economic growth with social justice became the proclaimed objective of the planning process under rural development. It began with an emphasis on agricultural production and consequently expanded to promote productive employment opportunities for rural masses, especially the poor, by integrating production, infrastructure, human resource and institutional development measures. Promoting development in rural areas is a slow and complex process. It requires simultaneous action in various sectors, in an environment undergoing rapid, sometimes volatile, change. The change comes from internal as well as external processes such as privatization and globalization, by forces appearing scattered and disparate (Bauman, 1998). When even well-informed researchers debate on the character of the present global processes, admitting that they do not yet fully understand what is happening in the global economy (Dicken, Kelly, Olds and Yeung, 2001), how can we then expect the rural poor to understand new global trends, respond to new challenges and tap opportunities? For this reason alone, it is important for all stakeholders to work together and identify which aspects of globalization will affect the livelihoods and welfare of the rural poor and how. But we need deep analysis. We must critically analyse global processes from the point of view of indigenous and endogenous knowledge systems, and ask whether local knowledge systems and social systems can cope with ever rapid change.

In their article Vander Ploeg et al., (2000: 399) suggest that a new model of rural development that emerges slowly but persistently in both policy and practice should be followed by a paradigm shift in associated theory. They suggest that:

> "there is a need for a new rural development paradigm that can help clarify how *new resource bases* are created, how the irrelevant is turned into a value and how, after combining with other resources, the newly emerging whole orientates to new needs, perspectives and interests."

They state that, the new rural development paradigm emerged as a set of responses to the old, modernisation paradigm—marking a clear divorce from the deterministic nature of the old order. Nevertheless, the new paradigm still has its roots in the past, since rural development is usually constructed on the back of existing production structures (Murdoch, 2000).

Development is the most complex concept in our social economical thought. It is the most critical factor also for mankind in search of a better and sustainable life in general.

The question of development has thus been examined from different angles by the scholars and thinkers in the respective field of investigation. Therefore, development is multidiscripency examination of finding ways and means of material and spiritual upliftment in development. Keeping in mind the proposition stated, it is pertinent to see the same challenge in some newer way and this is the objective of the present study. We have discovered the paradigm from economic philosophy, especially the finance and economics to identify the underlying problems and obstacles in the area of rural development. This is important in the sense that despite our commendable growth in the theory and practices of development and their positive impact in the standard of life of great number of people in India but also across the world. The rural population has mostly been left out getting fair share in the development pie. There is series of development taken up for their development all around but the result is not at all encouraging – the common answers provided for such a state of matter is corruption, lack of awareness and lack of political when and where social leadership and drive for catching up with the opportunities, provided by the development programme and projects. These are the simplistic explanations put forward and most of these are the social psychology of the intent group and benefitted for rural growth has mostly been ignored.

We can examine the problem using the present value paradigm for explaining lethargy on part of the rural masses in their response to the development programmes and efforts (an inner characteristics of rural masses despite their high demand for a better and decent life constituents). This is reflected in their preferences and choices made for the same. They ignore long-term benefits for the sake of short-term gains and compromises. Unless this dimension is taken care of the misery and underdevelopment in the countryside cannot be sorted out.

Present Value Paradigm

The present value paradigm is the social attitude that value presents more than the future and the future repercussions of the present choices. Though, in general, this is a common phenomenon of the human nature but more so in case of those social groups facing resource scarcity, asymmetric information, social exclusion, repression and low status in power matrix. Unfortunately most of these features are part of the social realities of the rural India.

The fundamental underlying assumptions of the present value paradigm are:

1. People prefer present gain to the future gain ($\alpha1$);
2. People prefer solution to the present problems to the future problems ($\alpha2$)
3. People prefer present claim over things to the future attainment ($\alpha3$);
4. People prefer present promises to the future achievements ($\alpha4$);
5. People see the future in the light of present and past contexts and achievements ($\alpha5$); and
6. People prefer tangible gains to the intangible benefits ($\alpha6$).

In the nutshell, the present value paradigm asserts that people in general discount the benefits derived from development programmes using present value paradigm as discounting factor. And this has very dramatic impact on the development initiatives, the people's participation and cooperation in this regard.

Paradox of planning in India for rural development centered around our poor understanding regarding the dichotomy of growth and development. Whole emphasis had been kernelled around the growth of rural economy led by agriculture and small scale industries and for that the plans were made in the light of investment and productivity of investment as an index of rural development without paying any attention to the fact that growth can be produced without creating broad based development. This thinking has created lopsided development and formed Iceland of centres of development within the widely spread poverty and underdevelopment.

The whole development plan ignored the imperatives of capacity and capability building in the rural India for more extensive and sustainable growth of the economy that only can ensure wide spread growth of rural economy. Only such kind of base can hold and promote sustainable development and reduce abject poverty in the country side. Capacity building depends on capability building and capability building get empowered through heavily investing in human capital, social rights, social equity and gender justice besides participatory democracy. India has measurably failed to address all these crucial planning objective for rural development in Indian context.

Unless masses participate and participate hopefully, nothing can be delivered in top down way because passive motives can dream but cannot realise the dream. Therefore, unless the rural masses attitudinal design is well understood and commensuration remedies are not developed, lasting solutions can not be provided for development in rural India. In this regard present value paradigm of rural masses can be at our help. Development requires growth but without having minimum development of human life capabilities in rural Indias, neither equitable growth nor the sustainable development goal can be realised.

INDIAN EXPERIENCE

Our point of view presented above has some support in the development experience in india. In one of the study by National Council of Applied Economic Research (1999) have brought forward some striking facts about the development indicator for the rural communities in rural india is the point in case at present.

1. About half of the population of rural India is illiterate and suffering from capability poverty.
2. About 40 per cent have extremely low income.

3. Over 50 per cent of the rural population cannot afford the cost of education and health care.
4. National policies and programme during the last half a century have not helped schedule cast and schedule tribes to emerge from the perennial poverty trap.
5. 63 per cent of the villages do not have all weather connecting roads.
6. About one-half of all the villages in India do not have any source of safe drinking water.
7. In many parts of India 25 per cent villages still waiting for in village primary schooling facility.
8. Only about 22 per cent of all villages have a health sub-centres within the village.

If we see the above eye opening facts in the light of 60 years of planning in India and majority of that period under the control of command economic planning at the top, for the bottom tells its own story. We have tried to create growth and supply of developments by a machinery which have only symbolic say in the decision-making and very myopic vision and thin capability receptors to demand and command the resources, commodities and socio-political power as per the requirements that merits. What was required actually was to create growth potentials and development motives at the bottom and supply security logistic support and political command to sensitivise the administration to work for the development of the needy at the grass root with sense of responsibility and accountability. This sense of responsibility and accountability was only to be ensured if the masses were of in a position and have a right to see their own requirements and benefits associated with planning and execution of their own destiny.

Resources should be planned and commanded by those for whom it is meant for and required for. The administrative machinery should play the role of facilitator and should enjoy least directive power and higher accountability for their directive. Specially the financial and other resources with due respect to the requirements of the federalism in finance should be in command of the stakeholder living in countryside in India.

What happened in India?

Integrated Rural Development Program IRDP for Rural Changeover[1]

First introduced in 1978-79, IRDP has provided assistance to rural poor in the form of subsidy and bank credit for productive employment opportunities

[1]This part is the summary view based on the study by Kashif Rajani on Rural Development in India retrieved from *http://ravi.lums.edu.pk/rwes/india.html* on 30th september, 2010.

through successive plan periods. Subsequently, Training of Rural Youth for Self Employment (TRYSEM), Development of Women and Children in Rural Areas (DWCRA), Supply of Improved Toolkits to Rural Artisans (SITRA) and Ganga Kalyan Yojana (GKY) were introduced as sub-programs of IRDP to take care of the specific needs of the rural population.

Wage Employment Programs

Important components of the anti-poverty strategy, Wage Employment Programs have sought to achieve multiple objectives. They not only provide employment opportunities during lean agricultural seasons but also in times of floods, droughts and other natural calamities. They create rural infrastructure which supports further economic activity. These programs also put an upward pressure on market wage rates by attracting people to public works programs, thereby reducing labour supply and pushing up demand for labour. It encompasses National Rural Employment Program (NREP) and Rural Landless Employment Guarantee Program (RLEGP) which were initially part of the Sixth and Seventh Five Year Plans.

Employment Assurance Scheme (EAS)

EAS was launched in October 1993 covering 1,778 drought-prone, desert, tribal and hill area blocks. It was later extended to all the blocks in 1997-98. The EAS was designed to provide employment in the form of manual work in the lean agricultural season. The works taken up under the program were expected to lead to the creation of durable economic and social infrastructure and address the felt-needs of the people.

Food for Work Program

The Food for Work Program was started in 2000-2001 as a component of the EAS in eight notified drought-affected states of Chattisgarh, Gujarat, Himachal Pradesh, Madhya Pradesh, Orissa, Rajasthan, Maharastra and Uttarakhand. The program aims at food provision through wage employment. Food grains are supplied to states free of cost. However, lifting of food grains for the scheme from Food Corporation of India (FCI) godowns has been slow.

Rural Housing

Initiated in 1985-86, the IAY is the core program for providing free housing to families in rural areas, targets scheduled castes (SCs)/scheduled tribes (STs), households and freed bonded laborers. The rural housing program has certainly enabled many BPL families to acquire *pucca* houses, the coverage of the beneficiaries is limited given to the resource constraints. The Samagra Awas Yojana (SAY) was taken up in 25 blocks to ensure convergence of housing, provision of safe drinking water, sanitation and common drainage facilities. The Housing and Urban Development Corporation (HUDCO) has extended its activities to the rural areas, providing loans at a concessional rate of interest to economically weaker sections and low-income group households for construction of houses.

Social Security Programmes

Democratic decentralization and centrally supported Social Assistance Programs were two major initiatives of the government in the 1990s. The National Social Assistance Program (NSAP), launched in August 1995 marks a significant step towards fulfillment of the Directive Principles of State Policy. The NSAP has three components: (a) National Old Age Pension Scheme (NOAPS); (b) National Family Benefit Scheme (NFBS); (c) National Maternity Benefit Scheme (NMBS). The NSAP is a centrally-sponsored program that aims at ensuring a minimum national standard of social assistance over and above the assistance that states provide from their own resources. The NOAPS provides a monthly pension of Rs. 75 to destitute BPL persons above the age of 65. The NFBS is a scheme for BPL families who are given Rs. 10,000 in the event of the death of the breadwinner. The NMBS provides Rs. 500 to support nutritional intake for pregnant women. In addition to NSAP, the Annapurna scheme was launched from 1 April 2000 to provide food security to senior citizens who were eligible for pension under NOAPS but could not receive it due to budget constraints.

Land Reforms

In an agro-based economy of, the structure of landownership is central to the well being of the people. The government has strived to change the ownership pattern of cultivable land, the abolition of intermediaries, the abolition of zamindari, ceiling laws, security of tenure to tenants, consolidation of landholdings and banning of tenancy are a few measures undertaken. Furthermore, a land record management system is a pre-condition for an effective land reform program. In 1987-88, a centrally-sponsored scheme for Strengthening of Revenue Administration and Updating of Land Records (SRA & ULR) was introduced in Orissa and Bihar.

Although these measures have been successful (to some extent) in curbing poverty, this model has a very basic flaw. Under this model resources are transferred from urban economy to rural economy just for short-term political motives. This is affecting both areas, not letting rural economy develop on its own and hampering growth and investments in urban economy. An ideal approach should include the Government, Panchayats and key village personals, NGOs and private companies. This will not only help reduce this imbalance but will have a multiplier effect on the overall economy. By aligning the goals of the two parts we can convert this seemingly zero sum game into a win-win situation. It would be a very long drawn and difficult battle with conventions but the reward is worth the effort.

We can make some critical observation over the results of the integrated efforts put into action as an ambitious attempt for changing prevailing sorry state of rural India.

Table 8.1: India's Global Position in Terms of Socio-demographic Parameters

Country	Life expectancy at birth (years)	Under-five mortality rate (per 1000 live births)		Infant mortality rate (per 1000 live births)		Maternal mortality ratio (per 1,00,000 live births)
	2001	1990	2001	1990	2001	1995
China	70.6	49	39	38	31	60
India	63.3	123	93	80	67	440
Nepal	59.1	145	91	100	66	830
Pakistan	60.4	128	109	96	84	200
Sri Lanka	72.3	23	19	19	17	60
Bangladesh	60.5	144	77	96	51	600
South Asia	62.8	126	96	84	69	427

Source: UNDP, Human Development Report 2003.

The striking features of Indian socio-demographic parameters presented in table 8.1 states that India is fairing closer to countries like Nepal, Pakistan, and Bangladesh and very near to the South Asia. After sixty years of ambitious planning we are lagging behind China and Sri Lanka. Generally corruption, nepotism, dominance of socially and politically raised class in planning and distribution of national resource and income are some of the explanations provided for such anomalies. Nothing can be said firmly but we can see the matter in the light of India's investment in the economy.

Table 8.2: Share of Agriculture GDP in Total GDP (at 1980-81 Prices)

(Percentage of total GDP)

Year	Agriculture, Forestry and Fisheries	Agriculture
1950-51	55.4	48.7
1996-97	26.1	24.4

Source: National Account Statistics of India 1950-51 to 1996-97, *EPW*, Research Foundation, Mumbai, 1998.

Table 8.3: Gross Capital Formation in Agriculture

(Rs. Crore)

Year	GCF in Agriculture			GCFA as % of GDP in Agriculture	GCF as % of Total GCF in Economy @
	Public	Private	Total		
		At 1980-81 Prices			
1960-61	589	1079	1668	5.8	13.5
1970-71	789	1996	2785	7.8	14.7
1980-81	1796	2840	4636	10.9	16.3
1990-91	1154	3440	4594	7.5	8.1
1991-92	1002	3727	4729	8.0	9.3
1992-93	1061	4311	5372	8.5	9.4
1993-94	1153	3878	5031	7.7	9.3
1994-95	1316	4940	6256	9.0	8.6
1995-96	1268	5693	6961	10.4	8.2
		At 1993-94 Prices			
1996-97	4689	11921	16610	6.5	6.4
1997-98	4240	12140	16380	6.6	5.5
1998-99p	3876	12581	16457	6.2	5.5
		Annual Average Growth (%)			
1971-79	10.0	7.2	7.9		
1980-89	–4.0	–0.1	–1.5		
1990-98	–1.9	8.1	5.6		

Note: P : Provisional
@ : Gross Capital Formation adjusted for errors and omissions
GCFA : Gross Capital Formation in Agriculture.

Source: 1. National Accounts Statistics, various issues, CSO, Government of India.
2. *Agricultural Statistics at a Glance*, various issues, Government of India.

When we examine the table 8.3 it is clear that over the years in agriculture GCF has come down and reduced to one-third of the total GCF in the economy as a whole. This shows the declining bargaining power of rural India in investment planning and lesser attractiveness of it to private capital to come to the countryside. This is reflected in the rural-urban economic divide and the disparities within rural India. This can be seen at region level also presented in Table 8.4:

Table 8.4: State-wise Percentage coverage of Irrigated Area under Principal Crops during 1997-98

State	Rice	Wheat	Pul-ses	Total Food-grains	Oil Seeds	Sugar-cane	Cotton	All crops
Andhra Pradesh	96.4	72.7	1.2	55.1	19.7	95.2	18.9	42.5
Bihar	40.4	89.0	2.1	47.8	20.2	30.6	—	46.6
Gujarat	61.2	75.6	10.7	32.2	26.0	100.0	37.7	34.3
Haryana	99.6	98.3	22.5	77.5	70.0	97.9	98.9	78.6
Karnataka	69.2	38.2	3.9	22.5	21.3	100.0	19.3	24.9
Kerala	52.2	—	—	49.3	16.0	100.0	—	14.0
Madhya Pradesh	23.6	69.2	18.5	30.4	5.7	98.6	39.4	25.0
Maharashtra	28.1	69.6	7.3	13.3	11.1	95.0	2.8	14.5
Orissa	36.2	100.0	5.0	26.7	11.0	100.0	—	26.8
Punjab	95.0	94.8	89.8	93.8	62.2	75.1	99.6	91.7
Rajasthan	41.5	94.7	7.7	23.6	43.9	100.0	98.0	29.9
Tamilnadu	93.2	—	6.4	62.0	40.9	100.0	34.6	53.7
Uttar Pradesh	62.7	91.7	27.7	64.7	39.5	95.0	91.7	65.9
West Bengal	25.9	73.0	4.5	27.6	63.5	30.8	—	27.1
All India	50.2	85.0	11.8	40.6	24.4	92.6	36.3	38.2

Source: Ministry of Agriculture, Government of India

Table 8.5 : State-wise Trend Growth Rates of Area under HYV Seeds and per Hectare Fertilizer Consumption

State	Area under HYV seeds	Per Hectare Fertiliser Consumption
1	2	3
Andhra Pradesh	1.15	6.21
Assam	2.74	10.63
Bihar	2.09	8.03
Gujarat	0.68	5.18
Haryana	1.09	6.80
Himachal Pradesh	2.12	3.97

1	2	3
Jammu & Kashmir	2.16	5.02
Karnataka	5.68	5.27
Kerala	4.83	3.51
Maharashtra	3.63	7.10
Madhya Pradesh	5.99	8.36
Orissa	6.14	7.40
Punjab	1.77	1.81
Rajasthan	2.72	9.26
Tamil Nadu	1.62	3.54
Uttar Pradesh	3.40	4.53
West Bengal	5.50	6.62
All-India	3.10	5.29

Source: The growth rates for area under HYV seeds pertain to 1980-81 to 1996-97.

Table 8.6: Percentage of school-going Boys and Girls aged 5-14 in 1987-88

State	Boys		Girls	
	5–9	10–14	5–9	10–14
Rural Areas				
All India	52.5	64.3	40.4	52.8
Bihar	33.0	54.6	19.7	28.7
Madhya Pradesh	43.9	61.6	26.3	29.9
Rajasthan	47.8	69.8	25.5	19.2
Uttar Pradesh	45.4	63.8	28.2	30.7
Urban Areas				
All India	73.0	79.9	67.8	71.9
Bihar	53.7	75.0	45.8	64.0
Madhya Pradesh	71.3	88.3	64.5	76.8
Rajasthan	68.3	83.2	54.7	64.0
Uttar Pradesh	58.9	71.3	49.4	60.8

Source: NSS data based on the 43rd round, 1987-88 published in *Sarvekshana*, Special No., during 1990 (all-India) and 1992 (state-series).

All the data given in tables 8.5 and 8.6 show that there are rural urban divide as well as inter-regional divide in the area of capital formation, infrastructure and education in rural India.This has led some more difficulties.

Agricultural growth failed to outpace the population growth (see Table 8.7). This resulted into poverty trap in the countryside.

Table 8.7: Population Growth *vs* Agricultural Growth

Year	Population growth		Agricultural Growth (Annual Compound Growth Rate)			
	Total Population	Annual Compound Growth rate (%)	Period	Area	Yield	Production
1951	361.1	1.25	1949-50 to 1964-65	1.61	1.50	3.13
1961	439.2	1.96	1967-68 to 1980-81	0.54	1.83	2.38
1971	548.2	2.20	1980-81 to 1991-92	0.05	3.16	3.21
1981	685.2	2.22	1949-50 to 1991-92	0.64	2.05	2.70
1991	844.3	2.11				
2000*	987.3	1.09				

Note: Estimated as on March 1, 2000.
While calculating agricultural growth, years 1965-66 and 1966-67 have been excluded as they were years of serious scarcity.

Source: Agricultural Statistics at a Glance, Government of India, New Delhi, 1998.

When agricultural growth remained struggling with the rural realities it was bound to be reflected in marginalisation of workers in agriculture. This is presented in the table 8.8.

Table 8.8: Indicators of Marginalization of Workers in Agriculture

Year	Population and Workforce (millions)					
	Total	Rural	Rural Workers			Total Rural Workers
			Cultivators	Agricultural Labourers	Others	
1951	361.1	298.6	69.9 (49.9)	27.3 (19.5)	42.8 (30.6)	140.0 (100.0)
1991	844.3	627.1	110.6 (38.8)	74.6 (26.1)	100.2 (35.1)	285.4 (100.0)

Figures in the bracket are percentage to total rural workers.
Source: Agricultural Statistics at a Glance, Govt. of India, New Delhi, 1993.

Land starvation and landlessness is another indicators of poor socio-economic power distribution in the rural India. Over the thirty years of drive for the same the situation has not improved much and whatever is left is already fragmented during the last fifty years of growing population and division of land in family division and no absorption of disguised unemployed in rural India (Table 8.9).

Table 8.9: Rural Landless Households

Year	Landless (Households owning less than 0.002 ha)	Near Landless (Households owning between 0.002 ha and 0.200 ha)	Total
1960-61	11.68	26.11	37.90
1970-71	9.64	27.78	37.42
1981-82	11.33	28.60	39.93
1991-92	11.25	31.15	42.40

Source: NSS, 17th, 26th, 37th and 48th rounds.

Problems

Numerous programmes have been implemented for soil and water conservation without enduring results. These programmes seem to be particularly difficult to implement when the development strategy relies on the top-down approach.

The present anti-poverty programmes give only a modest measure of relief to the poor without touching the system which has reduced them to poverty and frustrate their aspirations and efforts to move upwards. While policy-makers and researchers spend considerable time and energy to monitor the change in the proportion of population falling below poverty line, they do not seem to pay equal attention to the rapid marginalization which has occurred in recent years in population depending on the agriculture and the widening gap between the per capita income in agriculture and that in other sectors. There are clear indications that the sectors which are growing faster than agriculture do little to relieve the pressure of population on agriculture. The reasons for the low absorption of labour outside agriculture need to be sought in the development strategy influencing the overall growth of the economy and its pattern and composition (Rao, V.M. and Geromi, P.D., 2006).

When programme like soil conservation, wasteland reclamation and consolidation of holdings fail to achieve results, it is usual blame the implementation agency and/or the intended beneficiary of the programme. It is important to realize that land use is influenced by a host of factors like comparative advantage in alternative uses, policy regime for agriculture and farmer's perception attitudes. Hence, when considering improvements in the land use, it is most enough to look only at deficiency of the implementation agencies or lack of interest or motivation on the part of the intended beneficiary (Sharma, et al., 1995).

The second major problem we describe is agriculture in the semi-arid draught-prone regions with account for over a half of Indian agriculture. These regions are deteriorating into hardcore poverty areas with low crops yields, stagnant technology, meagre investment and continuing degradation of land based owing to erosion, loss of tree cover and indifference towards conservation of scarce water resources. Government show little interest in these arcas, farmers remain too weak to counter the oppressive poverty and rural communities subsist on periphery cut off from many dimensions of modernization. Technologies for overcoming degradation of land and loss of water resources are known. This is also true of technologies waiting in laboratories which could substantially raise crop yields. There are instance—regrettably few—of village communities achieving remarkable growth and modernization through local leadership, self-help and participation by using the programmes and resources made available by the government (Rao and Hanumappa, 1999). NGOs have also some successful cases to their credit. Barring these exceptions, village remain bypassed with a bewildering variety of schemes being implemented leaving behind nothing more than some dubious and statistics.

Hanumappa, (1999) observes:

> "Experience shows that even those watershed which were initially managed most efficiently have slowly degenerated due to lack of involvement of the participants. One of the reasons for this is the extra care taken by implementing agency (mainly government agencies which provided all the required technical and engineering help along with subsidies) and managing the projects from above. In the process participants become mere onlookers than stakeholders... even the efforts to form collective association and operationalise them have made with poor response".

Hanumappa also mentioned that NWDRA is targeted to cover only 3 million hectares by the end of 8th plan. It is important to note that even in this experimental phase there is no clear evidence of acceptability of the underlying strategy to the farmers.

The market environment marked by low and unstable prices adds to the woes of farmers facing draughts and scarcities. The policy regime instead of taking a corrective measure makes the situation worse by neglecting infrastructure, investments and institutions. This is evident in the case of oil seeds which were the source of a remarkable breakthrough in agricultural production. A recent study by Gulati and Kelly (1999) observes that:

> "farmers are responsive to profits and prices suggest that improvement in crop yielding input and output market and other infrastructure can bring about efficiencies in agricultural in the SAT (semi arid tropics), notwithstanding some degree of subsistence behaviour. There are several

constraints at the micro-level that may not allow farmers to go for the most efficient crop even when price incentives are given."

Despite having a wide network of rural branches in the country and implementation of many schemes and programmes for expansion of credit (targeted lending) for agricultural and rural development, a large number of people still continue to remain outside the fold of the formal banking system. The All India Debt and Investment Survey, 1991-92 shows that during the eighties there was a decline in the share of institutional agencies in cash due to rural households by 4.6 percentage points to 56.6 per cent as against a rise of 32 percentage points to 61.2 per cent during the seventies.

Solution

In the light of the experience gained so far in programmes like training for rural youth for self-employment (TRYSEM) run by the government and similar activities of NGOs attempt should be met to look ahead to identify the promising opportunities in different areas and to anticipate in advance the training and other assistance which could help the workers in agriculture to benefit from these emerging employment opportunities (Rao & Geromi, 2006).

Abundant funds are promised for agriculture but there is no matching readiness on the part of the government to take up task which are crucial for modernization of agriculture but have been grossly neglected so far. In social science analysis, it is important to look at government as one constituent in the total society. This is of help in understanding how social milieu helps/ inhibits capacity of governments to undertake tasks relating to goals like modernization of traditional societies. The development function to be handled by them and the responsibility for area-based planning assigned to them make them a key change agent in the process of modernization. What is important to note is that the government would be able to focus attention on these tasks only after it gets disentangled from its present numerous interventions of wrong kind motivated by populism, need to appease powerful lobbies and a strong urge to retain and if possible, further extent and strengthen its control over the economy.

Weak governance, poor work culture and professional ethics among elites and organized groups; gathering impatience among the lower strata with the social system and its inequities. These features would have to change for the society as a whole to move towards modernization. The future, indeed, looks green. But it is not necessarily without hope, crisis often help societies to get rid of accumulated toxicities and regain health and vigour. India could benefit much from such crisis.

Researcher have argued that the policy regime in India from independence right up to about the early nineties has had the effect of lowering the prices received by the farmer for their output while raising the prices paid by them for inputs purchased from industries [Singh, 1995; Economic survey (GOI), 1996-97; Parikh 1999].

The policy regime has favoured the better offs neglecting the development potential waiting to be tapped in the poorer part of agriculture. As a result a dualistic structure has emerged in agriculture with a small but dynamic part aligned with the main stream economy and policy and a large part languishing with inadequate access to the policy maker and to mainstream opportunities. With this view of agriculture, the natural next step is to regard farmers, and rural society in general, as people unwilling to change from the attitude, perception and lifestyles established over generation in the past. Hence, it is the position today that half-a-century after independence, few city dwellers—and the effluent in rural society—would want to live in villages. At the ground level, the personal finds that their conscientiousness, performance and rapport with the target groups in turn, remain cynical and passive. It is, thus, that the policy regime becomes ineffective from the top downwards (Rao and Jerromy, 2006).

In this context, the role of micro-credit comes into picture. Major reason for the lack of interest of formal financial institutions in extending rural credit are high transaction cost involved in small loan accounts and poor recovery of loans. As a solution, a new mode of delivery of credit through Self-Help Groups (SHGs) and voluntary organizations has been emphasized in recent times. In fact, micro credit is considered as the last hope for rural India. The early result of linking SHGs with banks, which was launched by NABARD during 1992-93, is very encouraging. By the end of March 1999, 32,995 SHGs have been linked with banks, and credits to the order of Rs. 57 crores have been dispersed. However, the linkage programme was highly skewed in respect of regions and institutions. The experience of some successful watershed projects in India and abroad shows that people's effective participation in the planning, execution, monitoring and maintenance of project is essential for success. The government should create a proper legal and political environment for people's effective participation, including those of women and the landless. But it should be basically people's programme, the role of government being limited to providing only technical guidance, basic infrastructure and limited finance, if necessary. Women have an important role in maintaining the household livelihood system. In poor families, they are largely responsible for collection of food, fuel and fodder.

National building is an outcome of numerous socio-economic and political processes and macro, regional and micro levels. The government's development role requires to influence, regulate and modify these processes, but, in a democratic polity, the government itself would, to an extent be a product of these processes. It is the fundamental responsibility of the government to ensure that its role and actions are guided by national perspective and by the long-term goals and interests of the nation as a whole. This is a difficult role to play for a government in a democratic policy where it has to continually respond to an innumerable sectional demands. This is particularly true in India where election threaten to become an annual chore. The development strategy so far has been centre-dominated with a metropolis-cum-elite bias and the philosophy underlying it favour a market-led strategy with the government playing a facilitating role, to promote growth, to make growth more broad-based, to improve the access to growth by the backward and the poor and to provide safety net to the weak and the vulnerable.

A remarkable feature of agriculture is the wide gap between what the technologist gets in the experimental farm and what a farmer gets on his farm and also a wide gap between the "best practice" farmer and the common run of farmers. The government's intervention through providing subsidies and organizing extension services have had an impact only in a few areas with large parts of agriculture remaining barely touched. The chief weakness in the present government role in agriculture is the inability of the top down approach to look after the development functions at the grassroots level which need a system based on devolution, participation and local leadership and initiatives (Rao and Jerromy, 2006).

Agricultural and rural sectors were expected to absorb the residual labour while leaving the other sector free to adopt capital-intensive technologies with meager labour absorption or permit entry only to highly skilled. Again, inequality in distribution of land and the economic gap between the haves and have-nots within agriculture and rural area attract considerable policy attention but not the pomp and vulgar show of effluence in the urban enclaves of rich proud of their western lifestyles, inevitably, agriculture become a "parking lot" of the poor and the marginalized.

Tamilnadu has been attributed to a programme of information, education and communication. The activity was reportedly added by the involvement of a great social reformer Periyer Ramaswami in creating awareness among the people to liberalize women from frequent delivery and to delay marriage. The adoption of a scheme of incentive and disincentive to delay marriage and to limit the number of children after marriage. (Visaria, 2006).

Some Success Story

MID-DAY MEAL AND ENROLMENT IN SCHOOL

Mid-day Meal Scheme has increased enrolment in schools. In 2007-08 the enrolment was 6,27,596 in both the primary schools and EGS centers and in the year 2008-09 it has increased to 7,37,413. There are reports from different parts of the state that more children are attracted to school with the introduction of cooked Mid-day Meal Scheme. As such attendance also has increased in schools.

The copy of the report of the monitoring institution on MDM Programme for the State of Meghalaya was received very recently. In the meeting held on the 12.02.2008 with the District Officers of Elementary & Mass Education, the findings and the observations of the monitoring institute was discussed as one of the agenda items. The district officers have been instructed to furnish their comments on the report. The points raised in the report like appointment of cooks and helpers so that teachers are not made to cook mid- day meals were explained and necessary advice was given on how to circumvent the particular problem highlighted therein. The district commissioners have also been requested to ensure that allotment and lifting of food grains is regular and timely.

It is a fact that there had been some disruptions in giving MDM to the school children during the rainy seasons due to the absence of good kitchen-sheds. With the construction of kitchen sheds in 2539 government L.P. schools and better convergence with the schemes like NREGS, this situation is expected to significantly improve. Another 5276 schools and EGS centres are yet to be provided with good kitchen sheds. Out of 2259 upper primary schools, only 468 upper primary schools in EBBs are being provided with kitchen sheds.

On the whole, Mid Day Meal Programme which has been implemented in the State has been able, to a great extent, to attract more children to schools. Dropout rate has come down considerably from 33.67 per cent to 24.06 per cent. Mid Day Meal Programme also helps the poor families by lessening their hesitation to send their children to school where they do not have to worry about providing food to the children during school hours. Mid Day Meal Programme will enhance the learning capacity of children as nutritious food is served to them every day although no study has as yet been conducted on this. At present the only problem that we are facing is the lack of *pucca* kitchen-sheds where Mid Day Meal can be cooked and served in spite of any kind of weather (Govt of Meghalaya, 2008).

MICRO-FINANCE, SELF-HELP GROUP (SHG) FINANCIAL INCLUSION

Micro-finance through SHGs has reached the un-reached rural poor. There is need to evolve an informal micro-financing through formal financial institutions. The massive growth of micro-finance has paved the way for immediate financial accessibility for the poor who are too far away from this accessibility and micro-finance. Micro-finance through self-help groups is an alternative system of credit delivery for the poorest of the poor groups. SHGs assist women to perform traditional roles better and to take up micro entrepreneurship (Rao, 2010).

A nation can be socially and economically strong only if none of their citizens are without work and basic necessities. Ideal position is practically impossible to derive for even the wealthiest country like USA. But any society itself should think and work that least of their citizens faces similar situation. Helping to reduce vulnerability poses a new set of challenges for public policy. A starting point understands the ways that communities and extended families try to cope with difficulties in the absence of public interventions. The idea emphasise one help himself. Coping mechanisms range from the informal exchange of transfers and loans within families and communities to more structured institutions that enable an entire community to provide protections to their neediest members. This paper describes ways to address the problem how to complement and extend informal and private institutions and emphasise on reaching and enriching poor. The most effective policies are discussed hereafter in this or subsequent article, that throw light on new institutions for providing insurance and credit and for generating savings be developed. The paper in its later part describes case of Indian situation and NABARD experience. A major constraint to the participation and contribution of poor and vulnerable households in economic growth is access to financial credit. Access to financial services permits individuals and households to better manage the risks and uncertainties they face—to save in secure ways, to invest in a business or home, or to cope with or insure against unexpected shocks (Sapovadia, 2008).

NREGA AND EMPLOYMENT GUARANTEE

NREGA's success is due to a vigilant group of civil society actors who have contributed to the Act becoming a role model for public service delivery in rural areas. In a very small number of cases, the administration has responded with equal enthusiasm. However, the murder of Lalit Mehta, an NREGA activist, and self-immolation of another activist Tapas Soren, are a grim reminder of the challenges of making this Act work.

The success of NREGA need not be measured on the singular parameter of employment generation, even though its record is far better than of its predecessors. As of now, 25 million households have benefited from 857 million of person days employment generated. Moreover, this Act has become a role model for innovation in many areas of public service delivery. This has implications for the important debate regarding public service provisioning in rural areas.

Starting from financial inclusion and social security provisioning for informal sector workers to identification of the poor, this programme seems to have done much better than most of the policies exclusively designed for the purpose.

Take the example of financial inclusion. By 2010, 27.1 million new bank accounts have been opened in the rural areas with zero balance requirements for wage payments under NREGA. Almost 80-90 per cent of these are for households that have been included in the financial network for the first time. This is an achievement—financial inclusion was not a stated objective of the programme.

Even in terms of participation of the marginalized sections in the number of workdays created, more than 50 per cent (29.4% scheduled castes and 24.1% scheduled tribes of total person days of employment generated have gone to SC and ST households.

Similarly, as against the stated objective of one-third of women participation in total person days generated, the actual numbers have been close to 50 per cent. An expected spillover has also been the rise in wages in almost all states since the initiation of the programme. According to the monthly wage figures from labour bureau, wages of unskilled labourers have increased between March 2006 and March 2008 in nominal terms by 7.4 per cent for males and 7.9 per cent for females. It would be naive to attribute all the increase to NREGA, but it will be equally foolish to ignore the role of this programme.

So, what has been done differently in NREGA that has ensured better targeting? Unlike other programmes which have been made toothless by anchoring them to below poverty line (BPL) cards, NREGA is a self-targeting programme. It is no wonder that the distribution of beneficiaries by social groups is almost similar to the distribution of poor obtained from the NSSO consumption surveys. Evidently, the self-targeting inherent in NREGA has a better score in targeting the poor than the officially conducted but flawed identification of BPL households. In fact, the self-selection nature of NREGA has persuaded the finance ministry to classify workers in the programme as poor, for inclusion in the Janashree Bima Yojana. Similarly, the case of extension of Rashtriya Swasthaya Yojana to the NREGA workers.

Although a programme of this magnitude will take time to be of any relevance in changing the landscape of rural India. Initial reports of evaluation studies by various institutions and individuals has documented the processes of revival and resurgence largely driven by NREGA as an axis of struggle by the rural poor. It has neither been claimed nor was envisaged that NREGA is the key to successful rejuvenation of rural areas. This requires many such efforts particularly towards ensuring the broken linkages of the growth process to include the rural areas as engines of growth. Nonetheless, it does offer an opportunity for the rural poor to stake claim to the fruits of the growth. Moreover, NREGA's success stories provide opportunities for mainstreaming and legitimizing the struggle for other social security legislation.

NREGA's success is as much a hope for civil society activists fighting for the rights of the poor as it is a critique of the development in case it fails to deliver (Himanshu, 2008).

GRAMIN SOUCHALAYA PROGRAMME

The Government of India through its flagship programme of Total Sanitation Campaign (TSC) has been able to enhance the sanitation coverage in rural areas from a mere one per cent in 1981to over 54 per cent in the current financial year. Through this programme in the year 2007-08 alone, more than 1.2 crore toilets have been constructed. The Government of India is committed to achieve hundred per cent sanitation coverage in all rural households by 2012 much before the Millennium Development Goal Target set by United Nations General Assembly of reducing by half the proportion of people without access to basic sanitation by year 2015. Besides, the government has also set a target of covering all Government Schools and Anganwadis with sanitation facilities by next financial year itself. Some of the states like Sikkim and Tripura have already achieved hundred per cent coverage.

Ms. Lizette Burgers, Chief (Water and Environment Section), UNICEF gave an informative presentation on "Sustainable Pathways to Attain the Sanitation Millennium Development Goals (MDGs)". She stated that out of the 2.6 billion peoples in world who are without toilet, 700 million belong to India. She explained the linkages of sanitation MDG 7 Target 10 of "reducing half the proportion so people without access to safe drinking water and basic sanitation facilities" and with other MDG goals of poverty and hunger, universal primary education, gender equality reduced child mortality rate, combating disease (HIV, malaria) and Global partnerships achievement and targets. She said India is likely to achieve MDG by 2010 and full coverage by 2016. Statewise sanitation coverage trends indicate that some of the states like Tamilnadu, West Bengal, will achieve hundred per cent coverage by 2011 and 2010 respectively, while states like Bihar will be able to achieve this target only by 2069 if the current rate of progress is maintained. She explained the various challenges that are being faced in the sanitation sector as being uneven progress across states and within states, quality in construction, locally suitable technologies and design adapted to needs. Effectiveness of current hygiene promotion initiatives: USE , Capacity of supply chain, Trained human resources, Management of NGP, Monitoring of inputs/outputs, Inclusive programming/technologies, Post ODF response, Issues of fatigue

To address these challenges she suggested the following pathways to sustainability:

- A system of delivery that promotes and reinforces commitment, participation, leadership, ownership, scaling-up/innovation and preparedness for next level of response. Adequate financial resources, technical resources, human resources, sustainable technologies, sustainable behavior/practices.
- *Adequate and sustained allocation of resources:* The resources include Financial Resources, Technical Resources and Human Resources. There should be commitment and action for sustained funding at national and state level. Base should be created for human resource for current and future response
- *Sustainable Technologies:* The technology should be affordable, available, useable, modern quality technologies. The technologies should be coupled with economic returns like improved leach pits Eco-san, Toilet linked bio-gas, Vermin-composting and cleaner technologies—Carbon Credits.
- *Sustainable Behaviour/Practices*: Sustained mobilization and monitoring for proper usage/maintenance by evolving communication strategy, continuous researched/benefit inputs on sanitation and hygiene. It should be seen as new business opportunity and as a sense of modernity. It should be made glamorous to break the taboos.

Concluding her presentation she mentioned that Sustainable Sanitation systems should be such that are safe, affordable and socially acceptable those encourage usage. Sustainable sanitation success stories are found in China, India, Ethiopia, Bangladesh, etc. Challenges in scaling up sustainable sanitation include know how, capacity, attitudes, demand, credit, financing, policies, etc.

Local governance should accommodate frameworks for Sustainable Sanitation. It also needs capacity development—training and education—for better understanding and more implementation, refined perspectives on O&M, including the economic opportunities and liabilities, ecosystem-based sanitation for agricultural reuse of products—food security and carbon sequestration, demand as a driver for sanitation promotion, cross-institutional collaboration for comprehensive initiatives and cost-efficiency.

Regarding provision of sanitation facilities in rural areas, she highlighted that the most critical element was that there are no monolithic magic bullet kind of technological solutions which would address all problems. The only one magic bullet solution is that of developing programmes, strategies and technologies that are demand driven and promote community ownership (Parikh, 2008)

MICRO IRRIGATION PROJECT

Small-scale Solutions

In part, it means rolling out large-scale irrigation schemes. But, with high costs per hectare and per beneficiary, large schemes are costly and slow to develop, and relatively few farmers would benefit from improved production.

For example, scenarios from the Comprehensive Assessment of Water Management in Agriculture suggest that even doubling the irrigated area in Sub-Saharan Africa would help provide only about ten per cent of the continent's food supply.

To improve water security for those who need it most—the rural poor—we need a broader range of solutions.

One place to start looking is the 'informal' water sector, which is especially vibrant in Asia. People who have not been well served by government water services have already taken matters into their own hands, often stimulating small-scale private sector development.

Motorised pumps, the most influential technology in water for agriculture in the last 20 years, are just one example. People buy a reasonably priced pumpset, go to a water source such as groundwater, a river or drain, and pump water to their fields when they need it.

Long flexible pipes are another. They are now found all over the Indian countryside, and also China, where they are called 'white dragons'. They allow people to pipe water over relatively long distances from the source and either use it on their fields or sell it.

While pumps and pipes require investment, operation and maintenance, the water itself is free, and there is little need to interact with others in the community or with the government. It sounds easy (Molden David, 2010).

The study was conducted to assess the impact of small-scale irrigation on agricultural production and poverty in marginal areas of Punjab, Pakistan Nine tehsils of Pothowar Plateau were selected as study area. Data were collected for the period 2002-03 and analysis was carried out with the help of various econometric techniques. The poverty head count index was found 33 per cent in the area. However, poverty headcount indices were 50, 34, 20, 37, 4, 43, 33 and 19 per cent for Jand, Pindi Ghaib, Fateh Jang, Attock, Gujarat Khan, Kahuta, Rawalpindi, Talagang and Chakwal, respectively. The poverty headcount was found 29 per cent, 23 and 37 per cent in irrigated, irrigated plus rain-fed and rain-fed categories of the farmers, respectively. Poverty estimates with respect to farm size were 33 per cent, 40 per cent and 27 per cent on small, medium and large farms, respectively. However when analysis of farm size with access to irrigation was carried out, it was revealed that the poverty headcount was 44 per cent, 40 per cent and 12 per cent for small, medium and large size farmers, respectively. It established the fact that irrigation reduces poverty. The access to irrigation through small-scale irrigation schemes must be encouraged to increase crop production in order to alleviate poverty. The land consolidation would improve the economies of scale for the installation of irrigation schemes. This would improve the agricultural productive potential of the Pothowar area. The access to irrigation through these small-scale irrigations schemes must be encouraged to increase crop productivity and hence reduce poverty. Land consolidation would improve farm size and facilitate the installation of small-scale irrigation. It would increase crop productivity and reduce the poverty. The establishment of agro-based industries is suggested to improve the off farm income and reduce poverty from the area. Agricultural machinery tools along with other agricultural inputs at union council level are suggested. Low cost technologies are needed to reduce production cost to reap the comparative advantage in the wake of WTO (Hussain..*et al.,* 2006).

GRAM VAN SAMITI

Village Forest Committee

In India Joint Forest Management (JFM) has emerged as an important intervention in management of forest resources. In many parts of India, small village groups have started to protect and reclaim degraded forestlands through collective action. The Joint Forest Management Programme seeks to develop partnerships between local community institutions and state forest departments for sustainable management and joint benefit sharing of public forest lands. The primary objective of JFM is to ensure sustainable use of forests to meet local needs equitably while ensuring environmental sustainability. The central premise is that local women and men who are dependent on forests have the greatest stake in sustainable forest management. The destruction of natural forests for timber, cropland, fuelwood, pasture, urbanization have had an impact on many poor rural families who are dependent on forest resources for fuel, fodder, food, medicine, housing etc. The deterioration of forests has accelerated soil erosion, sedimentation of rivers, increased flooding, and overtaxed the land's capacity to regenerate and sustain. It is now being recognised that local communities need to be involved in establishing sustainable forest management systems. Governments are opening a number of opportunities for sustainable forest management and biodiversity conservation by decentralizing authority and responsibility for resource management in different parts of the world. In the Asia-Pacific, attention is to community-based forest management programs and the devolution of management responsibilities on some forestry activities to local government units in the Philippines; land and forest allocation programs in China, Laos, Vietnam; transfer of use rights to forest user groups in Nepal; Joint Forest Management programs in India and privatization of forest plantations in New Zealand. Similar processes are underway in other parts of the world. The various initiatives have led to greater access and control of forest resources by local people, in turn resulting in improvement in forest protection and management and reducing pressure on resources. Substantial areas of degraded forests have been rehabilitated and new forests planted. Local people have started supporting forest conservation where they have been able to reap financial returns from benefit-sharing schemes. There are indicators of the positive impact of JFM across the country. In many states forests under JFM are regenerating. Remote sensing data are showing an improvement in quality and area of forests. Studies in Gujarat, Andhra Pradesh, Haryana, Madhya Pradesh and West Bengal have recorded improvements in productivity and diversity of vegetation and increased income to members of community institutions from non-timber forest products. Experiences from West Bengal, Haryana, Orissa, Himachal Pradesh, Andhra Pradesh, Gujarat, Uttar Pradesh, Jammu & Kashmir and Tamilnadu indicate that participatory forest management offers an important survival strategy for threatened Indian forests. However, for JFM to be successful, an essential condition is to convince people at the micro planning stage itself about the benefits likely to accrue. (Extension Digest, 2006)

General Discussion and Conclusion

The success story surveyed leaves us with no doubt that when peoples see things presently understandable and within reach to achieve; they participate, they achieve and they make things available to them by and for themselves. Small is beautiful is also find its meaning here when we see small irrigation projects, village level samiti managing local forest and water resources, NREGA for employment and capital formation in rural India and the Gram Souchalaya Yojona in different parts of India succeed and help reducing poverty in the countryside. This is not difficult to perceive the result in perspective of life concern as human efforts find its energy and motivation from tangible understanding and success of initiatives undertaken by the beneficiaries. Even small success keep zeal for hard work and series of disappointments create surrendering attitude forever and really very difficult to change. Life's urge when remains dream only in the distant future, the whole future growth becomes simply a dream only. Rural development lies in our ability to induce thought in the mind of the people, faith in the heart that their efforts will yield for them in time and reality. Fear of losing their rights and welfare had they not remained vigilant and united also play a vital role for enhancing work culture and productivity of human resources in rural India. This can only be possible if the representative government work for general security and defence, law and order, protection of weaker section and downtrodden; and provision and maintenance of mass public goods and services for the people. However, the remaining economic and social objectives should be left for decentralised units of public institutions spread across the nation working hard for making destiny realised. Government should provide logistic and administrative support but accountability should be conferred on the needy. Local government agencies should work with utmost accountability but with minimum of power to interfere in the wisdom of people and the people should also be made accountable for their own decisions and live up with their own creation. They should not be overly subsidised and spoon-fed otherwise also.

It is apparent now that keeping eyes off from the elemental realities of human thought, aspirations and attitude no science of development can either be developed or deliver results for the disadvantaged section of the economy and especially the rural economy of India. Thus I can recommend some policy measures in this regard for the betterment of life in rural India and efficient management of growth and development thereof.

1. In the rural development planning we have to accommodate those plans which are present concern of the people in rural India viz. gainful employment for whole year period; reasonable price for their produce and inputs used in agriculture; in village health and primary education facilities and affordable supply of food, medicine, water and cloths. All these things should be ensured using local resources and overdependence on market intermediaries should be limited.
2. People participation should be ensured in the administration and execution of plans at micro development goals which protects plans from biases and vested interests and at the same time it saves programmes to rhetoric and clever promises for some times in future.
3. There is another dimension to the problem here. People generally trade off short-term value with long-term benefits. People in this regard should be extensibly educated about the cost associated with their short-sightedness and benefits at stake with a better choice in their life and life-related matters, viz., child-mother health, girl child nutrition, health care and education, schooling for children for requisite number of years rather going short-term bonded and disguised employment; discriminating between male and female child; ignorance of women health and wasting vital voting power by selling

it or surrendering it for meagre money or minuscule cast and creed biases.

4. The Indian endeavour for rural development is in many a cases is limited by the depressed moral of rural masses. Besides the century of deprivation and oppression by foreign and domestic socio-political designs, it is the frustration built-up during the post-independent economic management by the political, bureaucratic and elite corporate nexus at the middle and lower level administration of development programmes due to skewed and fractured social and political base at the grassroot level in the rural India has squeezed out all the vital zeal to dream a decent life standard in the countryside and work for it and fight for it united, collectively and democratically. This has to be restored by revitalising local planning, local execution of plans, and empowerment of Panchayati Raj Instituions for more representative control of resources for local development. Local administration's power should be curtailed to the role of an facilitator and not the dictator.
5. There is a need for social audit of development programmes at the local level especially for the macro development programmes to curtail corruption, nepotism and inefficiency at the execution of the development programmes.

REFERENCES

1. *All India Debt and Investment Survey (1991-92)*, Reserve Bank of India Survey, February, 2010.
2. Bauman(1998), quoted in New Challenges and Opportunity for Rural Development by Vitanenak, paper presented at the IFAD Workshop: "What are Innovation Challenges for Rural Development."
3. Dicken, Kelly, Olds and Yeung (2001), quoted in New Challenges and Opportunity for Rural Development by Viitanenak, paper presented at the IFAD Workshop: "What are Innovation Challenges for Rural Development."
4. *Extension Digest*, 2006), Joint Forest Management (JFM).
5. Government of India, *Economic Survey*, various issue, Ministry of Finance, New Delhi.
6. Gulati, A and Kelley T. (1999), *Trade Liberalisation and Indian Agriculture*, Oxford University Press, New Delhi.
7. Hanumappa, H.G. (1999), "Watershed Management for Sustainable Development", paper presented to National Seminar on Watershed Management for Sustainable Development, Department of Economics, S.V. University, Tirupati, March 11-12.

8. Himanshu's column on, Rural Employment Generation and NREGA www.livemint.com/farmtruths retrieved on 3rd October, 2010.
9. Hussain. M et al., (2006), "Impact of Small Scale Irrigation Schemes on Poverty Alleviation in Marginal Areas of Punjab, Pakistan," *European Journal of Econonomics and Finance*, Issue 6, pp. 193-200.
10. McAreavey R, (2008), Development Agency of the United States, Department of Agriculture (USDA RD).
11. Molden David, (2010), "Small Scale Solution to Water Security", retrieved from *www.scidev.net/en/agriculture* and Development.
12. Ms. Lizette Burgers, Chief (Water and Environment Section), UNICEF, Address in Workshop on Rural Sanitation and Water Management, Ministry of Rural Development, Government of India, 2008.
13. NABARD (1999a), *Annual Report 1998-99*, National Bank for Agriculture and Rural Development, Mumbai.
14. Nagraj, N. (1996), "Peoples Participation in Karnataka Watershed Development Project," in *Watershed Development,* edited by Jensen et. al., WDCU Publication, p. 299.
15. Parikh, Kirit (1999), "Food and Agriculture Policy : The Challenges Ahead", Vikalpa, Vol. 24, No. 2, April-June, pp. 3-10.
16. Parikh.K. (2008), Member, Planning Commission, Address in Workshop on Rural Sanitation and Water Management, Ministry of Rural Development, Government of India.
17. Rao, V.M and H.G.Hanumappa (1999), Marginalisation Process in Agriculture: Indicators, Outlook and Policy Implications". *Economic and political weekly* (review of agriculture), Vol. xxxiv, No. 52, December 25,1999.
18. Rao, G.V.J. (2010), Micro Financing—A Boon for the Poor, *The Indian Journal of Commerce*, 63, 1, 81-88)
19. Rao, V. M. and Geromi, P.D. (2006), *Modernising Indian Agriculture. Indian economy since independence*, edited by Uma Kapila, Academic Foundation, New Delhi. pp. 285-286, 246-247, 281
20. Sapovadia, V. K. (2008), *Micro Finance: A Tool to Socio-economic Development*, NICM, India SSRN,
21. Sharma, V.P., Gajja, B. L., Shad, D. (1995), "Managing Land and Water Resources for Sustainable Agriculture Development: Issues and Options", *Artha Vijnana*, Vol. 37, No. 1.
22. Singh, K. (1999), *Rural Development : Principles, Policies and Management*, SAGE Publication, New Delhi.
23. Singh, Monmohan (1995), Inaugural Address delivered at the 54th Annual Conference of Indian Society of Agricultural Economics.
24. The Planning Commission (1997b) *Report of the Committee on 25 years Perspective Plan for the Development* of Rainfade Areas, Government of India, New Delhi,p. 310.

25. Van der Ploeg *et al.*, (2000), quoted in *New Challenges and Opportunity for Rural development* by Viitanenak, paper presented at the IFAD workshop: "What are Innovation Challenges for Rural Development.

26. Visaria, P. (2006), *Demographic Aspects of Development: The Indian Experience, Indian Economy Since Independence*, edited by Uma Kapila, Academic Foundation, New Delhi, pp. 177-178.

CHAPTER

9

Static and Dynamic Gains of Micro Finance

An Empirical Study in West Bengal

—Dr. Debashis Sarkar

ABSTRACT

Credit by origin is either institutional or non-institutional. The share of credit enjoyed by the non-institutional sources was of the order of 93.6 per cent in the year 1951-52 which was reduced to the level of 65.0 per cent in the year 1978-79. The credit is affected by both supply and demand side perspectives. Owing to accumulation of losses in the public sector banks the flow of credit to rural areas by banks in recent years has not been up to the mark. Appropriate institutional changes may be required to ensure necessary credit flow to agriculture. In view of this an attempt is made in this paper to examine the static and dynamic gains of bank finance on the farm sector in West Bengal. The static gains of bank finance pertain to its impact on the borrowers due to low rates of interest charged by the banks. The dynamic gains from bank credit are analyzed in terms of their effect on the selected stocks and flows pertaining to our sample households. The immediate effect of borrowing is on the fall in credit gap. It takes some time to get the asset formed and generate employment and income out of it. It has been observed that out of all 35 States/Union Territories in India West Bengal is in twelfth position with CD ratio of 56.29 per cent i.e. 16.10 per cent below the average CD ratio of 72.39 per cent for whole of India. Linking Self-Help Group (SHGs) of the rural poor with the banking system was launched initially in 1992. Thrift linked credit support is provided to the members of SHGs. Banks are in a position to reduce transaction costs as well as risk in delivering small loans. It has been observed from that West Bengal's share in All India SHGs number is 3.50 per cent whereas quantum wise bank loan it is still lower at 1.52 per cent for the commercial banks. It has been found that in West Bengal overall credit gap is 50 per cent and above in marginal and small categories of farms and above 80 per cent in case of medium and large category of farms. However, the gap is substantially lower in areas where self-help group has taken a root. This is the typical dynamic gains of micro-finance.

Introduction

Credit by origin is either institutional or non-institutional. Sources of non-institutional credit include village moneylenders, input dealers, friends and relatives etc. Institutional credit on the other hand is disbursed through multi-agency network consisting of Commercial Banks (CBs), Regional Rural Banks (RRBs) and Cooperatives. The Cooperative Credit Institutions, both short- and long-term structures (Agricultural Rural Development Bank) have emerged over the years as the prime institutional agencies for dispensation of rural credit. The share of credit enjoyed by the non-institutional sources was of the order of 93.6 per cent in the year 1951-52 which was reduced to the level of 65.0 per cent in the year 1978-79 (RBI Working Group Report, 1978). The credit is affected by both supply and demand side perspectives. On the supply side factors which influence credit are unbankablity of the persons seeking credit as perceived by the bankers, distance factor standing in the way of servicing the accounts, high transaction costs involved in dealing with a number of small accounts, inadequacy of manpower and lack of proper orientation of banking personnel, inadequacy of extension services to improve production efficiently etc. Similarly, on the demand side factors which stand in the way are high transaction costs owing to the necessity of repeated travel, wage loss and incidental expenses. Non-availability of products suitable to individual needs, lack of awareness, procedural hassles and prior experience of indifference are also regarded as impediments to growth of credit.

All the three basic objectives of economic development of any country, namely, output growth, price stability and poverty alleviation are best served by growth of agriculture sector. Growth in agriculture needs credit support. Credit is a 'pure service' transaction between two points of time rather than a spot market transaction in 'pure goods'. The time gap between sanction and realisation of credit give rise to several kinds of risks.

In terms of 4th Five Year Plan document over 30 per cent of the borrowings by cultivators are from institutional sources leaving a gap of around 70 per cent to be covered by the other financial institutions. Though there was fourfold increase in outstanding agricultural advances of commercial banks from Rs. 22,000 crores to Rs. 85,000 crores over the last decade (As observed by Vyas Committee set up by Reserve Bank of India in December, 2003) yet only five out of 27 public sector and two out of 29 private sector banks met the target of extending 18 per cent of net credit to agriculture. The share of agricultural lending in total credit halved from 21 per cent in 1970s to 11 per cent in 2001-02. Regional imbalance in credit disbursed to agriculture is also widening. Ironically, though production base in agriculture continues to comprise predominantly small and marginal farmers yet their share in credit is declining. Small and marginal farmers, who account for 80 per cent of the total number of holdings and 36 per cent of the total area, have only 27 per cent share in credit. Outsourcing certain preliminary credit-related tasks from development agents such as SHGs, NGOs would help banks expand their outreach without adding to their costs ultimately benefiting small and marginal farmers. Timeliness, adequacy of credit and concomitant costs of availing credit matters to the borrower. Measures to reduce costs of funds, transactions and risks, could lower the cost to borrowers without impairing viability of RFIs. Banks system and procedures should lead to cost-effective lending to step-up flow of credit in agriculture.

RRBs get credit from their sponsor banks at the rates of interest higher than the market rates. To compete with commercial banks RRBs need to bring down their rate of interest in line with commercial banks. The multi-tier co-operative structure adds its own costs and margins aggregating 5 to 6 per cent to the basic cost of funds, which is higher than that of commercial banks. The customers who use credit efficiently subsidise those who use credit inefficiently, represented by NPAs. This also raises the transaction costs in the system, thus denying the diligent credit to customers the benefit of lower interest rates. Inadequate flow of credit to agriculture can be viewed in two different ways. Owing to accumulation of losses in the public sector banks the flow of credit to rural areas by banks in recent years has not been up to the mark. Appropriate institutional changes may be required to ensure necessary credit flow to agriculture. Clearly, there is a need to examine the issue of rural credit and rural credit delivery systems in an objective as well as transparent way.

Under this background an attempt is made in this paper to examine the impact of bank finance on the farm sector in West Bengal.

SCENARIO OF CREDIT IN WEST BENGAL

As per 2001 Census West Bengal's population was 801.76 lakhs with density of population 903 per sq.km, highest amongst all the states in the country. Percentage of urban population to total population is 27.97. However, average population per bank branch is 19 thousands. In West Bengal share of primary sector in State Domestic Product (SDP) declined to 24.20 per cent in 2004-05 from the level of 35.90 per cent in 1993-94. On the contrary share of secondary and tertiary sector moved up to 21.31 per cent and 57.15 per cent respectively.

Table 9.1: Deposits and credit of commercial bank in India, 2006

(Rs. in crores)

Sl. No	Region/State/Union Territory	Deposits	Advances	CD Ratio
I. Northern Region		**492588**	**318318**	**64.62**
1.	Haryana	49365	28329	57.39
2.	Punjab	72797	41320	56.76
3.	Rajasthan	48900	37781	77.26
4.	Chandigarh	18468	14184	76.80
5.	Delhi	269754	181846	67.41
II. North Eastern Region		**33034**	**13454**	**40.73**
1.	Manipur	1218	610	50.08
2.	Mizoram	966	494	51.14
III. Eastern Region		**237954**	**117015**	**49.18**
1.	Orissa	32715	21605	66.04
2.	West Bengal	126035	70940	56.29
IV. Central Region		**252317**	**111643**	**44.25**
1.	Madhya Pradesh	55516	33603	60.53
V. Western Region		**608256**	**559365**	**91.96**
1.	Gujarat	105120	58462	55.61
2.	Maharashtra	486022	496908	102.24
VI. Southern Region		**467024**	**394046**	**84.37**
1.	Andhra Pradesh	117198	95336	81.35
2.	Karnataka	133376	101258	75.92
3.	Kerala	80435	49391	61.40
4.	Tamilnadu	132700	146613	110.48
	All India	2091174	1513842	72.39

Note: Figures in bracket indicate total number of states/union territories under the region

Source: Extracted from Table 1.5, *Basic Statistical Return*, Reserve Bank of India, March 2006.

The growth in share of tertiary sector in State Domestic Product to 57.15 per cent from the level of 42.79 per cent is certainly an encouraging phenomenon for the state economy. However, on further analysing tertiary sector, it is observed that Banking and insurance which is a component of producer services (other services in the tertiary sector next to producer services are consumer services and government services) registered a rate of growth of 7.51 per cent in State Domestic Product in 2004-05. This is significantly on the lower side as the compound annual growth rate of State Domestic Product from the sector during the period 1993-94 and 2003-04 was 17.81 per cent (*Economic Review*, West Bengal, 2005-06)

Since agricultural credit is a sub-component of total advances which in turn is related to deposits, a glimpse of the summarised position as on March 2006 on three base parameters like deposit, advance and CD ratio of all the regions, States/Union Territories and whole of India is given in Table 9.1 for easy comprehension of the prevailing situation. The table contains summarised figures for all the regions comprising 35 states/union territories and individual states whose CD ratio is 50 per cent and above.

It has been observed from the Table 9.1 that out of all 35 states/union territories in India West Bengal is in twelfth position with CD ratio of 56.29 per cent i.e. 16.10 per cent below the average CD ratio of 72.39 per cent for whole of India. While Tamilnadu occupies number one position with 110.48 per cent, Maharashtra comes next with 102.24 per cent. States/union territories whose CD ratio is above country's average are Rajasthan – 77.26, Chandigarh – 76.80, Andhra Pradesh – 81.35, Karnataka – 75.92. Had the state attained country's CD ratio of 72.39 per cent its quantum of advance would have increased by another Rs. 20,000 crores? CD ratio is important because target of agricultural advance follows from it.

Static and Dynamic Gains

The gains from bank finance to borrowers may be divided into static and dynamic gains. There are a variety of definitions and interpretations of economic statics and dynamics (Hicks, 1937). One of the most widely used concepts of statics and dynamics is that the former is concerned with equilibrium and the latter with disequilibrium and change (Ackly, 1985). The former involves a cross sectional analysis as well as the shift of the economic variables from an initial equilibrium to a new equilibrium in which case it becomes a matter of comparative statics. The latter method involves a time variables between one equilibrium position and another. In other words it is concerned with the path rather than the destination itself. Generally speaking equilibrium is a situation in which each individual agent is doing as well as it can for itself, given the array of actions taken by others and given the institutional framework that defines the options of individuals and links their actions (Kreps, 1992). The static gains of bank finance pertain to its impact on the borrowers due to low rates of interest charged by the banks. There is an element of subsidy in the borrowings from the banking system and this also confers a static benefit on the borrowers. Overdues to the banking system have become an important feature of the expense of banking system. In the case of dynamic gains a host of variables appear on the stage and undergo a change due to bank financing.

The dynamic gains from bank credit are analyzed in terms of their effect on the selected stocks and flows pertaining to our sample households. The immediate effect of borrowing is on the fall in credit gap. It takes some time to get the asset formed and generate employment and income out of it. We have analyzed the dynamic gains to the different categories of farmers.

Micro-finance and Self-help Groups

It is fact that the outreach of traditional institutions for providing credit has certain limitations on various grounds. There lies the need for a completely new type of credit institution which will be owned by the beneficiaries themselves. Thus, the importance of Self-Help Groups as new generation credit institutions which were formed out of necessity by the beneficiaries from amongst homogeneous groups where each and every one can open up their mind and participate in the affairs of the group. 'Microfinance' the word is associated with small finance. It will be very difficult to quantify the amount. Normally credit limit within Rs. 5000.00 may be regarded as microfinance.

Linking Self-Help Group (SHGs) of the rural poor with the banking system was launched initially in 1992. SHG-bank linkage programme has emerged as the major microfinance programme. 560 banks including 48 commercial banks, 196 RRBs and 316 co-operative banks are now actively involved in the operation of this programme. The rural poor can now have access to the formal banking system. Thrift linked credit support is provided to the members of SHGs. Banks are in a position to reduce transaction costs as well as risk in delivering small loans. The number of SHGs linked to banks reached 10.79 lakh by March 31, 2004 out of which 90 per cent are exclusively women groups. By end-March, 2004 average loan per SHG stands at Rs. 36,179.00 and average loan per family is Rs. 2,412.00.

It has been observed from Table 9.2 that West Bengal's share in All India SHGs number is 3.50 per cent whereas quantum-wise bank loan it is still lower at 1.52 per cent for the commercial banks. Southern region occupies 60 per cent share of SHGs in number and 79.4 per cent share in loan quantum for the commercial banks.

Table 9.2: Development of SHGs linking with institutional credit as on 31 March, 2007

(Rs. in million)

Institution	SHG No.	Bank Loan	Institution	SHG No.	Bank Loan
Northern			**Central**		
CB	85926	3063.88	CB	154216	5735.41
RRB	61418	1868.52	RRB	153416	4550.35
Co-op	34674	1243.06	Co-op	25097	643.16
Total	**182018**	**6175.46**	**Total**	**332729**	**10928.92**
North-Eastern			**Western**		
CB	37619	1563.06	CB	139332	5339.03
RRB	46414	912.89	RRB	49253	1941.25
Co-op	7721	162.96	Co-op	81862	1868.71
Total	**91754**	**2638.91**	**Total**	**270447**	**9148.99**
Eastern			**Southern**		
CB	221054	7794.09	CB	956640	90480.17
RRB	208097	6141.03	RRB	392209	34896.08
Co-op	96730	2110.79	Co-op	173295	10092.99
Total	**525881**	**16045.91**	**Total**	**1522144**	**135469.24**
All India			**West Bengal**		
CB	1594787	113975.64	CB	55862	1728.93
RRB	910807	50310.12	RRB	50953	1241.88
Co-op	419379	16121.67	Co-op	74748	1514.35
Total	**2924973**	**180407.43**	**Total**	**181563**	**4485.16**

Source: (Down loaded from NABARD web site)

NEW GENERATION RURAL FINANCIAL INSTITUTIONS IN WEST BENGAL

It has been felt that the three tiers of cooperatives, commercial banks and Regional Rural Banks could not meet the credit requirement of rural India and there exists a substantial gap which needs to be bridged. Accordingly, the concept of Self-help groups surfaced toeing the lines of Grameen Bank of Bangladesh. Self-help group is a unique approach to financial intermediation which combines access to low cost financial services with a process of self management. Essentially, a woman groups constituted and managed by themselves is given much encouragement. In many a cases SHGs are formed and supported by non-government organizations (NGO) or by government agencies. They are linked not only to banks but also to wider development programmes.

Table 9.3: Self-help group – bank linkage –upto 31 March, 2007

(Rs. in millions)

Region/State	No. of SHG	Bank Loan	Region/State	No. of SHG	Bank Loan
All India			**West Bengal**		
Cooperative Bank	1594787	113975.64	Cooperative Bank	55862	1728.93
RRB	910807	50310.12	RRB	50953	1241.88
Co-op	419379	16121.67	Co-op	74748	1514.35
Total	**2924973**	**180407.43**	**Total**	**181563**	**4485.16**

Source: NABARD

A consolidated report on development of SHGs in India vis-a-vis West Bengal is presented in the Table 9.3. It has been observed that average loan per SHG in West Bengal is Rs.24703 whereas it is Rs. 44342 in all India level. Furthermore, 22014 SHGs in West Bengal received repeat bank loans amounting Rs.884.40 million. A further analysis of the progress of SHGs in West Bengal as a percentage to all India and eastern region has been made with respect to institutional financial intermediaries i.e. commercial banks, regional rural banks and co-operatives. The results are furnished in the Table 9.4.

Table 9.4 : Progress of SHGs in West Bengal and India

Particulars	Within West Bengal		WB % to Eastern Region		WB % to All India	
	SHG No %	B. Loan %	SHG No %	B. Loan %	SHG No %	B. Loan %
CB	30.77	38.55	25.27	22.18	3.50	1.52
RRB	28.06	27.69	24.49	20.22	5.59	2.47
Co-op.	41.17	33.76	77.27	71.74	17.82	9.39
Total	**100**	**100**	**34.53**	**27.95**	**6.21**	**2.49**

It has been observed that West Bengal occupies 3.50 per cent share of SHGs number but the share in commercial bank loan is only 1.52 per cent. In respect of Regional Rural Banks share in number is 5.59 per cent but the loan from RRBs is only 2.47 per cent. In case of co-operatives the picture is even more dismal – with 17.82 percentage share in number loan figures at 9.39 per cent. Comparing West Bengal as a percentage to eastern region the position improves a little but never the bank loan share exceeds the share in percentage of SHGs number.

Comparing the performance of institutional agencies within West Bengal it has been observed that co-operatives occupy the major share of 41.17 per cent in number of SHGs with 33.76 per cent share in loan. Next comes the commercial banks with 30.77 per cent in number of SHGs achieved 38.55 per cent share in loan component. Last is RRB with 28.06 per cent sharing in number of accounts shared 27.69 per cent of total loan disbursed by all the three institutions.

It has been observed that Southern region occupies 60 per cent share of SHGs in number and 79.4 per cent share of bank loan which is the highest in the country. Table 9.5 provides the details of number of SHGs and loan component.

Table 9.5: Performance of southern region as on 31.03.2007

(Rs. in million)

Financial institutions	Number of SHGs	Loan component
Commercial banks	956640	90480.17
Regional Rural Banks	392209	34896.08
Co-operative Banks	173295	10092.99
Total	**1522144**	**135469.24**

EXISTING CREDIT FLOW GAPS AND REASONS THEREOF

Credit gap in agriculture is a matter dealt with since long and from the period of pre-independence. A study by Reserve Bank of India in the years 1935 and 1936 revealed that credit in agriculture was primarily supplied by village moneylenders and institutional credit was negligible. Thus inadequate agricultural credit had a significant role in founding both Reserve Bank of India and transforming Imperial Bank of India to State Bank of India.

Even then the flow of credit was found to be inadequate. As a result the concept of Priority Sector came into being in 1969 to highlight the need of agricultural lending. All said and done agriculture continue to starve of credit due to lack of resources of co-operatives and unfamiliarity of commercial banks to local needs especially to the needs of small and marginal farmers. The solution was sought to be found in establishing Regional Rural Banks out of Narasimham Working Group (1975) recommendations and National Bank for Agriculture and Rural Development (NABARD) in 1982.

Even then and initiating a lot of corrective measures, Vyas committee set up by Reserve Bank of India in December 2003 observed that only five out of 27 public sector and two out of 29 private sector banks met the target of extending 18 per cent of net credit to agriculture. The share of agriculture in total credit halved from 21 per cent in 1970s to 11 per cent in 2001-02.

Credit Deposit (CD) ratio determines level of deployment of credit. It is observed from the secondary information that CD ratio in India moved from

58 per cent in 1992 to 72 per cent in 2006 whereas in West Bengal CD ratio in 1992 was 51 per cent which increased by 5 per cent to reach 56 per cent at the end of 2006. Thus, the State could not reach the targeted level of 60 per cent CD ratio. In agricultural credit where the target is 18 per cent of net bank credit, the picture is even more dismal. In India, credit to agriculture went down from 15 per cent in 1992 to 11 per cent in 2006. However, in West Bengal there was no deterioration in percentile achievement. It was 8 per cent either in 1992 or in 2006. The reason behind such dismal performance is that agricultural credit could not pace up with other sectors to attain such heights.

Table 9.6: Credit profile of the sample farms

Source	Marginal			Small		
	Nos	% Nos	% Loan	Nos	% Nos	% Loan
SHG	13	16	30	3	20	42
Bank	9	11	51	3	20	55
Private	17	21	19	1	7	3
No Loan	41	52	0	8	53	0
	Medium			**Large**		
SHG	0	0	0	0	0	0
Bank	1	25	100	1	100	100
Private	0	0	0	0	0	0
No Loan	3	75	0	0	0	0

The information collected through the survey of farmers in Malda district, West Bengal reveals that combined institutional credit of banks together with new age financing agencies i.e. self-help groups covers 30 per cent of the population out of which Banks share is 14 per cent. Private sources cover 18 per cent of the population. Therefore, majority of the population i.e. 52 per cent have no access to formal source of credit. Table 9.6 gives a fair idea of institutional coverage of agricultural credit.

Credit gap is arrived at with reference to actual holding in cultivation, scale of finance recommended for various crops by District Level Technical Committee under the chairmanship of Malda District Central Co-operative Bank and the quantum of credit actually received from various sources.

It will appear from the Table 9.7 that overall credit gap is 50 per cent and above in marginal and small farmers' category and above 80 per cent in case of medium and large category of farmers. However, the gap is substantially lower in areas where self-help group has taken a root. This is the typical dynamic gains of micro-finance.

Table 9.7: Credit gap among the size of farms

Category	Cost of cultivation (Rs.)	Credit entitlement (Rs.)	Credit received (Rs.)	Credit gap (Rs.)	% of credit gap
Marginal	607235	399800	198085	201715	50
Small	236750	158733	67812	90921	57
Medium	220320	165217	20000	145217	88
Large	57275	43623	2500	41123	94

The reasons for credit gap are multi-various. The reasons may be broadly attributed to two factors. One is Institutional and the other is functional. About 20 per cent of lands are cultivated by oral tenants who do not have access to formal source of credit. A review of Land Tenancy Acts may permit the tenants to obtain credit from institutions. The 18 per cent target of flow of credit to agriculture based on the aggregate credit of the bank is misleading. As a good recovery in agricultural credit will substantially lower the outstanding in agricultural advance thereby pulling down otherwise a good achievement.

Lack of infrastructural facilities such as market yards, godowns, connecting roads from farmer's place to market stands in the way of flow of credit to agriculture. Farmers are wary of marketing their produce when there is a good harvest. Unless the produce fetches a good price there will be little desire to borrow for raising crops. The multi-tier co-operative structure leads to additional costs for each tier adding its own costs and margins to the basic cost of funds. Hence, there is the need to consider elimination of one of the tiers.

Inadequate flow of credit to agriculture can be resulted from accumulation of losses in the public sector banks. The same institutions that have been responsible for providing agricultural credit for the last twenty years or so not necessarily should continue to do so. Appropriate institutional changes may be pursued to ensure necessary credit flow to agriculture. Clearly, there is a need to examine the issue of rural credit and rural credit delivery systems in an objective as well as transparent way.

Timeliness and adequacy are critical to increasing the credit flow to agriculture. Delay in processing the loan applications as well as allowing lower quantum of loan than what is required causes detrimental effect on credit flow. Local bodies' involvement to create awareness amongst farmers for availing institutional credit as well as technological upgradation is wanting.

Documentation and requirement of supporting papers proves to be working against the increase in flow of credit to agriculture. Such requirement of paper documents should be kept to the bare minimum possible. Scale of finance stands in the way of flow of credit. Fixing scale of finance should be left to individual banks that should be flexible enough in applying the same keeping an eye to the requirement of the concerned farmer-borrower.

In time of bumper harvest farmers even cannot realize the costs of their operations due to low Market prices. More so if for any reason the crop fails the farmer is lead to default in repaying their debts. Such unforeseen circumstances can be guarded by raising the level of minimum support price and crop insurance schemes which cover risks of market fluctuations and yield variations to an extent.

The situation worsens when the farmer dies and the family is lead to default. Hence, the farmers in a group should be covered for life by group insurance to take care of such extra-ordinary events. Production credit or short-term loan do not take care of immediate consumption needs of the farmers. This causes some impediment in effective utilization of loan component and may lead to diversion of funds for non-productive purposes. Thus, while considering short-term credit need assessment of the farmer should include all requirements directly and indirectly related to production, post-harvest and household expenses. Simultaneously, repayment capacity needs to be assessed on the basis of aggregate household income from all sources.

Micro Finance Institutions (MFIs) are known to charge high rates of interest to their borrowers. Lenders to MFIs may ensure that these institutions charge interest to their clients on a cost plus reasonable margin basis. The village level branch of a commercial bank/regional rural bank finds it easier to access funds from its own headquarters than the primary agricultural credit societies. There are no easy solutions to this dilemma of easy credit adversely affecting the relationships of primary societies with their members and their federal structures which affects flow of credit.

Policy Implications of the Study

The foregoing findings of micro-level investigation have several implications for the design and formulation of micro-finance projects in the farm sector. Despite the persistence of top-down bureaucratic process in the administration of micro-finance by the commercial banks, the static and dynamic benefits are quit visible and tend to benefit the hitherto disadvantaged sections and vulnerable groups of the rural economy. The benefits accruing to those covered by different programmes and there is a pro-poor bias built into the credit system and it needs to be strengthened, if the fight against extreme poverty is to be a success. Micro-finance as an instrument of fighting poverty has come of age and international micro-credit summits are regularly held for dissemination of knowledge and replication of successful experiments like that of Grameen Bank of Bangladesh.

REFERENCES

1. Ackly, Gardner, 1985, *Macro Economic Theory*, Prentice Hall of India Private Limited, New York.
2. Basu, Kaushik, 1984, *The Less Developed Economy*, Oxford University Press, Delhi.
3. Griffin, Keith, 1979, *The Political Economy of Agrarian Change*, Macmillan, London.
4. Hicks, J. R., 1937, *Value and Capital*, Oxford University Press, London.
5. Kreps , David, M., 1992, *A Course in Microeconomic Theory*, Prentice Hall of India Private Limited, New Delhi.
6. Reserve Bank of India, 1991, *Report of the Committee on the Financial System*, Mumbai.

CHAPTER

10

Land Reforms for Alleviation of Rural Poverty

—Dr. K. Somasekhar
—Dr. G. Venkata Naidu

ABSTRACT

India is a land of villages wherein three-fourths of populations lives in rural areas. These people are facing many problems like poverty, unemployment, underemployment lack of infrastructural facilities and so on. It has been well recognized by the government that without development of rural areas it is not possible to attain the country's development. One of the main aspect of development of rural areas is to elimination of poverty by providing employment opportunities. Several policies and strategies adopted to provide employment opportunities during the plan period.

In spite of it, poverty could not be completely eradiated. Even after 63 years of Independence still more than one-forth of rural population lives in below poverty line. Evaluation studies conducted by research institutions identified that the root cause for not being elimination of poverty due to the people does not possess land. As per the data available 31 per cent households does not have land contrary to it few percentage of the people are having thousands of acres in their hands. In this backdrop, land reforms policy introduced by the Government to distribute the surplus land among the landless people to eliminate poverty. This paper examines implementation of rural development programmes and progress of distribution of land. Further hurdles for poor progress of land reforms, finally strategies to be adopted to implement land reforms effectively for elimination of rural poverty.

Introduction

Land reforms assume greater significance in a country of India where three-fourths of population live in rural areas. Rural India is known for a number of problems of poverty, illiteracy, unemployment and under-employment, malnutrition, poor health coverage, lack of education facilities, poor housing, non-availability of protected water supply, poor physical infrastructural facilities like roads, transport, communication, electricity. Keeping in view of these problems ever since the independence of the country, rural development and alleviation of poverty have been accorded high priority in plans for economic development. Every plan documents, right from the First Five Year Plan, has spelt out the Philosophy, the programme content and the financial allocation for the different schemes including those means for providing the basic minimum services of the rural community.

The term rural poverty is the opposite term of rural development. It implies lack of development or under-development. There is no university acceptable definition of poverty in spite there are several connotations and definitions in vogue. Poverty implies a condition characterized by deprivation of some sort by the other and perceived as undesirable by the persons concerned or others. It is a multi-dimensional concept and phenomenon. Generally there is a consensus among scholars about poverty being concerned and defined as a person's lack of access to objectively determined, reasonably adequate quantities of goods and services to satisfy his/her material and non-material basic needs.

ANTI-POVERTY PROGRAMMES

On 15th August 1947, India got political independence but still it was in economic bondage and faced with the acute problem of poverty (mainly rural) when almost half of its population was below poverty line. In the first three Five Year Plans (1951-1966), the dominant thinking in the policy planning was that poverty could be effectively tackled through general growth process and that the benefits of higher growth would automatically trickle down to poor masses and alleviate their poverty. In the First Plan the emphasis, therefore, was placed on agriculture development which shifted to industry in the next two plans. During this period, emphasis was also placed on land reforms, community development and cooperative movements but many things went wrong and hence no specific attempts were made to tackle rural poverty directly. But nonetheless, various anti-poverty programmes were put to experiment around this period. It was during the Fourth Five Year Plan that the focus shifted from growth to the direct attack on poverty; and special attention was given to poverty alleviation i.e. *'Garibi Hatao'*. It is sufficient to note here that alleviation of rural poverty has been centered on the development agenda of the country since independence. The rural poverty alleviation schemes which are now being implemented by the Ministry of Rural Areas and Employment, can be grouped in four categories viz. (*i*) wage employment schemes; (*ii*) self employment schemes, (*iii*) area development and land reforms schemes and (*iv*) the social benefit schemes.

Wage Employment Schemes

The Rural Manpower Programme (RMP) was started in 1960-61 in 32 community development blocks on a pilot basis for utilizing rural labour force, which was later extended to 1000 blocks by 1964-65 and remained in operation till 1968-69. The objective was to generate employment of 100 days to at least 2.5 million persons during the Third Plan, but could generate only 137 million mandays of employment. In the Fourth Five Year Plan, the Crash Scheme for Rural Employment (CSRE) was started (April, 1971) for three year period for generation of 315 million mandays for 1000 persons in each of 350 districts of the country every year through labour intensive works. Along with CSRE, a Pilot Intensive Rural Employment Programme (PIREP) was started in November 1972 in 15 selected community blocks for a three year period, to provide additional employment opportunities for unskilled labour. 18.16 million mandays of employment were generated under PIREP. Drought Prone Area Programme (DPAP) was launched as Rural Works Programme (RWP) in 1970-71 in 54 DPAP units spread over 13 states in the country. Towards the end of Fourth Five Year Plan the programme was changed to an Area Development Scheme on the recommendations of the task force on Integrated Rural Development Programme (1973). In the Fourth Five Year Plan, Small Farmers Development Agency and Marginal Farmers and Agricultural Labour were started in 85 districts and later expanded in 160 districts in the Fifth Five Year Plan. The emphasis in both the schemes was on self-employment through diversification of farm economy of small and marginal farmers and agricultural labourers.

Culmination of earlier experiences was in the Food for Work Programme (FWP) which started in 1997, as Wage Employment Scheme, and Integrated Rural Development Programme (IRDP) in 1976. The FWP aimed at generation of employment by utilizing available stocks of foodgrains. Employment of 979.32 million mandays were generated during the year 1977-78 to 1979-80 (September). This scheme became very popular in the rural areas and came to be recognised as a major instrument of rural employment. FFW was restructured and renamed as National Rural Employment Programme (NREP) in October, 1980. The programme became part of Sixth Five Year Plan from April, 1981 and was implemented as a centrally sponsored scheme on 50:50 sharing basis between the Centre and states with the objectives of generation of additional gainful employment, creation of durable community assets and raising of nutritional standards of the rural poor. During Sixth Plan the total expenditure on implementation of NREP was Rs. 1873.00 crore and the employment generation during the period was 1775.18 million mandays. To supplement NREP and also to provide employment to at least one member from each landless household for 100 days in a year, Rural Landless Employment Guarantee Programme (RLEGP) was launched in August, 1983, as 100 per cent Central funded programme covering the entire country. During the Seventh Plan, an expenditure of Rs. 7809.93 crore was made and 3496.30 million mandays were generated under NREP and RLEGP. It has however, not been possible to provide 100 days of employment to at least one member of each landless household in a year as was envisaged under RLEGP.

It was found in the evaluation of NREP that about 53 per cent villages of the country were such that not a single work was taken up under NREP in its implementation of nine years or so. In spite of the clear guidelines that the felt needs of the village people should be reflected in the works programme, there was not much involvement of the people at the grassroots level in identifying the works and implementation of these programmes. It is in this background in 1989-90, a massive programme of Jawahar Rozgar Yojana was launched by merging NREP and RLEGP. The expenditure under JRY is shared between the Centre and the states on 80:20 basis. Apart from the commitment of Government to empower the village level institutions, one of the reasons for the launching of JRY was to take to wage employment programmes to each and every village in the country. In 1993-94, the element of assurance was added in the wage employment programmes by launching Employment Assurance Scheme (EAS) in 1746 blocks and to supplement the efforts of JRY to generate additional gainful employment. EAS is quite similar to JRY except that an assurance of 100 days of employment is provided under EAS is quite similar to JRY except that an assurance of 100 days of employment is provided under EAS in the form of casual manual work to all those rural poor who need and seek employment in lean season. The worker who wants to get employment has to register with the village panchayat and when 10-20 such persons demand work, the block level officer provides employment by opening up new works or on the existing work. Under JRY and EAS employment is provided in the form of casual manual work on minimum wages in the rural areas, by taking up useful community and social assets. Sampoorna Grameena Rojgar Yojana (SGRY) was launched in 2001 by merging JGSY and EAS in order to provide additional wage employment and food security to rural poor.

A new era has begun in rural India as historic programme Mahatma Gandhi National Rural Employment Guarantee Scheme (MGNREGS) launched in 2006. The objective of the scheme is to provide to every registered rural household a guarantee of at least 100 days of employment during a financial year. The scheme also envisages if employment is not provided after registration he will be entitled to unemployment allowance of 25 per cent of wage rates for first 30 days and for rest of the days 50 per cent of the wage rates for which legal guarantee is given.

Self Employment Programmes

We have noted that in the first three Five Year Plans (1951-66), the dominant thinking in the Policy Planning was that poverty could be effectively tackled through the general growth process. Emphasis was, therefore, given to the projects and policies which were expected to have higher growth rate. In the Fourth Five Year Plan (1969-74), special attention was given to alleviation of rural poverty. Special programmes were introduced for the benefit of the poor, relatively less privileged classes and backward areas. The objective of these programmes was creation of assets, skill development and creation of infrastructure as well as to take up development works in the backward areas. Beneficiary oriented programmes like small Farmers Development Agency (SFDA). Marginal Farmers and Agricultural Labourers Agency (MFAL) aimed at helping the specific target groups of beneficiaries were started.

For taking up any economic activity one needs capital. People living in poverty find it difficult to save and invest in economic activity. Credit to poor is rarely available and if available it is on very high rate of interest which affects the profitability of the project taken up with this credit. All India Rural Credit Survey (Gorwala Committee) found that in 1951-52, institutional credit covered about 7 per cent of the rural households. The supply of credit at reasonable rate of interest to poor becomes important for taking up self employment schemes. It is in this background that the integrated Rural Development Programme (IRDP) was initially started in 1976, in 20 selected districts of the country with the aim to providing subsidized credit to the rural poor for taking up self employment micro enterprise. The programme was reviewed in 1978-79 to integrate the methodology and approach of the three major on-going special programmes of SFDA, Community Area Development (CAD) and Drought Prone Area Programme (DPAP). The underlying contents of these three major programmes were integrated into a new programme of IRDP and taken up in 2300 blocks of the country in 1978-79. Upto 1978-79, IRDP was a Central sector scheme and 100 per cent funds were provided by the Central Government. During 1979-80, this programme was made a centrally sponsored scheme in which funding was shared on 50:50 basis between the Centre and the states. IRDP was extended to all the blocks in the country, w.e.f. 2nd October, 1980. Since then IRDP continues to be a major instrument of poverty alleviation in the rural areas. IRDP, a self employment scheme, aims at enabling the identified rural poor families to augment their income and cross the poverty line through acquisition of credit based productive assets. Assistance is given in the form of subsidy and credit. Under this scheme 50 per cent of the assisted families are supposed to be from SC/STs. More than 50 million families have been assisted under IRDP. The programme is being further strengthened by promotion of group activities and cluster approach where 5 beneficiaries can secure a subsidy of upto Rs. 1.25 lakh for a project costing Rs. 2.5 lakh.

In 1999 a new programme in the name of Swarnjayanti Gram Swarozgar Yojana (SGSY) launched by integrating six existing programmes called IRDP, DWCRA, TRYSEM, SITRA, GKY and MWS. Its main objective is to improve family incomes of rural poor by formulating schemes keeping in view of the local needs and resources. It also aims to provide sustainable income through micro enterprise development.

PREVALENCE OF RURAL POVERTY

In spite of several programmes implemented by earmarking crores of rupees right from First Five Year Plan onwards still around one-fourth population are in below poverty line (Table 10.1).

Table 10.1: Percentage of Rural Population Below Poverty Line in India

Year	In Lakhs	Percentage
1973-74	2,612.90	56.44
1977-78	2,642.47	53.07
1983-84	2,519.57	45.65
1987-88	2,318.79	39.09
1993-94	2,440.31	37.27
1999-00	2,392.00	27.09
2004-05	2,209.24	26.10

Source: Tenth Five Year Plan, Vol. 1, Planning Commission, New Delhi.

Table 10.1 shows that as a result of anti-poverty programmes there has been decline in poverty from first year plan onwards. During the last ten Five Year Plan period half of the population only crossed the below poverty line, remaining half of the population remain in poverty. The reason is that the most of these people does not possess land. In the rural areas agriculture being the mainstay of the people, unless the people own's a land it will be difficult to meet their basic needs as the anti-poverty programmes alone can't help them.

IMPORTANCE OF LAND REFORMS

Agrarian relations do influence the levels of production and productivity and also the income and wealth distribution in the agricultural sector. The pre-requisite for a productive land tenure system are direct ownership of land, absence of intermediaries, reasonable land rent, consolidation of holding and efficient land record system.

Land reforms refer to measures taken by the Government with regard to ownership, tenancy and management of land. Thus, land reforms encompass the whole agrarian structure. It is not desirable having a ownership on land in few people. The ownership pattern on land should be efficient both socially and economically.

The term land reforms includes not merely redistribution of land but also tenancy and other land management aspects measures to conserve land use, prevention of its degradiation etc., land reforms provide a real sense of participation in rural life for the rural poor.

In the rural context in India land is not only means of livelihood, it is also a source of prestige and social identity. Social status in the society can be attained through the landownership and tenure. Indeed, evaluation studies relating to poverty alleviation programmes have revealed how the very poor, without any support, are marginalized. Hence, a blind emphasis on growth without eliminating exploitative elements in the agrarian structure is not economically socially desirable.

Poverty is the end product of the process of monopolization of means of production. The problem has to be tackled on two fronts—curbing the monopolization process and improving the capacity of the poor to participate and share in the development.

It was soon realized that absence of landlordism had resulted in agricultural stagnation. The landlords were content with receiving rents. They did not show any interest in land improvement. The actual tillers of the soil had neither means nor the incentive to invest as they did not own the land under these circumstances. The best way to increase agricultural production was the transfer of technology of land to the actual cultivator. However, land reform is not only a reform of the way the land is held and maintained but just as much reform of the man who tills the land.

The objective of land reforms is removal of poverty and improving the socio-economic status of the rural poor in order to make them effective in participation in the process of development of rural areas. Land reforms also aim at restructuring the agrarian relations to achieve egalitarian social structure in the future of landownership and cultivation continues perhaps the most fundamental issue in national development. To a large extent, the pattern of economic and social organization will depend upon the manner in which the land problem is resolved sooner or later, the principles and objectives of policy for land cannot but influence policy in other sectors as well.

In these words, the First Five Year Plan (1951-56) enunciates the importance of land reforms. Even with the passage of time this observation has attained the significance. There is close relationship exists between the pattern of land ownership and power structure in a village. Furthermore, the fruits of rural development will continue to be cornered or substantially controlled by those who possess land.

Since the beginning of planning in India various programmes of rural development have mostly benefited those who own land and thus command resources. The Panchayati Raj institutions too have been dominated by the rural land elite, and so the case with cooperative societies. Due to various reasons in India ownership of land invests one, with social prestige and is thus abroad measure of persons status in rural society, second, agriculture is the dominate occupation in the village and so land becomes an input of critical significance in survival and success. Thus, India is a country which has an extending skewed distribution of landholdings which points to an urgent need for reform.

According to the 59th round (for the reference year 2003-04) of NSSO data the ownership of land in rural India was as follows:

Table 10.2: Ownership of Agricultural Land in Rural India

Ownership in ha	% of households	% of land owned
No land	31.0	Nil
<1	49.1	22.9
1-2	10.8	21.3
2-5	7.0	30.0
>5	2.1	26.5
	100	100

As per table 10.2 it may be noted that around one-third of rural households does not possess land. 60 per cent of households are having below 2 hectares of land which means they belong to small and marginal farmers. Whereas remaining 10 per cent of the farmers are having above 2 hectares of land. It clearly shows that large proportion of the rural population either they does not have land or lower rungs of land ownership. It also shows that very few of the households posses high portion of land.

Thus, in the rural India there is a dichotomy that small percentage of the households owns huge portion of land, huge portion of population owns either small portion of land or without land. Hence, there is a need of redistribution of land through land reforms in favour of the poor which will enable them to make their lands emerge as source for greater agricultural production. Land reforms aim at achieving the twin objectives of growth through optimum utilization of land and equity by means of redistribution of ownership holdings and security tenure.

Land Distribution

The agricultural sector has, no doubt, experienced technological changes. But, in the absence of institutional changes, these have only accentuated the economic disparities between those who own land and other productive resources on the one hand and those with little access to productive assets. The case for land ceilings arises from the absolute and permanent shortage of land, land ceiling in more urgent than other kinds of ceilings.

There is a need to support the landless by distributing the surplus land among them after fixation of a ceiling on landholding. It would definitely help in removal of poverty as eventually step up agricultural output along with employment opportunities. In the rural areas there is found to be tension between the landless labourers and landowners due to the shortage of land as ownership of land is concentrated in a few hands. Therefore make land reform a task of very high priority in any scheme of rural development. Rural development without land reform is found to remain hollow.

In 1948, "Agrarian Reforms Committee" was appointed under the chairmanship of J.C. Kumarappa by the Congress party to examine the land reforms. The Committee submitted its report in 1949 and its recommendations become the party's policy on land reforms in independent India. The Committee recommended that all intermediary interests should be abolished, land should belong to the tillers, leasing of land should be prohibited except in the case of widows, minors and other disabled persons; and those cultivating land continuously for a period of six years should be granted occupancy rights.

In the First Five Year Plan government has announced its policy on land reforms. It divided the tenants-at-will into two categories. Those cultivating land belonging to large landholders, and those belonging to middle and small owners. The plan recommended that all landholders should be allowed to resume tenanted land for personal cultivation. However, the limit upto which land could be resumed by large cultivators was very vaguely defined and this question was left to the states to determine. As regards middle and smaller farmers, they should, said the plan, resume the land for personal cultivation within a period of five years. Thus only the land belonging to large holders over and above the ceiling limit, was available for distribution among the tenants-at-will.

The Second Five Year Plan discerned on definite trend towards the ejection of tenants and attacked to the ignorance on the part of the people of legislative provisions regarding security of tenure, possible lacunae in the land, inadequate land records and defective administrative arrangements. The Third Five Year Plan too admitted that the total impact of land reform has been less than was hoped for. The Fourth Five Year Plan noted in 1969 that the tenants and sharecroppers continued to be subject to the landlords right to resume the land and that they constituted as much as 82 per cent of the total number of tenants. The Fifth Five Year Plan reported that the existing legislation fell far short of the accepted policy and concluded that the objectives of tenancy reforms still remain to be attained. The observation of the Sixth Five Year Plan concerning land reforms were not significantly different. During the subsequent plans VII, VIII, IX and Tenth Plan period also the land reforms as poverty alleviation measure remained on the developmental agenda. During these plan period legislation have been enacted to eliminate exploitation by providing security of tenure and regulation of rent for tenants and sharecroppers bring direct contact between the tiller and the state and give social and economic status to the landless by distributive measures.

The progress of distributions of surplus land among the poor is presented in table 10.3.

Table 10.3 indicates that the distribution of surplus land among the landless is not at all satisfactory. This is due to the defects in the Land Ceiling Act and also the lethargy on the part of the administrators. Besides too much of political interference is also obstacle for implementation of land reforms effectively.

Implementation of Land Ceiling Programme

The objective of land reforms could not be achieved to a desired extent due to the loopholes in the ceiling laws. Those are, transfers have been permitted under the law as well as those indulged in a clandestine manner. Besides, several exemptions were granted to various states. The ceiling limits are also open to question. They were fixed at a time when farm productivity and prices were low. The advent of new agricultural technology, the policy of support prices and the exemption of agricultural income from taxation have altered the situation and strengthened the case for lower earnings.

State governments fixed a land ceiling limit, these ceiling limits were based on the basis of individual holder as a unit instead of a family. This

Table 10.3 : Distribution of Surplus Land Among the Poor

Sl.No.	State	Total cultivable area (in acres)	Ceiling surplus area distributed	% of cultivated area
1.	Andhra Pradesh	39476640	571880	1.45
2.	Assam	8007920	479878	5.99
3.	Bihar	2222217	303217	1.09
4.	Gujarat	4147999	133999	0.43
5.	Himachal Pradesh	2055920	87259	0.93
6.	Jammu & Kashmir	2596560	3340	—
7.	Karnataka	31977120	117147	0.37
8.	Kerala	6175200	64283	1.04
9.	Madhya Pradesh	56521680	185313	0.33
10.	Maharashtra	52117200	554870	1.06
11.	Manipur	406720	1682	0.41
12.	Orissa	20080560	154298	0.77
13.	Punjab	10661520	103487	0.97
14.	Rajasthan	63683920	452174	0.71
15.	Tamilnadu	20812160	182369	0.78
16.	Tripura	773760	1599	0.21
17.	Uttar Pradesh	51827040	390501	0.76
18.	West Bengal	14711360	965293	6.56
19.	D & N Haveli	59520	6851	11.51
20.	Delhi	1483	394	0.22
21.	Pondicherry	84320	1022	1.21
	Total	**449943920**	**5190856**	**1.15**

Source: Annual Report 2002-03, Government of India, Ministry of Rural Areas and Employment.

paved the way to retain as much as 1000 acres by a large family. Exemption were available for plantations, sugarcane farms operated by sugarcane factories, cattle breeding forms, gazing lands, efficient farm, mechanized farms, religious and charitable institutions and trusts and cooperative farms etc. Thus the very purpose of land ceilings is being defeated.

After deliberations with the state governments it was decided to re-enter dealing legislation, fixing a limit on the size of ownership holdings. These are:

1. 10 to 18 acres was the limit of perennially migrated land capable of yielding two crops a year.
2. In the case of a single crop the ceiling was 27 acres.
3. In a household of more than five persons, additional land was allowed for each extra member over 18 years age.

The concept of both sufficient irrigation as well as quality of land were subject to different interpretation. The individual may also asset that he cultivates only one crop, by using their power the landlords could easily make illegal transfers. In the absence of birth registration, minors claimed that they were above 18 years so as to enable a family to acquire more land.

Apart from this loopholes, there are weaknesses in the system of land ceiling. The allottees had suffered because of the procedural delays in judicial decisions, lack of inputs, capital and technical know-how and the overall indifference towards the comparatively weaker sections.

The Ten member task force on Agrarian relations, headed by P.S. Appu was appointed by the Planning Commission in 1972. It submitted its report in 1973 where in committee observed "That in the context of the socio-economic conditions prevailing in the rural areas of the country, no tangible progress can be expected in the field of land reform in the absence of the requisite political will. When there is lack of will among the politician, definitely it reflects in policy and legislation and its implementation.

Ceiling laws can be effective when the bureaucracy itself favour and by proper setup at administrative level. In the implementation of the land ceiling this is also one of the problem noticed by committees appointed by the government to examine the implementation of land ceiling. Further, these committees also noticed absence of correct and up-to-date record of rights.

The land reform programme lacked an integrated approach. Consolidation of holdings was conceived of and undertaken without providing for village roads, irrigation and drainage channels, land shaping, soil conservation etc. There is also no effective political conservation at the grassroot levels to minimize and eliminate the tensions that are found to emerge with the implementation of land reforms.

Against this backdrop, in order to implement land reforms effectively so as to alleviate rural poverty there is need to take following initiatives:

1. There is need to fix time-frame to settle all the disputes which are pending with the courts as there are about 60-70 per cent agricultural land is locked-up in court cases in various states.
2. Since the land reforms is a state subject there is need to encourage the states by allocating more funds to the states which have created favourable conditions for land reforms.
3. Mere land distribution may not solve the problem of poverty, therefore, it is necessary to provide backward linkages such as credit inputs and other agricultural inputs as these beneficiaries cannot afford on their own.
4. There are instances that some of the beneficiaries of land distribution either selling or mortgaging the land. So to check from selling, a specific undertaking may be obtained from the beneficiary.
5. Implementation of land reforms relies on the administrators and administrative setup. If the administrators with commitment and dedication posted in the administrative setup then only there will be scope to attain desired results.
6. As there is no proper database on different aspects including land records, it is becoming hurdle to identify the beneficiaries. Hence, there is need to pay much attention to update land records properly.
7. There is need to give priority in distributing land to the landless persons more particularly SC's and ST's.
8. It should be ensured that there are no escape routes for the vested interests to transfer land and thus indirectly retain possessing of surplus land illegally.
9. Micro-level administrative machinery at the village and taluka/mandal level needs to be strengthened. The Panchayati Raj should also be actively involved to enforce land reforms as superscribed to then under XI schedule of the Constitution.
10. Above all sensitization of the public, youth and women organization, is essential in order to enlighten them about the whole concept of land reforms and to make them to participate in the implementation.

Conclusion

Poverty has been one the major challenging problem which is confronting the country. In spite, several policies and programmes executed for elimination of poverty but, so far poverty completely eradicated. There are so many factors why we have failed in this direction. One of the major factor is around 40 per cent of the population does not possess land. Several evaluation studies shows that there was less impact of the development programmes on the landless poor. Hence, it is need of the hour to implement land reforms effectively by distributing surplus land among the landless labourers in order to elimination of rural poverty completely.

REFERENCES

1. R.K. Sharma, Anil Kumar and S.K. Chauhan, "Impact of Land Reform on Farm Production", *Kurukshetra*, 1993, p. 8.
2. FAO (1953), Inter-relationship between Agrarian Reform and Agricultural Development, p. 63.
3. G. Parthasarathy (1971), *Agricultural Development and Small Farmers: A Study of Andhra Pradesh*, Vikas Publishing House, New Delhi, p. 25.
4. M.P. Mathur, 'Distribution of Surplus land: Impact on Beneficiaries, *Financial Express*, June 7, 2006.
5. S.R. Maheswari (1985), *Rural Development in India*, Sage Publication, New Delhi, p. 144.
6. Ministry of Rural Development (GOI). Annual Report for the year 2003-04.
7. Karalay, G.N., 2005, *Integrated Approach to Rural Development—Policies, Programmes and Strategies*, Concept Publishing Company, New Delhi.
8. R.K. Singh, 2005, *Poverty and Sustainable Development—Third World Perspective*, Abhteei Publication, Delhi.

CHAPTER

11

Politics of Rural Development

—Trilochan Dash

ABSTRACT

*India is predominantly a land of villages, out of which 76 per cent of the people are living in 6,00,000 villages across rural India. Since independence, different policies and programmes were introduced in order to uplift their socio-economic status of living by different governments both at centre and states. The most alarming worry is that all the noble policies were in the air due to high bureaucratic in nature, change of government and their shifting of the ideologies, external pressures from the supra-national agencies and most important one is lack of understanding in the masses in rural India. Many vested interest people took advantage out of it. The slogan '**Garibi Hatao**' remained immortal in Indian soil. The present paper tried to analyze the certain important arguments in this regard which may give further investigation in the field of research.*

Introduction

Mahatma Gandhi rightly said, "India lives in the villages". The demographic picture of the country reveals that over 76 per cent of India's population still lives in 6,00,000 villages across rural India. Out of these 89 per cent have no access to telephones, 52 per cent do not have access to power, 10 per cent have no access to drinking water, 91 per cent have no access to toilet facilities, average distance to all weather roads is 2 km and 244 million rural people are "poor" compared to 80 million urban poor. Around 100 districts are under the constant threat of drought and semi-famine like situation every year. Other districts face floods and torrential rains every year. About

25 per cent rural households are landless and bonded labour and have no income generating assets. About top 39 per cent own 80 per cent and lowest 30 per cent own only two per cent of the assets in rural areas. About 50 per cent of the villages have very poor socio-economic conditions. In spite of that rural India still contributes about half of the national income. Agriculture is the primary occupation which sustains the rural areas. The relevance of rural development is all clear when one realizes that 29 per cent of India's population still lives below the poverty line both in the rural and urban areas, earning less than US $1 per day. Since India's independence, concerted efforts have been made to ameliorate the living standard of rural masses. Realizing the noble objectives, the Government of India has launched various five year plans to rural development programmes. Various approaches and strategies have applied to rural development. In the beginning of 1950's the community development programme was introduced to involve popular participation in rural development. Basically, it emphasized on the building of infrastructure in rural areas with the participation of the rural people. In the 1960's, it was seen that community development programmes had not resulted in increased agricultural production since plan outlays for rural development were spread thinly over several programme. The report of Ford Foundation Team (1959), India's food crisis and steps to deal with it outlined the need for agrarian reorganization. Approach to rural development took a new direction in the Third Five Year Plan with more emphasis on agriculture production. In the 1970's, the approach of 3rd Five Year Plan continue to Fourth Five Year Plan with some of the variation. The main focus was on covering bigger farmer and fertile state/district in the country and also the focus was on under-privileged farmers and areas to Drought-Prone Areas Programmes (1970), Cash Scheme for Rural Employment (1971), Tribal Area Development (1972), Minimum Need Programme (1975), Small Farmers Development Agency (SFDA), and Marginal Farmers and Agricultural Labourer Development Agency (MFAL, 1971) were introduced. Later on integrated approach toward rural development wage introduced in 1978-79 in order to fulfill various goals such as Training of Rural Youth for Self Employment (TYRSEM), Development of Women and Children Rural Areas (DWCRA), Supply of Improved Toolkits to Rural Artisans (SITRA) and Ganga Kalyan Yojana (GKY) were introduced as sub-programs of IRDP to take care of the specific needs of the rural people. It is an anti – poverty programme. The important components of the anti-poverty strategy, Wage Employment Programme have sought to achieve multiple objectives. These programmes not only proved employment opportunities during lean agricultural seasons but also in times of floods, drought and other natural calamities. They create rural infrastructure which supports further economic activity. These programs also put an upward pressure on market wage rates by attracting people to

public works programs, thereby reducing labour supply and pushing up demand for labour. It encompasses National Rural Employment Programme (NREP) and Rural Landless Employment Guarantee Program (RLEGP) which were part of the 6th and 7th Plans. Employment Assurance Scheme was launched in October 1993 covering 1,778 drought-prone, desert, and tribal and hill areas in the country. It was later extended to all the blocks in 1997-98. The EAS was deigned to provide employment in the form of manual work in the lean agricultural season. The works taken up under the program were expected to lead to the creation of durable economic and social infrastructure and address the felt-needs of the rural people. Food for Work Programme was started in 2000-01 as a component of the EAS in eight notified drought-effect states of Chhattisgarh, Gujarat, Himachal Pradesh, Orissa, Rajasthan, Maharashtra, and Uttaranchal. The program aims at food provision through wage employment. Food grains are supplied to states free of cost. Rural Housing was initiated in 1985-86 and it is the core program for providing free housing to families in rural areas, targets scheduled castes (SCs), scheduled tribe(ST) household and freed bonded labourers the Samagra Awas Yojana (SAY) was taken up in 25 block to ensure convergence of housing, provision of safe drinking water, sanitation and common drainage facilities. The National Social Assistance Programme (NSAP), launched in August 1995 marks a significant step towards fulfillment of the Directive Principles of State Policy. The SAP has three components: (*a*) National Old Age Pension Scheme (NOAPS); (*b*) National Families Benefit Scheme (NFBS); (*c*) National Maternity Benefit Scheme (NMBSM). The Act came into force on February 2, 2006 and was implementing in a phased manner. In phase one it was introduced in 200 most backward district of the country. It was implemented in additional 130 districts in Phase two 2007-2008. As per the initial target, NREGA was to be expanded country wide in five year. However, in order to bring the whole nation under its safety net and keeping in view the demand, the scheme was extended to the remaining 274 rural districts of India from April 1, 2008 in Phase III. The Act is also a significant vehicle for strengthening decentralization and deepening processes of democracy by giving a pivotal role to the Panchayati Raj institutions in planning, monitoring and implementation (Sarma, 2005). The unique feature of the ACT include: time bound employment guarantee and wage payment within 15 days, incentive-disincentive structure to the state governments for providing employment or unemployment allowance at their own cost and emphasis on labour-intensive works prohibiting the use of contractors and machinery. The Act also mandates 33 per cent participation for women. Over the last two years, implementation trends vindicate the basic objective of the Act. Thus, the Indian polity has been trying to change gears from mere survival to performance; from the economic growth to political Justice—and it has been encountering stubborn resistance from a variety of entrenched interests. The latter have held out against a government which had won the political battle for a newer of policies but had given little thought to what was involved in putting them through. In consequence, of faced arising Tide of popular discontent which, however, remained largely unorganized and unstructured (Rajni Kothari, 1990).

In order to achieve the above approaches towards rural development, the various strategies were adopted such as collective strategy, reformist strategy and market-oriented strategy. The first approach emphasizes the use of land, agricultural, technological and employment policies. The aim is to bring about fundamental changes in the organization of productive forces in the rural areas. It has also emphasized the importance of land reforms to bring about socio-economic change in rural areas. The second strategy emphasizes on the need for reciprocity in rural development policy. So, local institutions such as co-operatives are given great importance in this strategy of rural development. The village community play a crucial role in Gandhian scheme of rural development and people's participation is being increased through Panchayati Raj. Lastly, this strategy gives primary importance to the use of market forces in shaping rural development. It has been advocated for the growth of the agricultural sector which in turn is expected to lead to rural development. The example of 'Green Revolution' in the 1960's in Punjab is the use of this strategy.

POLITICS AND RURAL DEVELOPMENT

Politics and development are the two sides of the same coin because power and authority are to govern through a social process. Political parties and their ideologies have a significant role while framing policies for the development of a nation and welfare of the people. As a result, the issue of development is above politics but in reality, politics is often more important to political parties. Such fallacy is observed across the countries in different periods. The nature of political interference differs according to the context and motive and on many occasions, greater development goals are sacrificed for the benefit of a few or an individual. Many argue that political ideology of development is very important from the point of social justice and equity. It is the ideology of development issues which bring about sustainable development. Another school of thought feels that the political interference is a reason for under-development. Post-globalization, the belief is shared also by multilateral development agencies and they prescribe minimal state role in development initiatives. Thus, it is necessary to know the rationale behind the meaning and significance of the two terms.

Politics is a process by which groups of people make collective decisions. The term is generally applied to behavior within civil governments but politics has been observed in other group interactions, including corporate, academic, and religious institutions. It consists of "social relations involving authority or power" and refers to the regulation of public affairs within a political unit, and to the methods and tactics used to formulate and apply policy. The word "politics" comes from the Greek word (*politick*), modeled on Aristotle's "Affairs of the City", the name of his book on governing and governments, which was rendered in English mid-15 century as Latinized *"Polettiques"*. Politics is the art as well as science of government. It consists of social relations involving authority of power. It is a process by which groups of people make collective decisions and is not restricted to behavior within civil governments alone. Politics has been observed in all group interaction including corporate, academic and religious institution. Thus, politics is that part of itches which has to do with the regulation and governance of the nation and state, the preservation of its safety, peace, development and prosperity, the defence of its existence, the augmentation of its strength and resources and the protection of its citizen in their rights with preservation and improvement of their morals. In other words, political institution express and embody the wisdom of the people of the time and the route to good political and social institution is by deepening of wisdom and by broadening of vision.

On the other hand, Development implies change (Thirlwall, 2003). It is also an act or process, a step or growth, progress, advancement (Datta, 2010). It is a process of gradual change of people and society from the existing state to a better one. It aims at releasing the broken, restoring the marginalized and transforming the present exploitative and oppressive economic, political, social and cultural structures into a just society. In this vision of a just society, exploitation of man by man, and the domination of man over man, and men over women, must be stopped. Pit has defined development in more general terms in perceived increased effectiveness of social and economic activities and functions of the society and situations and in the range of options open to people. In this sense, development is perceived as improvement in the quality of life even when this means fewer goods and services. Defined in these terms development inevitably becomes a normative concept. It connotes the direction that development has to follow. In the modern context, development has been referred to as overall process of transforming men and societies in to a social order in which every human being can achieve moral and material well being. In a broader sense, the concept of development has been referred to as a whole, integral, value-loaded cultural process encompassing the natural environment, social relations, education, production, consumption and well being (Pitt, 1971). Thus, development has been described as a generic term meaning growth, evolution, stage of improvement or progress. The concept of 'development' gained currency after World War II and has been defined by most economists, in the operational sense, as growth of the per capita gross national product (GNP). It is a relative term and is comparable to different countries, different sectors, and different time periods. The scope of development is vast and all encompassing—social, economic, industrial, technological and so on. However, development is strongly linked to economic growth and usually leads to other types of development.

Development practitioners and experts have evolved different indicators for measurement of sectorwise development, for example, increase in annual GDP is an indicator of the economic growth of a country. Literacy level among women is considered as an indicator of social development. Basing on the frequently found difference in development between urban and rural areas, development is also commonly understood as rural development, i.e. the status of development in rural areas of a country.

To understand development in the rural context it is not simply an economic proposition but it has social, psychological and cultural dimensions as well. It is a multi-dimensional concept. To be precise, rural development is a programme designed to improve the socio-economic living conditions of the poor. It aims at raising their cultural level and re-orienting their rich traditions. It seeks to achieve increase rural production and productivity, greater socio-economic equity and a higher standard of living for the rural poor. It is partly ameliorative and partly development-oriented. Development is interlinked with motivation, innovation and the active participation of the beneficiaries, inter alia, calls for organization and management. Rural Development recognizes the importance of such basic services as health, housing, education and expanded communications. This is required for enhancing the productivity of the rural poor. Moreover, it aims at providing gainful employment, so that the rural people too may contribute their mite to the national product. Further, rural development implies a fuller development of existing resources, including the construction of infrastructure, such as roads and irrigation works, the introduction of new production technology, the revival of traditional arts and crafts, and the creation of new types of institution and organizations.

Rural development in general is used to denote the actions and initiatives taken to improve the standard of living in non-Urban neighborhoods, countryside, and remote villages. These communities can be exemplified with a low ratio of inhabitants to open space. Agricultural activities may be prominent in this case whereas economic activities would relate to the primary sector, production of foodstuffs and raw materials. Rural development actions mostly aim at the social and economic development of the areas. These programs are usually top-down from the local or regional authorities, regional development agencies, NGOs, national governments or international development organizations. But then, local populations can also bring about endogenous initiatives for development. The term is not limited to the issues for developing countries. In fact, many of the developed countries have very active rural development programs. The main aim of the rural government policy is to develop the undeveloped villages.

Rural Development implies both economic betterment of people and greater social transformation. In order to provide the rural people with better prospects for economic development, increased participation of people in the rural development programmes, decentralization of planning, better enforcement of land reforms and greater access to credit are envisaged (Datta, 2010). Rural development is an old theme, but has been evolving to incorporate new contents and fresh concerns. To substantiate it, Copp has defined rural development as a process aimed at improving the well being and self-realization of people living outside the urbanized area, through collective efforts. He further contents that the ultimate target of rural development is people and infrastructure. According to him, one of the objectives of rural development should be to widen people's range of choices. The World Bank defines rural development as a strategy designed to improve the economic and social life of a specific group of people, the rural poor. It involves extending the benefits of development to the poorest among those who seek a livelihood in rural areas.

REFORM FOR WHOM

Economic reforms were launched in 1991, almost two decades ago; the successive governments talked about 'first generation' and 'second generation' reforms and even now talk about 'Third Generation'. The reform packages that the different governments had come up with might have varied in terms of the language used, but were identical in content. Not much of public debate had ever taken place on any of these reform models, as they came from the west and got transplanted on to the Indian soil. The 'reformists' saw the reforms as an end in itself. No attempt was ever made to understand the human development concerns that permeated the countryside. No changes were initiated to mitigate them. The daily gyrations of Sensex and the sentiments on the Dalal Street seems to excite the reformists in Delhi, more than the muted wail of the millions who are inherently disadvantaged, exploited and unable to articulate. The latest budget, though more sensitive to these concerns in some ways, is no more exception to this. It is disconcerning to see successive governments, while presenting their budgets, seemed more anxious to seek approbation from the cheerleaders of the industry and trade, rather than reach out to those that can not help themselves (Sarma, 2005).

SHIFTING OF POLICY PARADIGM

With the shifting of the cultural and socio-economic environment, policies and theoretical thinking about rural development have been continuously changing overtime. Rural Development is, therefore, an opaque concept used by various interests with different meanings. No agreement exists as to what development as a process, as a goal or as an achievement is, or what should be considered 'special' about rural-development, as opposed to other types of development (Buller and Wright, 1990). At the end of the last millennium, emerging socio-economic changes in the countryside could no longer be understood within the old paradigm. The rural economic employment issues and the aims and circumstances of agricultural production all changed considerably. Therefore, a new rural development paradigm started to take shape, trying to explain current socio-economic changes in India. Thus, rural policies should be pro-active and should go hand in hand with socio-economic changes of the society.

The literature on the development and transfer of public policies is large in India. In their reviewed article, Dolowitz and Marsh (1996: 344) define Policy Transfer as

> "a process in which knowledge about policies, administrative arrangements, institutions etc. in one time and/or place is used in the development of policies, administrative arrangements and institutions in another time and/or place".

This seems to be a good, widely accepted working definition for the subject. However, there is some confusion concerning those policies introduced within an international organization, such as the EU or the WTO, and disseminated throughout all participating countries. Another definition by Stone (1999: 53) provides an answer in saying that:

> "Policy transfer occurs at the sub-national level: between states in federal systems and across local governments, municipalities and boroughs. Policies sometimes develop from particular local practices—either through pilot schemes or the innovations of street level bureaucrats—and are transferred to other local areas or settings".

A usual approach to policy transfer is a pluralist one saying that it brings new ideas to inward-looking states and bureaucracies and opens up possibilities for change. However, as Dolowitz and Marsh argue (1996: 355, 356)

> "if policy transfer occurs within relatively closed International policy communities, instead of introducing new ideas, lesson drawing simply reinforces the existing system, maintaining the status quo".

They continue stating that: policy making is not inevitably, or perhaps even usually, a rational process. Rather, it is often a messy process in which different policy, solution, and problem streams need to combine at the appropriate moment for a policy to develop. There are certain factors such as political conflicts, lobbying power; the dysfunction of bureaucracy and the ruling policy paradigm have a great influence on the process. The main agents of policy transfer are elected officials, political parties, bureaucrats, pressure groups, experts, supra-national organisations, NGOs, academics and even entrepreneurs. The objects of policy transfer can be: policy goals, administrative techniques, institutions, ideology, attitudes and ideas, approaches and philosophies. The most transferring agency is the institutions, political culture and financial resources of the transferring country.

Another important area need to be examined is the nature of policy transfer. Broadly it is two types such as hard (Stone, 1999) or coercive (Dolowitz and Marsh, 1996) transfer, or by others instrumental learning (Stone, 1999) or legitimation (Bennett, 1997). In this type, legislation, standard procedures, bureaucracies, rules and regulations are transferred from one place (one country) to another, mainly by centrally controlled bureaucratic institutions. The policy transfer is compulsory; local actors are usually obliged to comply with new regulations but are also entitled to aid and benefits, delivered by the policy. The other type is called variably soft or voluntary transfer, social learning or harmonization. In this case it is not simply bureaucratic institutions and legislations that are transferred, but approaches, development philosophy, broad policy ideas, new technologies or management techniques are also transferred. Another important area needed to understand is social learning and explores the change of policy paradigms. Hall suggests that policy-makers should work within a framework of ideas and standards that specifies not only the goals of policy and the kind of instruments that can be used to attain them, but also the very nature of the problems they are meant to be addressing. Hall distinguishes first, second and third order changes in policy making. First and second order changes are the results of 'normal policy development', usually responding to policy failures rather than simply the challenge of emerging problems. These changes can bring in new policies, new objectives and ideologies, but do not change the policy paradigm. They are usually most strongly advocated by experts and the civil servants who have to operate and implement the policies, in other words they are the results of the autonomous action of the state. Lastly, third order changes involve the significant alteration of basic principles and could be considered as a shift of the policy paradigm. They respond to the changing circumstances and anomalies that are impossible to deal with through the old paradigm and hence have resulted in repeated policy failures. Thus, the paradigm shift occurs backed by political transition (change of government and bureaucrats) and is driven by overwhelming political authority, rather than expertise.

MYTH AND REALITY

1. IRDP Disaster

The Integrated Rural Development Programme (IRDP) is a grim reminder of how mechanically trying to meet targets can completely undermine the very integrity of a veritable social revolution, that a counter-revolution can be set into motion. Arguably India's worst-ever development programme, the IRDP aimed at providing income-generating assets to the rural poor through the provision of cheap bank credit. Initiated in 1978 as a pilot project, the IRDP was rapidly expanded to cover all rural blocks by 1980. It became the lynchpin of India's anti-poverty effort in the 1980's. It peaked to cover 4 million households by 1987. Several independent evaluation studies based on micro-surveys across 11 states showed substantial mis-classification of beneficiaries under the IRDP, with better-off families being selected (Rath, 1985). Little support was provided for skill formation, access to inputs, markets and necessary infrastructure. In the case of cattle loans, for example, a majority of cattle owners reported that they had either sold off the animals bought with the loan or that these animals were dead. Cattle loans were financed without adequate attention to other details of fodder availability, marketing of milk, etc. (Shah et al., 1998: 311). As Dreze (1990) has pointed out, the IRDP promoted a very deep dependence on corrupt government officials at every stage. It was principally an instrument for powerful local bosses to opportunistically distribute their largesse. There was no attempt made to ascertain whether the loan being provided would truly lead to the creation of a viable long-term asset. No attempt was made to work out the necessary forward and backward linkage to ensure that the loan was a success. Little information was collected on the intended beneficiary. In chasing targets of high credit supply, what we may term as the "quality of lending" was completely undermined. Working for the poor does not mean indiscriminately thrusting money down their throats. Unfortunately, IRDP did precisely that.

The abiding legacy of the programme for India's poor has been that millions have become bank defaulters for no fault of their own. Today, they find it impossible to rejoin the formal credit sector. The IRDP alone accounted for 40 per cent of the losses incurred by commercial banks in rural lending in 1988 [RBI, 1995]. The final nail in the coffin was the official loan waiver of 1989, which destroyed whatever semblance of credit discipline there was.

By the end of the 1980, great concern began to be expressed about the low capital base, low profitability, high non-performing assets and inefficiency of public sector bank. They were seen as being burdened with huge arrears, since their earnings were invariably lower than their loan losses and transaction costs. They required continual refinancing and recapitalization by apex institutions. Loans recovery was regarded as an especially serious problem. Loan collected as a percentage of total amounts due was between 50 and 60 per cent throughout the 1980s and early 1990s. Of the 196 RRBs, 173 report losses in 1993. A 1993 survey of rural households showed that only 12 per cent of borrowers made regular repayment of those who take loans for buying assets. 16 per cent never bought the asset, 50 per cent had sold the asset and 27 per cent said that their asset had been stolen or had died [Meyer and Naagarajan, 2000: 179-81]. A study in Orissa found that loans were disbursed without assessing the feasibility, viability and entrepreneurial experience of borrowers [Rajasekhar and Vyasalu, 1993]. An RBI study of 300 rural financial institution across the country in 1984-85 found that they were unable to cover their costs [Satish and Swamination, 1988]. The study argued that break-even nominal interest rate were 27 per cent, 28 per cent and 34 per cent for commercial bank, cooperatives and RRBs respectively. Low interest rates, high transaction costs and low loan recovery rates were depressing bank profits.

It must also be recognized that the expansion of the formal credit sector, even in the period of social banking, showed a great imbalance, being concentrated in the hands of the rich and the already developed regions. The poor still depend on the informal sector in a big way (Shah, Mihir et al, 2007).

2. Farmer's Movement and Marginalised World

Rural agitations today are no longer between agricultural labourer and landlord as used to be the case as late as the 1970s. During this period there were a large number of organizations with political allegiance to left wing national parties that were active in rural India campaigning for the landless labourer and poor sharecropper. Such mobilizations have become historical anecdotes in most rural regions of contemporary India. Except for certain pockets in Bihar and Andhra Pradesh, the concerns of the agricultural workers do not get political expression anywhere else. Even in these areas, such as Bihar, it is not clear to what extent the Naxalite brigades are actually Maoist in their orientation and to what extent they are now extortionate group feeding off poorly organized state machinery. The simple reason why such organizations have lost their initial focus is because agricultural labour is no longer a critical issue that involves masses of rural Indians. As most holdings are family farms, the need for wage labour is intermittent during peak seasons. This has reduced the scope for left wing organizations to be active on their own terms.

By the 1980s it was clear that landless labourers had no viable future in the economy of the village. The increasing incidence of family farms made hired labour less critical for agricultural prosperity in the years following the green revolution, such as Punjab and Haryana; labour could be hired from among migrants who came from east India in search of employment. Agricultural prosperity among capitalist farmers almost always meant a scarcity of local labour. This is primarily because even in large farms the amount of labour required percent decreased substantially owing to mechanization. Increased prosperity of the region also meant greater opportunities outside the farm which is where the local labour set off for in search of employment. This left the field open for migrants from east India who was happy to get some employment even though they were far from home.

In this context it must also be kept in mind that in many parts of India, particularly in Punjab and west UP, those who worked earlier as aggressive labour are no longer willing to work in the same capacity. As we mentioned earlier, *harijans* and *adi-dharmis* of UP and Punjab respectively had more or less set their minds against laboring on others fields. Cumulatively, this led to the diminution of the agricultural labourer's presence in rural India. By the time the 1980s came around agricultural labourer movement that involved huge rural unions and supra-local organizers became more or less a thing of the past. Now was the turn of Mahendra Singh Tikait and Nanjudaswamy to lead agitation espousing the interests of owner cultivators? In these mobilizations it was clearly stated that any one who did not own land was not really a farmer. There was no room now for agricultural labourers in theses movements which the Bharatiya Kisan Union of Uttar Pradesh and Haryana articulated most cogently.

Even as the owner cultivators were getting restive, anew configuration was taking place in rural politics, in the past when agricultural labourers mattered most in rural uprisings the target was always the local landlord, *jotedar* or *thanedar*. With the shift to owner-cultivator brand of agitation the enemy was no longer local, but supra-local, even the government of India. Not surprisingly, BKU and Shetkari Sangathan were constantly moving into cities to impress upon the public, and upon recalcitrant politicians, the authenticity of their demands. Thus while they were still agriculturalists, in the main, already the link between town and country was being strongly established [see Gupta, 1997]. Concurrently there was the demand among the same category of owner–cultivator for reservation in urban jobs and in educational institutions. The Mandal recommendations of 1990 were timed just right to coincide with the urban aspirations of cultivating castes such as Yadavas, Gujars, and Jats. An urban job was clearly a prize catch for communities that for generations prided themselves in being farmers first and last. There is a play on a famous couplet in west UP that captures this sentiment rather nicely. The famous Urdu poet, Ghagh, had once eulogized rural life when he wrote; *'Uttam Kheti, madhyam baan: nishidh chakri, bhikh nidam'*. Translated it means that agriculture is the best, followed by business, salaried jobs and beggary. Today, the villagers have recast the ditty along the following lines: '*Uttam chakri, madhyma baan: nikrisht krishi, bhik mahan.*' In this case a politician who begs for vote is on top, followed by salaried job, and at the bottom of the heap is the agriculturist.

Most of the political debates in the country do not have a rural character at all. This is rather surprising given the fact that a large number of politician in and legislatures have rural origins. Occasionally a Mahender Singh Tikait or a Nanjudaswamy will stir things up in the villages, but in the main, political ideologies that inform most of the national parties do not have a strong rural component. The usual concessions are made in terms of subsidies or minimum price for agricultural produce, but the kernel of political ideologies do not reflect any major pre-occupation with the village. Even Laloo Prasad Yadav and Mulayam Singh Yadav demonstrate little by way of rural concerns. Playing the arithmetic of caste does not necessarily mean committing oneself to the chemistry of the village.

Yet, because it is also a question of arithmetic, politicians often vie against each other in appearing as champion of the beleaguered owner-cultivators. Current political discourse shows little concern towards the interest of agriculture labourers. But even here there is a strong element of political gamesmanship at work. In the name of protecting the poor farmer, political parties have in general opposed the institution to tax on agricultural incomes. Yet, as many owner-cultivators have told me repeatedly, this tax concession makes no difference to them as their incomes would be below the taxable amount any way. These farmers argue that the exemption on agricultural tax is to help the rich entrepreneurial farmers and those in cities who want to escape the burden of taxation by diversifying into agricultural production, or in animal husbandry, or poultry farming, and so forth. At the same time politician are alive to the fact that the opening up of agricultural imports would ruin the owner-cultivators who are in substantial numbers. As this would lead to political and economic instability, they are obviously cautious about it. Even so there are peasant activist like Sharad Joshi of Shetkari Sangathan who welcomes an open market, for he believes that the peasants in Maharashtra would do very well if they could take their produce abroad. Sharad Joshi's calculations need to be looked at closely, for he is obviously not keeping his books very carefully. To imagine that the Indian farmer could compete against the west where agriculture is industry is quite difficult to conceive. Indeed this is precisely the reason why India constantly opposes moves in international forums to let market dynamics control Indian agriculture.

While the owner-cultivators are protected politically, their futures are left unplanned. In 2000, the National Agricultural Policy formally recognized that agriculture has become "a relatively unrewarding profession," and that efforts to revive it had to be multi-pronged in character. Horticulture, floriculture, the cultivation of aromatic and medicinal plants, over and above animal husbandry and fisheries are some of the alternatives they have presented to improve agriculture. While these recommendations sound good on paper, there are vast infrastructural deficits that have to overcome. To begin with, the conditions of owner-cultivators do not in general favour heavy investments in chancy cash crops. The suicide of farmers in Andhra Pradesh and Punjab is most alarming. In search for a better economic future they had take loans to upgrade their agricultural production which they could not repay. According to reports, the overwhelming number of suicides among farmer is on account of their inability to pay back loans. Further, this happens with those agriculturists who are ambitious and want to move on, but are suddenly pulled up because the empirical structures are far too unyielding which makes their attempts to take off back drive and thrust. Further the village lacks other kinds of basic facilities like transportation system, cold storages, and a sound marketing framework.

Without this kind of infrastructural back up, the hope that the production of non-food crops will revive the village is not very realistic. Regardless of how feasible this strategy will eventually be, there is no gainsaying the fact that agricultural production of food is far from being either romanticized or valorized for its own sake any longer. Though the majority of Indian live in villages, the village leaves little impress upon the national culture today.

Conclusion

Thus, development is bound to be in egalitarian, as Nobel laureate Arthur Lewis pointed out long ago, because it does not start in every part of the economy at the same time. However, the diffusion of economic and social development across sub-national unit once the economy growth process is initiated has important implications for future growth and well-being. The structure of employment growth and variation across states in India is a key outcome of this unfolding development process. Since we are on the subject of devolution as the means to improve the quality of expenditure in government, it needs to be emphasized here that the Planning Commission and the central government should review the utility of all centrally sponsored schemes and devolve as many schemes as feasible, along with funds, to the states, as the first step of reform of the planning process. It is the states and the local bodies that should have predominant presence in social sector spending. Transfer of resources from the center to the states should be entirely rule-based and discretionary flows should discontinue. This is the only way to improve the efficiency of public expenditure in the social sectors (Sarma, 2005).

The social sector-related problems faced at the ground level are best known to the local community itself. It is therefore imperative that the schemes meant to address such problems are designed and implemented in consultation with the local community. Local community is capable of managing its own affairs. It has the ability to innovate and solve its own problems, provided it is allowed to do so. There are innumerable examples of how local leadership has led to more in innovative and cost-effective solutions to local problems, than what the top-down approach could deliver. There are many examples of how villagers built roads, schools, wells etc., on their own, without seeking financial support from the government and without having to depend on contractor. Wherever the villagers had the responsibility of overseeing a school, the teachers would be more careful in attending to their duties and the parents would be more conscientious in ensuring their children's school attendance. Where the village community had to supervise the local public health care facility, the doctors and their staff would be more regular in attending to the patients' need. Community participation has reduced the scope for corruption, wherever it has been encouraged (Sarma, S.A.E. 2005).

The sensitivity of public representatives towards their constituency should have a profound influence on rural development. Though it is difficult to judge the sensitivity of public representative's vis-à-vis their respective constituencies, as a rough measure, we have examined their frequency of visits and also the nature of development activities initiated through MP's and MLA's local area development funds. More than 31 per cent of the visits fall in the category of more than one year in the case of visits by there MP implying that 69 per cent of villages were not visited by there MPs even once in a year. In the case of MLA's visit, more than 42 per cent of the visits fall within the category of more than one year. What is striking is that for both MPs and MLAs, a large part of the rural population failed to specify anything about the visits of their representatives to their villages. The nature of development schemes run by the public representative, broadly classified, reveals that these are in nature of raising the village infrastructure by the provision of public water supply, village roads, community hall, etc. More than 75 per cent of the village could not report the nature of any development schemes run by their respective representatives either by the MPs or MLAs. Among the other schemes reported, these are mostly concentrated in the construction of rural roads (12.05%), followed by public hand pumps (6.25%) and community halls (4.04%) (Srivastava, D.K. et al.; 2007).

However, rural development includes not just economic betterment but also social transformation with particular emphasis on educational facilities to bridge the rural-urban divide. Education plays a pivotal role in achieving development and sustainable livelihoods in a competitive economic environment. Higher educational levels contribute to local economic development in several ways. Thus, educational initiatives and programs were designed by various organizations to promote literacy and develop skills amongst the poorer sections of the society.

It is against this background that the culture surrounding agriculture must be understood. This culture is not a stable one. History has not left behind a consistent legacy, nor does rural culture have a temporal overhang, that is, safely cantilevered on present commitments. Agriculture is an economic residue that generously accommodates non-achievers resigned to a life of sad satisfaction. The villager is as bloodless as the rural economy is lifeless. From rich to poor, the trend is to leave the village, and, if that entails going abroad, then so be it. All this may sound a trifle alarming, but this is what India's villages are telling us whether or not we are inclined to listen to this rustic murmurs (Gupta, 2005).

REFERENCES

1. Datta,Tathagata (2010), "Politics of Development", in B.M. Dash (ed.) *Rural Development in India*, New Delhi Publishers, New Delhi, pp. 22-26.
2. Dolowitz, D. and Marsh, D. (1996), "Who learns from whom—a review of the Policy Transfer Literature" In, *Political Studies*, XLIV, pp. 343-357.
3. Gupta, Dipankar. (2005), "Whither the Indian Village: Culture and Agriculture In 'Rural' India", *Economic and Political Weekly*, Feb 19-25, Vol. XL, No. 8, pp. 754-757.
4. Gusztav, Nemes (2005), *The Politics of Rural Development in Europe*, Institute of Economics Hungarian Academy of Social Sciences, Budapest, pp. 3-39.
5. Hall, P.A. (1993), "Policy Paradigms, Social Learning, and the State—The Case of Economic Policy Making in Britain" In, *Comparative Politics*, April, pp. 275-296.
6. Pitt, Devid (1971), *The Social Dynamics of Development*, Oxford, Pergsmon Press, p. 9.
7. Rajni, Kothari (1990), *Politics and The People: In Search of Humane India*, Ajanta Publications, New Delhi, Vol. 1, p. 216.
8. Ramaswamy, K.V. (2007), "Regional Dimension of Growth and Emplyment", *Economic and Political weekly*, Dec 8-14, Vol. XLII 49, p. 55.
9. Roy, Sanjoy (2010), "Approaches and Strategies of Rural Development During Five Years Plans", *Rural Development in India* (ed) B.M. Dash, New Delhi Publishers, New Delhi, pp. 1177-181.
10. Sarma, S.A.E. (2005): "Social Sector Allocations", *Economic and Political Weekly*, April 2-8, Vol. XL, No. 14, p. 1417.
11. Shah, Mihir, *et al.*, (2007) "Rural Credit in 20th Century India: Overview of History and Perspectives", *Economic and Political Weekly*, April 14-20, Vol. XLII, No. 15, p. 1356.

12. Srivastava, D. K. et al., (2007), "Rural Poverty In Madhya Pradesh : Looking Beyond Conventional Measures", *Economic and Political Weekly*, Feb. 3-9, Vol. XLII, No. 5, p. 386.

13. Stone, D. (1999), "Learning Lessons and Transferring Policy Across Time, Space and Disciplines" *In Politics* 1999/19 (1) pp. 51-59.

14. Thirlwall, A.P. (2003), *Growth and Development: With Special Reference to Developing Economies*, Palgrave Macmilan, New York, seventh edition, p. 19.

Chapter

12

Involvement of Women in Panchayati Raj Institutions in India

—Gurupada Saren

ABSTRACT

Empowerment of women through one-third reservation under the 73rd amendment is an important facet that involve the women in participation in the political system in Panchayati Raj Institutions (PRIs). It has ensured the better accountability and more transparency in the local affairs of the community and increased the self-sufficiency of women representatives. The noteworthy factor is that Non-Governmental Organizations (NGOs) often provide important training and support to the elected women representatives towards smooth functioning of the Panchayats. It also looks forward towards the social transformation in rural areas through the involvement of women.

Introduction

The Local Self Government (LSG) existed since time immemorial in India. It is the process to manage local affairs by local bodies who have been elected by the local people. The local government includes the Panchayati Raj Institutions (PRIs) in the villages and the Municipal and Metropolitan Councils in the cities. The local self government performs as an instrument of democratic self government in India. Through these institutions the local people can participate in political system under PRIs and deliberate on various development activities. These democratic institutions are based on the principle of self-government and should represent people's desires and strengths. The 73rd Constitutional Amendments Act, 1992 have broadened the scope of local self-governance.

The rural local government operates through Zila Panchayats, Taluka Panchayats and Gram Sabha/Panchayats are known as Panchayati Raj Insitutions (PRIs). Women are important stakeholders in the PRIs to perform in the day to day activities, practice the better democracy and bring the development to the people's hand. The participation of women in PRIs has broadened through the 73rd Constitutional Amendment Act which guaranteed the 33 per cent reservation in the local body. But due to age-old practice in developing countries, especially in India, Women have been kept in only household chores and strict various social taboos which impeded the participation in various social and development activities; only the men folk managed the affairs outside the home. However, the 73rd amendment encouraged the women to participate in various activities pertaining to development activities in community, e.g. arrangement for drinking water, smooth functioning of primary school *Anganwadi* centres etc. But they lack the proper education and training in comparison to men for which they have to struggle for day to day activities in panchayat work. However, there are tremendous zeal from NGOs who have entrusted the proper functioning of their activities which really ensures the dream to come true in their real life.

Brief History of PRIs in India

If we look back to previous century, the existence of PRIs in India was very informal and the participation was minimal and women's participation was negligible. Panchayats means councils of five persons. Panchayati system has been in existence since ancient times; there are also evidences from the Vedic period. It was a people's institution with the aim of grass roots governance and better practice of democracy in every village. The village panchayat had powers in terms of judicial and executive to govern the village administration and development activities. The main activities were to collect the taxes out of the produces in the village and paid the government's share on behalf of the village (Nehru, Jawaharlal, 1964). During the Mughal rule, the self government system in village battered and new class of feudal chiefs emerged and revenue collectors become apparent between the ruler and the people. The British government declined the local government system to a large extent and established local civil and criminal courts, revenue and police organisations, increase in communications, the growth of individualism and the operation of the individual *Ryotwari* (landholder-wise) system as against the *Mahalwari* or village tenure system.

Lord Mayo took a decision in 1870 towards the local government in the colonial policy with the aim of providing needed momentum to the local institutions and decentralizing the power to bring about administrative efficiency in meeting the demand of people at the village level. On May 18, 1882 the famous resolution of Lord Ripon recognized the twin consideration of local government: (*i*) administrative efficiency and (*ii*) political education. But he abandoned the rural decentralization for its administration, growth and development. The Royal Commission on Decentralization (1907) recognised the importance of panchayats at the grass-root level and recommends that it is most desirable to govern the village administrative system. The Montague Chemsford Reforms (1919) tried to decentralize the power to the local people but could not able to provide the feasibility towards vibrant and democratic through which they can practice the democracy at the grassroot level. The British administrator concentrated on rural governance but they were not concerned with the decentralised democracy and they were aiming only the colonial objectives.

During 1920s to 1947, the Indian National Congress emphasized the issue of all-India *Swaraj* but there was lack of consensus among the top leaders regarding the status and role to be assigned to the institution of rural local self-government. However, the Rural Self Government Bill, 1925 provided for a nine-member village authority elected on the basis of restricted adult franchise. The successful village authority was to be given more powers to practice the democracy. The panchayat could include more than one cadastral village. It could be entrusted with certain functions such as water supply, education, medical relief and sanitation. There was even single member village authority could also be put in place where no recognised forms of village organisation existed.

Panchayati Raj After Independence

After Independence, an enormous effort has been given to introduce the Panchayati Raj Institution (PRIs) as an Act so that the grass root peoples can utilize its benefits towards their betterment in terms of participation in the decision-making process for the development of themselves. However, various committees have been constituted to study the feasibility of local self governance.

In 1957, the Balwant Rai Mehta Committee was appointed with the chairmanship of Balwant G Rai Mehta to study and assess the community development and national extension services towards ensuring the improvement of economic and social condition of the rural areas. The committee had argued for the involvement of the local people in planning, decision-making and implementation process of any development projects. The committee had suggested that: (*i*) to establish the elected local bodies at the village level i.e. gram sabha and devolution the power, authority and resources; (*ii*) the block/samiti level should be the inter-mediatory stage so that proper follow-up could be done for the various development projects; (*iii*) the zila parishad should play a advisory role in the process of development and the benefits should trickled down the development to the lowest level i.e. village; (*iv*) the body must be constituted for five years by indirect elections from the village panchayats; (*v*) the PRIs' functions should cover the development of agriculture and its allied activities, the promotion of local industries and other services such as drinking water, road building, etc.

Due to political and bureaucratic resistance at the state level to share power and resources with the local institutions etc. the democratic momentum could not able to develop towards the betterment of the people in the rural areas. However, there was trend to establish the political ideology among the people rather than to provide an opportunity for its people.

K. Santhanam Commmittee was appointed by the Planning Commission in 1963 with the aim of decentralization of the financial matters. As the state government control over the resources, the PRIs were not able to carry out the performance of various development activities as expected of the local people. The committee studied how to determine the issues related to sanctioning of grants to PRIs, gift and donation, handling over revenue in full or part to PRIs. However, the committee recommended that: (*i*) the special powers should be enshrined to the panchayats to levy the taxes on land revenue and home tax etc.; (*ii*) all grants at the state level should be mobilised and sent in a consolidated form to various PRIs; (*iii*) to set up and establish a Panchayat Raj Finance Corporation with the aim of management of financial resources of PRIs at all level, provide loans and financial assistance to these grassroot level government and also provide non-financial requirements of villages.

However, the State Finance Commission has taken over the responsibility to collect taxes and determine the level of grants and recommends the final distribution of resources to the local authorities.

After coming to power, the Janata Party, in 1977 had appointed a high level committee with the chairmanship of Ashok Mehta (1978) to strengthen the various measures of functioning of PRIs. The committee examines and suggests that: (*i*) the district administration has sufficient manpower who have technical expertise and can be involved in planning, coordination and mobilization of resources; (*ii*) PRIs has two-tier system, with Block/Mandal Panchayat at the base and Zilla Parishad at the top; (*iii*) the PRIs are confident enough to take decision in planning and implementation for the development of themselves; (*iv*) the district administration should play a role of linkages between rural and urban development; (*v*) there should be proper representation of SCs and STs in the election to PRIs on the basis of their population; and (*vi*) the term of PRIs should be for four years. However, only Andhra Pradesh, Karnataka and West Bengal had passed the new legislation based on this report.

In 1985, V.K. Rao Committee was appointed to evaluate various aspects of PRIs. The people should take the responsibility for their own development in planning and implementation of the various development projects. However, the committee recommended that: (*i*) PRIs have to be activated and provided with all the required support to become effective organisations at the grassroot level; (*ii*) PRIs at the district level and below should be assigned the work of planning, implementation and monitoring of rural development programmes; and (*iii*) the block development office should be the spinal cord of the rural development process.

L.M. Singhvi Committee (1986) was appointed to study the feasibility of the PRIs. The gram sabha is the base for local self governance and facilitate the participation of the people in the process of planning and development. However, the committee has suggested: (*i*) the grass roots democracy should be constitutionally recognized, protected and preserved under the Constitution of India; and (*ii*) there should not be involvement of political parties in panchayat elections.

However, Sarkaria Commission was opposed the recognition of the Constitution; but the momentum gained in the late 1980s with the initiatives of late Prime Minister Rajiv Gandhi. Due to political compulsion it was not materialized for the implementation of PRIs.

Panchayati Raj and Women

The panchayats had its existence in India since the ancient times. Panchayati Raj (PR) as an institution came into being after Independence and takes a shape of local self-government. During the colonial rule the female members were not allowed to franchise their vote and contest the elections (Neema Kudva, 2003). After late fifties, several states did set up PR bodies at village, block and district levels and participation of women was encouraged in the process. PR was seen as a means of ensuring democratic participation for rapid rural development and social transformation. There were no provisions for financial resources and lack of constitutional support, these PR bodies started suffering. However, there were hardly any women participated on these bodies, except as co-opted members who were accorded little power, respect or political status. There was lack of political will and zeal to bring its importance in nation's agenda. Several commissions were set up to examine the prospects and consequences in which could be reinforced, such as the Balwant Rai Mehta Committee (1957), the Ashok Mehta Committee (1977), the G.V.K. Rao Committee (1985), and the L.M. Singhvi Committee (1987).

During 1988, a parliamentary sub-committee recommended that Panchayati Raj bodies be given constitutional recognition for the betterment of the people and to ensure the participation of women to practice the democracy. However, it was only in 1992 that Parliament gave constitutional status to Panchayati Raj. On December 22 and 23, 1992, two amendments to the Constitution—the 73rd Constitution Amendment for rural local bodies and the 74th Constitutional Amendment for urban local bodies—made them 'local self-government' (LSG). After that all the states passed their own Acts within a year to conform the amended constitutional provisions. As a result India moved towards 'multilevel federalism', which has broadened the scope of democratic base of the Indian polity (Mathew, 2003).

There were some major forces in the constitutional amendments for women's political empowerment has the reservation of one-third of the seats for women in local bodies, along with reservation of seats for Scheduled Castes (SCs) and Scheduled Tribes (STs) according to their proportionate in regional level. Women were reluctant to enter this new political gamut because of which political parties and vested interest groups try to exploit the situation. In the process of women's participation in PRIs, the vested interest peoples and upper castes dominate and they (women) became only rubber stamps and grabbed the power by the dominated local elites. This was called the proxy rule. A new group of *sarpanch patis* also emerged where the husband of the woman sarpanch managed the affairs of the panchayat, while the woman acted only as a rubber stamp. However, things have changed over time to some extent and transparency and accountability became more visible. It has been proved that wherever women hold positions in local bodies there is greater efficiency and transparency in the running of public affairs.

Over the past decade women have proved to be not just passive but disinterested participants in the political processes. More women, who are from the marginalized section of society, have entered the battle of PRIs and showed the result which really brings the development in their hand. Through the provision of reservations, in the system of local self governance in India, has empowered the process for women, since it has not only brought women out of their houses and into the public place but also ensured their participation, raised the voice etc. It has ensured the achievement of a platform and delivered the public goods in the hands of people and try to uplift their family in particular and community as a whole.

Micro Finance and Women

Micro-finance is used as an effective tool to fight against the poverty across the globe. Few years prior to 1997, a series of meetings were held to design an approach that can be followed by all under-developed and developing countries across the globe for the betterment of women folk in the rural areas. These meetings have been worked towards the preparation for the World Micro-Credit Summit Campaign, held in Washington, DC, February 1997, where more than 2,900 people, representing 1,500 institutions from 137 countries, participated (For details please see *www.microcreditsummit.org/uploads/socrs/SOCR2009_English.pdf)* The Summit proclaimed a global target of supporting 100 million of the world's poorest families, especially women with micro-finance for self-employment and other financial services by the year 2005. The Summit declared that it target to reaching the poorest and these form the group from where most of the Micro-finance Summit's target of 100 million poorest would be tapped. It also promotes the use of quality poverty measurements to identify the poorest across the globe. It would also try to reach and empower the women though various economic activities. Since women are supposed to be good credit risks, and women-run enterprises benefit their families, micro-finance is seen as a tool to empower women.

Through the building of financially self-sufficient institution, the experience of developing countries have shown that micro-finance programs can improve their efficiency to become self sufficient. The involvement of women would help to structure their interest rates and fees to eventually cover their operating and financial costs. It was also to publicize and ensuring a positive, measurable impact on the lives of stakeholders, their families and the community.

Women's Participation in PRIs: A Challenge

The social transformation in India that have contributed towards generating process of empowerment for women is the 73rd Constitution Amendment Act that makes it mandatory for a 1/3rd (one third) reservation of seats in local self governing bodies and the other the formation of self help groups of women around micro finance. This paper raises questions about the processes of empowerment generated under PRIs.

The participation of women in panchayati raj institutions (PRIs) ensured their development and empowerment through the practice of democracy. The perceptions of women's participation in PRIs further reinforced the self-perceptions of present elected women members for themselves and develop their outlook towards the society. Majority of them were remained punctual and regular in attending panchayat meetings, and spoke there, but neither participated in deliberations, nor considered capable to undertake panchayat work. Internal development of the elected women representatives was poor due to lack of formal education and proper orientation and training. There was also lack of awareness about PRIs among them. In general, improvement in participation was viewed empowering for women. Male members of panchayats and unsuccessful women candidates have broadly endorsed the views expressed by outgoing women members regarding role in election process and participation in panchayat meetings. Interestingly, male members had better appreciation of women's participation in deliberations, awareness about PRIs, empowerment through participation and declining influence of social obstruction. However, they approved the dependence on husbands or relations for help, support and advice with little role played by caste leaders, political parties, NGOs and local influential. Most unsuccessful women candidates also contested panchayat elections at the instance of their husbands/family members and involved in door-to-door publicity. They attributed their failure mainly to lack of awareness, own indifference and non-cooperation of family as well as the communiuty.

Majority women now contesting elections, entering into panchayats, feeling encouraged to participate in meetings, taking part in decision-making and their views receiving greater attention. But they are still observing *purdah*, seeking advice from family male members and attending meetings with them. Low education, lack of confidence, *purdah* system and dependence of males were cited as main impediments.

Roles of NGOs and Responsibility of Women in PRIs

The role of NGOs has substantially contributed to strengthen the democracy through elected representatives especially the women. After getting the proper orientation, training and education from various national NGOs, the women have tried to focus on the welfare of their respective community and family. They were engaged themselves for the basic needs of the community, e.g. construction of roads, arrangement for drinking water facilities etc. Through the participation of various workshops/seminars the women representatives of PRIs had an opportunity to acquire the knowledge, skills to look after the day to day activities of panchayats. The urban exposure has given a positive modern outlook and tries to facilitate the same in their real life situation. During the process they have been learning to take part on various deliberations at the panchayat level and prepared themselves to take the responsibility as elected members of the concerned panchayat.

However, the women folk have become much more committed towards their duties and responsibilities of PRIs. Their participation in local affairs in their respective community under the PRIs has ensured a significant difference. Reservation has been used as a tool for empowering the women to ensure their adequate representation and delivery of public goods. They are also trying to fight the prejudices that the women are not capable of being independent leaders. They have developed various managerial skills and acquire knowledge for various day to day activities in their home as well as in the panchayats. As a result they are now better manager for community and involve in various development activities which really concerned them. For instance, women can demand for pure drinking water and attendance of teacher in primary school where the education of their children matters.

There is a need for the policy of reservation for women PRIs headed by women and definitely the participation and leadership has made an impact on grass-root governance. It has also fought back many myths such as inability to handle power and responsibility outside their homes. The political empowerment and assumption of leadership role had an impact in socio-political areas. It has ensured the visible improvement in the administration and delivery of services at Gram Panchayat (GP) level mainly through the focus on the felt needs of the people, greater transparency, greater reliance on horizontal linkages and greater participation of people particularly women members of the village community (Mathew, 1994; Palanithurai, 2002). Besides the amendment has made possible the creation of political space for women and enabled them to gain physical, economical and socio-cultural status to boost the confidence and to alter the age-old strong hold of repressive tradition.

Women Need a Space in Politics

For every sphere there is a need of space. The elected women representatives also need to create political space through which they can improve their situation as an individual and family as a whole. However 73rd constitutional amendment Act has ensured their political space through 1/3rd reservation in the local body under PRIs.

There is need for physical space of her body and its mobility across spaces outside her house. It also includes the house, land, commercial space (like a shop), school, place of work, etc. Women also need a space for economic activity for which she should be allowed to ownership, access and control of goods and services, which enhance economic activities which bring her liberty. There is a need of socio-cultural space that can enhance women's power within the domestic sphere. This space broadens the scope of women's position within kin-based hierarchies is relatively higher than others. The access and control to socio-cultural space that a woman can have which will enhance her position within the household, is intimately connected to various religious performances, caste factors and ethnic origins etc. The important space is political space for which women has been guaranteed under 73rd amendment act perceived at two level, private political space and public political space. The political situation exists within the domestic unit.

Conclusion

The participation of women in local affairs under the political system has ensured the space for the practice of democracy in rural India. The implications of 73rd Constitutional Amendment have positive initiatives towards the empowerment of women in the guise of PRIs. There is a need to delve into the areas through which the women bring forth the social transformation in rural areas and emancipated themselves from the clutches of power grabbers at the village level. Under the PRIs the participation of women have ensured the smooth functioning of panchayats which is reflected in transparency and accountability at the community level. There is pretty clear about the women's situation before Independence and how the situation has changed over a period of time through the involvement of women in various local bodies. However, the participation of women in PRIs and involvement in various micro-finance activities empower them. The initiatives taken by various NGOs to train/orient and educate the elected women representatives are appreciated and how to function smoothly in panchayat level and broaden the scope of democracy among the women in India.

REFERENCES

1. Baluchamy, S. (2004): *Panchayati Raj Institutions*, Mittal Publications, New Delhi.
2. Bardhan, Pranab and Mookherjee, Dilip (2007), *Decentralization and Local Governance in Developing Countries*, Oxford University Press, New Delhi.
3. Barik, Bishnu C. and Sahoo, Umesh C. (2008), *Panchayati Raj Institutions and Rural Development: Narratives on Inclusion of Excluded*, Rawat Publications, Jaipur.
4. Hooja, Rakesh and Hooja, Meenakshi (2008), *Democratic Decentralization and Planning*, Rawat Publications, Jaipur.
5. *http://www.unescap.org/huset/lgstudy/country/india/india.html#links* accessed on 10.11.10.
6. *http://www.waterforfood.org/gga/Lecture%20Material/MSVani_CustomaryLaw.pdf* accessed on 13.11.2010.
7. Jai, LC (2005), *Decentralisation and Local Governance*, Orient Longman, New Delhi.
8. Mathew, George (1994), *Panchayati Raj—From Legislation to Movement*, Concept Publishing Company, New Delhi.
9. Neema Kudva (2003), "Engineering Elections: The Experiences of Women in Panchayati Raj in Karnataka, India," *International Journal of Politics, Culture and Society*, Vol. 16, No. 3, Spring 2003.
10. Palanithurai, G. (2002), *Dynamics of New Panchayati Raj System in India*, Concept Publishing Company, New Delhi.
11. Pinto, Marina (2000), *Metropolitan City Governance in India*, Sage Publications, New Delhi.
12. Singh, K.K. and Ali, S. (2001), *Role of Panchayati Raj Institutions for Rural Development*, Sarup & Sons, New Delhi.
13. *www.indianetzone.com/24/growth_local_self_government_india.htm* accessed on 10.11.2010
14. *www.microcreditsummit.org/uploads/socrs/SOCR2009_English.pdf* accessed on 23.11.2010

CHAPTER

13

Rural Development with a Feministic Approach

Issues and Alternatives

—Dr. Nishu Bala

ABSTRACT

The term rural development connotes overall development of rural areas to improve the quality of life of rural people. In this sense, it is a comprehensive and multi-dimensional concept, and encompasses the development of agriculture and allied activities, village and cottage industries and crafts, socio-economic infrastructure, community services and facilities and, above all the human resources in rural areas. As a phenomenon, rural development is the end-result of interactions between various physical, technological, economic, social, cultural and institutional factors. As a strategy, it is designed to improve the economic and social well-being of a specific group of people—the rural people. In the Indian context, rural development assumes greater significance as 72.22 per cent (according to 2001 census) of its population still live in rural areas. In absence of adequate employment opportunities in rural areas, male members of most of the rural families are forced to migrate to the cities. Therefore, female members of the families become the primary bread winner of the family. These women are always seen to be engaged vigorously in familial and farm activities, home-based industrial occupation and contribution, to a great extent, to the family's economy. Therefore, any strategy for rural development must include women as the primary agents. It is with this background that the present paper tends to highlight the role of women in rural development which is often ignored altogether of underestimated.

Introduction

There are no universally accepted approaches to rural development. It is a choice influenced by time, space and culture. The term rural development connotes overall development of rural areas to improve the quality of life of rural people. In this sense, it is a comprehensive and multi-dimensional concept, and encompasses the development of agriculture and allied activities, village and cottage industries and crafts, socio-economic infrastructure, community services and facilities and, above all the human resources in rural areas. As a phenomenon, rural development is the end-result of interactions between various physical, technological, economic, social, cultural and institutional factors. As a strategy, it is designed to improve the economic and social well-being of a specific group of people—the rural people. As a discipline, it is multi-disciplinary in nature, representing an intersection of agriculture, social, behavioral, engineering and management sciences.

In the Indian context, rural development assumes greater significance as 72.22 per cent (according to 2001 census) of its population still live in rural areas. Most of the people living in rural areas draw their livelihood from agriculture and allied sectors (60.41% of total workforce) and poverty mostly persists here (27.1% in 1999-00). At the time of independence around 83 per cent of Indian population was living in rural areas. Accordingly, from the very beginning, our planned strategy emphasized rural development and will continue to do so in future. Strategically, the focus of our planning was to improve the economic and social conditions of the underprivileged sections of rural society. Thus, economic growth with social justice became the proclaimed objective of the planning process under rural development. In Indian planning strategy, it began with an emphasis on agricultural production and consequently expanded to promote productive employment opportunities for rural masses, especially the poor, by integrating production, infrastructure, human resource and institutional development measures. In absence of adequate employment opportunities in rural areas, male members of most of the rural families are forced to migrate to the cities. Therefore, female members of the families become the primary bread winner of the family. These women are always seen to be engaged vigorously in familial and farm activities, home-based industrial occupation and contribution, to a great extent, to the family's economy. Women of landowning families undertake the supervision of pre-harvest and post-harvest operations throughout the year, shoulder the responsibilities of looking after the cattle, e.g. feeding, milking, converting of milk for *ghee* for sale and home consumption, in addition to the upbringing of the children and general maintenance of the family.

It is with this background that this paper has been written with an emphasis that we have to recognize women as the driving force for rural development. This paper has been divided into three sections. The present section gives the introduction of the theme of the paper. The second section highlights the challenges and problems of rural women while the last section concludes the discussion by giving policy implications. Women farmers are the main food producers in developing countries and yet they are one of the most vulnerable groups. Their economic empowerment to produce more and to participate in policy formulation is critical to addressing poverty in rural areas. Since the 1990's women have been identified as key agents of sustainable development and women's equality and empowerment are seen as central to a more holistic approach towards establishing new patterns and processes of development that are sustainable. The World Bank has suggested that empowerment of women should be a key aspect of all social and rural development programs (World Bank, 2001). Although a considerable debate on what constitutes empowerment exists, in this paper we find it useful to rely on Kabeer's (2001) definition: "The expansion in people's ability to make strategic life choices in a context where this ability was previously denied to them." For women in India, this suggests empowerment in several realms: personal, familial, economic and political.

Women as Agents of Rural Development: The Challenges

"You can tell the condition of a nation by looking at the status of its women."

—*Jawaharlal Nehru*

Women comprise half of human resources, they have been identified as key agents of sustainable development and women's equality is as central to a more holistic approach towards stabilizing new patterns and process of development that are sustainable [Mishra, 1996]. The contribution of women and their role in the family as well as in the economic development and social transformation are pivotal. Women constitute 90 per cent of total marginal workers of the country. Rural women who are engaged in agriculture form 78 per cent of all women in regular work. Experience of NIRD (National Institute for Rural Development) action research projects reveal that, the operational aspects, such as the extent of enabling that goes into the community self help processes and sharpening the mindset of women. Empowering women, particularly rural women, is a challenge. This is because of the fact that they have to face various types of problems. Women from the landless families work as agricultural labourers during all the seasons and in various agricultural operations. This way, they put in 10-11 hours of work per day in the agricultural fields. In cash crops like potato, rice and cotton, in particular, female labour force is found to be high. The payment in grains during harvest of wheat and rice and cash for other crops form the major part of the resources for the family's survival. They also look after the cattle which brings them an extra income from sale of milk besides improving the dietary standards of the family. If we take the example of Punjab, apart from shouldering the responsibility of looking after the cattle, cleaning of cattle-sheds and milking of cattle, the female members of the family have to face abuse, sexual assaults and accusations by the landowners. Many women work with men in 'home-based' work and provide any help required by their brothers and husbands. These tasks are performed along with the usual 'women's work' such as cooking, washing utensils and clothes and upbringing of children. Their work outside the home does not permit any change in the role expectations of the family and the males. All these multiple roles of women are supposed to be a part of their role as 'ideal mothers', 'ideal wives' and this deprives their right to an independent economic status. Further the culturally and socially defined role of women is in direct conflict with their role as 'bread-winner' and it is customary for the women not to seek gainful employment.

Since social, cultural and familial constraints deprive women of their freedom, i.e. empowerment and mobility in the outdoor activities, they are therefore only in small numbers in the organized sector. This forces them to accept whatever work is available within the village, denying them exposure to the outside world. This is due to the fact that women's roles and work as workers are not considered to be primary. Also, they are pushed into the category of secondary workers like 'helpers' in spite of their hard labour and briskness (factors acknowledged even by the landowners) at work.

The landowning classes prefer to employ more women as agricultural workers as they can be easily paid much less when compared with their input in terms of work. The women are employed for all types of agricultural work such as sowing, transplanting, weeding, leveling, picking, harvesting etc. They brave all severe climatic conditions like men in pre-harvest and post-harvest operations of rice and wheat. During peak seasons, female labour is in maximum demand and when the demand for labour decreases, it is the woman who has to face unemployment crisis. They, therefore, form the majority of the reserve force of labour. This way, their lives are one of continuous insecurity of employment within the village in the primary sector, i.e. agriculture.

The women have also to bear the brunt of discrimination in wages. The principle of 'equal pay for equal work' is not strictly adhered to in the fixation of wage rates for male and female labour in agriculture. A tendency prevails to exploit female labour because of their poor bargaining power and this fact lowers their dignity as labour. In one of the villages, when the scheduled caste agricultural women workers demanded equal wages, they were pushed back to their homes. Unfortunately, these women do not have any other alternative except to get back to the work after a few months for their own and family's survival. According to a reliable source at the government sponsored Potato Research Institute in Punjab, women agricultural labourers are neither given permanent employment nor equal wages in the institute, whereas men are enrolled as permanent ones. Women are treated as casual labourers and are paid as much less as can be.

In industries and tanneries etc., the women are rarely employed as permanent and are offered low paid jobs ignoring their skill potential. These employers appreciate women's aptitude for work in terms of discipline, honesty and high output, yet they continue to be biased against female employment. This adds to barriers in women's opportunities to work outside the village.

Since the strict socialization of a woman starts right from her early childhood to prepare and prove herself to be 'an ideal wife', 'an ideal woman' and 'an ideal home-maker', she is seldom encouraged for education and economic independence. These patriarchal attitudes and practices are reflected in the local folk songs and folk tales in the area. The woman is supposed to pass on her earnings to the male members in the family, who squander it either on gambling, and/or liquor thus leaving the 'wife or woman' totally powerless and helpless. This powerlessness and lack of control over her own earned income results in other evils like 'dowry', 'alcoholism', and 'wife-beating', 'desertion' and they have to face limitless hardships. Very seldom, they can raise their voice against these evils.

Conclusions and Policy Implications

From the ongoing discussion, we can conclude that rural women play a vital role in farm and home system. She contributes substantially in the physical aspect of farming, livestock management, post-harvest and allied activities. Her direct and indirect contribution at the farm and home level along with livestock management operation has not only help to save their assets but also led to increase the family income. She performs various farm, livestock, post-harvest and allied activities and possesses skills and indigenous knowledge in these areas. The women were empowering themselves technically to cope with the changing times and productively using their free time and existing skills for setting and sustaining enterprises. They were engaged in starting individual or collective income generation programme with the help of self-help group. This will not only generate income for them but also improve the decision-making capabilities that led to overall empowerment.

1. The government should abolish the legally based discrimination on the basis of gender fixed in inheritance rights; give them equal access to land, livestock, and means of production; make it possible for them to participate in business activities; and guarantee them a right to membership and voting in labor organizations, credit associations, and similar organizations.

2. The number of women in training and extension programmes should be increased, especially in posts from which they have been excluded until now. The contents and subjects of training and extension programmes should be expanded so that the role of women in production, processing, and marketing can also be taken into account.

3. To achieve participation equal to that of men in public institutions, the women's cooperative activities should be promoted. To achieve this goal, it will be necessary to create a system for ascertaining the obstacles hindering the participation of women in schools, health services, employment, and general development. Statistical data showing women's contribution in production should be compiled and published. Measures facilitating household work and care of the children increase the chance for women to participate in economic, training, and political activities. Men should also be obligated to do their share of household work.

4. Training facilities of equal quality for girls and women, with the same subject matter as for men, should be established and made attractive by offering scholarships. These institutions should be followed up by possibilities of earning an income with the guarantee of an equal salary for equal work. Training possibilities for women are especially important not only in the fields of agriculture and in non-agricultural gainful employment, but also in the sectors health, nutrition, children's education, and family planning. It is necessary to make sure that, during the transition from a traditional economy to the modern technologies, the negative implications for women are minimized.

5. The face of the farmer and natural resource manager is primarily a a female in most of the developing world. Knowledge, technology, policies, institutions and programmes must therefore be developed by putting women at the centre to orient structures and processes to address their needs as food producers and environmental managers through gender mainstreaming and investing in women and girls to bridge the existing gender gaps. The prevailing misunderstanding and neglect of this fact has contributed to a significant loss of opportunities and investments in women farmers and thus has had major consequences for security and poverty alleviation. Rather than being regarded as a vulnerable group, women's knowledge, experience and substantial roles make them experts in agriculture and natural resource management; they are key agents in the way forward for sustainable development.

6. As women bear the brunt of poverty, it is just and fair that the bulk of our programmes be targeted towards them. We have to ensure that they also enjoy the fruits of freedom. We need to formulate tangible programmes that will take women issues to the centre of our agenda. The consolidation of democracy in our country requires the eradication of social and economic inequities, especially those that are systematic in nature, which were generated in our history.
7. Though agriculture has a central role to play in the rural community, it is not an end in itself but a means to an end which is rural development. It remains one of the important ingredients which include access to health care, education and other government services. Therefore the project planning for rural development needs to take these factors into account. Although significant progress has been made in restructuring and transforming our society and institutions, systematic inequalities and unfair discrimination remain deeply embedded in social structures, practices and attitudes, undermining the aspirations of our constitutional federal democratic republic. This needs the complete uprooting of discrimination against women in rural areas.

REFERENCES

1. Registrar, Census of India, Government of India, New Delhi.
2. Kabeer, Nail (2001), "Reflections on the Measurement of Women's Empowerment", in *Discussing Women's Empowerment—Theory and Practice*, Ida Studies No. 3. Novum Grafiska AB: Stockholm.
3. Mishra, S.P. (1996), Report "Factors Affecting Women Entrepreneurship in Small and Cottage Industries in India" International Labour Organisation, Swedish International Development Cooperation Agency.
4. World Bank (2001), *Engendering Development: Through Gender Equality in Rights, Resources, and Voice*, New York: Oxford University Press.

CHAPTER

14

Micro-Finance
An Instrument for Rural Development

—Dr. Y. Ashok Kumar
—P. Venugopala Rao

ABSTRACT

Among its multifarious services, the women centered micro-financial service is among the most prominent ones. The economic status and development of women and children critically depend on the savings and productive investment of the poor households. The traditional models development assume that saving are heavily concentrated in the high income groups and the poverty groups do not save significant amounts. The traditional models also presuppose that the propensity to invest in the poverty groups is low. These models further assume that expansion of the formal institutional credit sources would eventually lead to the development of the poor.

The institutional credit markets have never been very friendly with the poverty groups. The amount of credit advanced by the organized financial institutions to the poor has been inadequate. The rate of account the peculiarities surrounding the economic activities undertaken by the poor. As a result, the record to repayment performance has been bad. The exploitative informal credit sources such as the moneylenders, pawn brokers etc., have only worsened the economic well being of the poor. The SHG movements has so far shown that the outcomes have gone beyond thrift, credit and economic well being. The movement had served as instrument of social change essentially out of empowerment of women, improvement in literacy levels and children's education, particularly girl education, housing facilities, abolition of child labour, decline in family violence and banning of illicit distilleries in the villages have all been reported in different studies.

Introduction

It is axiomatic to say that India lives in rural area and that India's economic destiny is linked up in excitably with the development of its rural areas. Rural India is important because that is where 76.29 per cent of her population lives. The poor always need credit. As the income situation worsens, supply of cash gets tightened, the interest rate of the money-lending bares its claws with all its ugliness, it goes for 5 to 10 per cent per day. The poor needs credit because he has no caution to tide over the adverse situations which too often arise in meeting social obligations in carrying on productive enterprises and at times of total disaster. One can reasonably make a statement that people are poor today because of the failure of the financial institutions to support them in the past. The basic reason for the poor being poor is that they have separate from a very slim economic base, with a very little economic maneuverability's.

Though *Garibi Hatao* as a slogan has caught the attention of the people since the mid-term elections to the Lok Sabha in March 1971, the objective contained in the slogan is not a new on removal of poverty and raising the standards of living of the people have been the twin objectives of our economic policy since independence. The fact that a vast majority of Indian masses has been condemned to very low level of living for many past decades, in a matter of common knowledge. Poverty in India is so obvious that it should need no proof. A cursory glance at living conditions of people in rural areas and cities provided ample evidence of the extent of poverty in our country. The ill-fed people in rural areas and cities provided ample evidence of the extent of poverty in our country. The ill-fed people living in dilapidated houses, wearing shabby and torn clothes, all give enough indications of our poverty. But these are the days of scientific methods and statistical analysis. Professor Dandekar and Rath have therefore, done yeoman's service in providing a statistical measurement of the extent of poverty in India (1971: 106-146).

In recent years accumulation of considerable statistical evidence, pertaining to the trends in income distribution, as economic development proceeded in different countries point to the fact that there is no unique relationship between the rate of growth in numbers living below the poverty line. Observed in the case of some developing countries, these trends highlighted the need for only integrating distributional considerations with the growth strategy in any meaningful planning exercise but also tackling the problem of poverty by incorporating a set of policy instruments within the frame-work of planning, considerable efforts are being developed in recent years to make the planning possible.

Perpetuation of Poverty

The extent of poverty generally depends upon the extent of ownership of productive assets and the access to gainful employment opportunities. It is well established that due to lack of such productive assets and regular employment, poverty falls mainly on the rural people. The question that arises is how do the poor, who by definition, lack adequate purchasing power, make both ends meet and survive. The gap between current income and consumption is usually bridged through occasional having loans from relatives and friends. In some cases, the rural poor are even compelled to borrow on extremely exploitative terms making them bonded laborers to the creditors. The dependence of the rural poor on the informal sources of credit for meeting their production/consumption needs on exploitative terms is one of the courses that perpetuates poverty. Such dependence restricts their power to generate a surplus from their small economic enterprises as also their potential to participate effectively in the production process. The links the poor establish with the suppliers of credit are often used to siphon off the meager surplus generated by the poor.

The poor are not unproductive. In truth, they are the productive segment of the population. But unfortunately fruits of their labour are usurped by the better segment of the population through economic social and political manipulations. Availability of credit to the poor greatly enhances economic strength and maneuverability of the poor. It immediately improves their income situation. Credit alone is useless. It must necessarily be packaged with training, marketing, transportation facilities, technology and education.

By encouraging the poor to take up independent professions, a shortage will be created in the supply of wage labour, as a result wage rate will shoot up increasing the cost of production. And adversely affecting agricultural production. The success of credit programmes also depends on the wider national policy framework in which they are implemented. Institutional preparation is extremely important for credit to become useful. Conventional methods of credit dispensation have themselves to be inefficient and inadequate to reach the poor.

Savings plus credit can be a good starting point for group formation. There is a great incentive to form a group if people see that it is the only way one can have access to the credit. Credit programme for the poor should not be designed for only a handful of people. It may start with a handful of people to gain experience and gradually expand to cover more and more people. Contrary to popular belief, credit programme for the poor requires only a very small amount of money. Combating money-lending by only mobilizing group savings will be possible but it will be very hard and an uphill task. Simple way to de-capacitate the moneylenders is to bring in the institutional credit. Both of them are in credit business.

Group Savings

It imposes a discipline on the group member in developing a saving habit which was not there. Saving enhances self-confidence. Being a non-saver all of his life an individual in a group finds it a great source of encouragement to become a habitual saver.

Group savings of the poor can demonstrate the strength in the largeness of their number. Even if each poor person saves a vary small amount each week regularly, it adds up into an unbelievable large amount in no time.

Multiplier effect of investment can be vividly demonstrated in a credit programme for the poor through continuous expansion of the economic base of poor as his income rises with additional investment through borrowing. Vicious cycle of "low income-low saving–low investment–low income" cannot be broken by injecting credit in the cycles: "credit more income-more savings-more investment–more income".

Role of Voluntary Agencies

These agencies have come into existence as a result of an urge to help and improve the lot of the poor. They believe that group effort is the key to generating peoples' participation in any project. Some agencies concentrate on literacy and skills training in order to expand the range of economic opportunities open to the people with whom they work. Other programmes follow an integrated primary health care strategy, targeted at women and children in particular.

NGOs undertake this challenging task broadly the following modalities are adopted.

1. NGOs act as quasi Bank help groups in stabilizing credit activities. Once the groups are organized they act as intermediaries and facilitate in obtaining loans from the financial institutions.
2. The NGOs are certainly capable of performing a number of tasks which are crucial to the poor and which the banks are unable to undertake, such as travel to remote regions to reach the poorest who are largely ignored, any official development schemes play a vital role in mobilizing people; live with villagers and interact closely with them; act as guide, philosopher and friend to the groups.

Voluntary agencies using their experience, they have so far gained, can play a significant part in assisting banks, government authorities and donor agencies to shape new credit policies that are beneficial to the poor and to implement them. They try to bridge a gap where the people cannot reach their leaders and the leaders cannot reach their people. They try to do or get done what the government does not do, cannot do, will not do or should not do.

Poverty Scenario—A Statistical View

Both the rural and urban poverty ratios which are fluctuating until 1973-74 have been declining since then. The earlier phase was broadly characterized by the pre-green revolution era. During this period poverty levels were determined mainly by weather fluctuations and partly by (primary and secondary) consequences of institutional reforms such as land reforms and spread of co-operatives. In several states such as Andhra Pradesh, Maharashtra, Orissa, Rajasthan, Uttar Pradesh and West Bengal, the rural poverty ratio was higher than the all-India level during 1957-58 and 1973-74. During 1966-67 and 1967-68, the years of the consecutive droughts, poverty level shot up to 80 per cent in Uttar Pradesh.

In the second phase, which coincided with the post-green revolution phase and the poverty alleviation programmes era, poverty levels in rural and urban sectors declined considerably in almost all the states/UTs. The lower levels of poverty in a majority of the regions during 1987-88, a year of drought compared to the previous drought in 1983, only confirms the effectiveness of poverty alleviation programmes and food security measures. During this period, rural and urban poverty levels registered a sharp decline. The intensity of poverty also declined considerably in both the rural and urban India.

Systemic View

Move towards the systemic view of poverty begins with conceptualization of poverty reduction much more in line with the social science perspective than the conceptualization underlying the statistical view. We look at poverty reduction as a process beginning providing relief to the hard-core poor but continuing to help them to progress towards human development and empowerment. The approach would have to focus not so much on poverty numbers and changes in them as on the social, economic and political trends and relationships revealed by the poverty data. As illustrations of 'systemic view', we describe two scenarios which are in progress but are still in the beginning phase of unfolding.

Micro-finance programmes are chosen as the illustrations of economic path to help the poor to acquire productive livelihoods and a status of dignity in society. The illustration of political path is drawn from rural West Bengal and Bihar where a confrontation between the politically mobilized poor and their oppressors has brought some modest gains to the former. In neither case is the eventual outcome for the poor predictable with an acceptable degree of confidence. This adds urgency to the need to adopt a 'systemic view' in research on poverty and policy-making for poverty reduction.

Micro-finance as a Poverty Reduction Strategy

The micro-finance movement in India has shown significant potential, with intensive official support, its coverage has significantly expanded. RBI has also expanded its scope by giving freedom to institutions to change interest rates at their own discretion and more importantly to cover the credit needs of housing and shelter improvements. SHGs involve thrift as well as credit arrangements. National Bank for Agriculture and Rural Development (NABARD) and Small Industries Development Bank of India (SIDBI) have provided for SHGs and their members funds for capacity building through training. Peer monitoring helps better credit recovery. The SHG movements has so far shown that the outcomes have gone beyond thrift, credit and economic well-being. The movement had served as instrument of social change essentially out of empowerment of women, improvement in literacy levels and children's education, particularly girl education, housing facilities, abolition of child labour, decline in family violence and banning of illicit distilleries in the villages have all been reported in different studies. Women have acquired better communication skills and self-confidence, they have also acquired better status within families.

Government Programmes for Alleviation of Poverty

The government of India formulated policies and programmes for helping certain specified categories of the poor section of rural community included as part of the National Plan. Integrated Rural Development Programme (IRDP) primarily related to the unified or integrated approach for the socio-economic development of the rural communities. It is designed to eradicate the rural poverty and generate more income especially for the poor sections of the rural community.

The main objective of the IRDP was to bring the identified rural families target groups above the poverty line and to create substantial opportunities of employment for these people in the rural sector through productive programmes at block level and generate more income. The main thrust of IRDP was to transfer of productive assets and thus broaden the resource base of the poorest of the poor rural families. The IRDP Programme aimed at integration of five major sectors viz:

(*i*) Agriculture including animal husbandry, fishery, forestry and horticulture.

(*ii*) Village cottage and small industries;

(*iii*) Tertiary sector which would cover artisans and requirement of skilled workers in several rural activities;

(*iv*) Employment in various services that was necessary for the achievement of production and distribution in the fields of comprehensive agriculture and rural industries;

(*v*) Labour mobilization training in skills and organized mobility to tie up labour with opportunity.

REFERENCES

1. Dandekar, V.M., and Rath, Nilakantha, 1971, "Poverty in India", *Economic and Political Weekly,* VI (No.1) 106-146
2. NABARD Annual Report 1990-91, Resolution of Declaration and Plan of Action of Micro-credit Summit, Washington 1997.
3. SASY Guidelines, 1999, Ministry of Social Justice and Human Rights, Government of India, New Delhi.
4. NABARD Annual Report 2003, and 2004, Annual Report of Commission Rate of Rural Development, Govt. of Andhra Pradesh 2003-2004.
5. DPIP Guidelines, 2000 and 2002, A.P. Mutually Aided Co-operative Societies Act, 1995.
6. AP Rural Poverty Reduction Programme (APRP) Guidelines-2002.

CHAPTER

15

Historical Perspective of Panchayati Raj in India

An Overview

—Dr. V. Venkateswarlu

ABSTRACT

Land reforms, co-operatives, panchayati raj and community development movements, are supposed to be the four solid pillars on which a prosperous, dynamic and genuinely democratic rural social system is attempted to be built by the Government of Independent India. Panchayati Raj is also claimed as a real democratic political apparatus which would bring the masses into active political participation and also would establish a genuine political control from below, from the vast majority of the weaker, poorer sections of Rural India. According to some it will "decentralize democracy".

The starting point of local self-government in India is the Resolution of Lord Ripon of 1882 which urged the setting up of local self-governing bodies at the sub-divisional level and a supervisory and coordinating body at the district level. In accordance with these recommendations, laws were enacted during 1883-1885 but their implementation could not make much headway. The Royal Commission of 1908 on Decentralization re-emphasized the usefulness of these bodies and recommended measures to strengthen them. However, nothing concrete emerged. Local self-government received a new stimulus under the Diarchical System, introduced by the Government of India Act of 1919 under which some provinces passed Village Panchayat Acts.

The recommendations of the Mehta Committee were approved by the National Development Council in 1958. Later, the Central Council of Local Self Government in 1959 laid down the following principles for establishment of rural local self-government, namely Panchayati Raj: (1) It should be a three-tier structure of local self-governing bodies from village to the district, the bodies being organically linked up. (2) There should be genuine transfer of power and responsibility to them. (3) Adequate resources should be transferred to the new bodies to enable them to discharge these responsibilities. (4) All developmental programmes at these levels should be channelled through these bodies. (5) The system evolved should be such as will facilitate further devolution and dispersal of power and responsibility in the future. This paper aims at highlightening historical perspective of Panchayati Raj System in India and also analyzes the structural functional system of Panchayati Raj Institution.

Introduction

Land reforms, co-operatives, panchayati raj and community development movements, are supposed to be the four solid pillars on which a prosperous, dynamic and genuinely democratic rural social system is attempted to be built by the Government of Independent India. Panchayati Raj is also claimed as a real democratic political apparatus which would bring the masses into active political participation and also would establish a genuine political control from below, from the vast majority of the weaker, poorer sections of rural India. According to some it will "decentralize democracy".

The inspiration for Panchayati Raj is derived from the tradition of *Panch Parameshwar*, where God speaks through the Five, and official publications speak of 'Village Republics' as established historical facts, but do not list any sources for this well-established myth. By January 1957, every state had a Panchayat Act, and by September of that year 73 per cent of India's villages were covered by statutory panchayats with powers to enforce sanitation laws, to maintain the roads and protect the water supply. These were not autonomous bodies, and their activities were checked by state officials.

In India, most indigenous local consultative bodies seem to have had a caste origin. Within most castes, there were panchayats, meeting to hear cases and arbitrate between fellow caste members involved in disputes, and punish offenders against caste rules and customs. Inter-caste panchayats were also formed to hear disputes between members of different castes. There were also regional caste courts in some places, hearing cases in which the people involved were from different villages. Disputes were also referred to *Doras, Deshmukhs* and *Jagirdars* for arbitration, and this was often paid for, an additional source of income to landlords. Before the introduction of British courts, justice was administered by the masters, or one's caste fellows.

The Indian Constitution deals with government at the centre and state levels, and does not foreshadow Panchayati Raj as a form of political organization, except that states are directed in the Directive Principles to 'take steps to organise village panchayats ... to enable them to function as units of self-government'. The declared aim, then, was the decentralising of democracy. There was also a more practical, immediate reason.

The main consideration which prompted their introduction seems to have been the need for provoking public co-operation and participation in national construction and development, in view of the slow momentum of economic growth compared with such countries as Israel, Yugoslavia and China.

The starting point of local self-government in India is the Resolution of Lord Ripon of 1882 which urged the setting up of local self-governing bodies at the sub-divisional level and a supervisory and coordinating body at the district level. In accordance with these recommendations, laws were enacted during 1883-1885 but their implementation could not make much headway. The Royal Commission of 1908 on Decentralization re-emphasized the usefulness of these bodies and recommended measures to strengthen them. However, nothing concrete emerged. Local self-government received a new stimulus under the Dyarchical System, introduced by the Government of India Act of 1919 under which some provinces passed Village Panchayat Acts. Keeping the above aspects in view this paper aims at highlightening historical perspective of Panchayati Raj in India.

Origin of Panchayati Raj

In independent India, the framers of the Constitution included Panchayats under the Directive Principles of State Policy under Article 40 as follows: "the State shall take steps to organise village panchayats and endow them with such power and authority, as may be necessary to enable them to function as units of self-government." Panchayats were thus established in a number of States.

Introduction of the Community Development Programme in 1952 was a major step for ushering in an era of economic development and social welfare in rural India. The National Extension Service (NES) followed the Community Development Programme, was to be implemented in the newly created 'Block' consisting of a number of villages. It was, however, soon realized that peoples involvement was not representative enough, and as such not effective. Accordingly, the Balvantray G. Mehta Committee was appointed in 1957 to study the Community Development Projects and assess the extent to which the CD programme was succeeded in utilizing local initiatives and creating institutions to ensure continuity in the process of improving economic and social conditions in rural areas. With this objective, it is recommended an early establishment of statutory local bodies and devolution to them of the necessary resources, power and authority.

The committee submitted its report in November, 1957 and stated: 'So long as we do not discover or create a representative and democratic institution which will supply the local interest, supervision and care necessary to ensure that expenditure of money upon local object conforms with the needs and wishes of the locality, invest it with adequate power and assign to it appropriate finances, we will never be able to evoke local interest and excite local initiative in the field of development'. The substance of the recommendations centred on the concept of 'democratic decentralization' envisaging replacement of the erstwhile district boards and other executive bodies such as District Planning Committees and Block Advisory Committees by an organically interlinked popular set-up at the district and lower levels. The main recommendation of the committee was as follows:

> Development cannot progress without responsibility and power. Community Development can be real only when the community understands its problems, realizes its responsibilities, exercises the necessary powers through its chosen representatives and maintains a constant and intelligent vigilance on local administration.

The recommendations of the Mehta Committee were approved by the National Development Council in 1958. Later, the Central Council of Local Self Government in 1959 laid down the following principles for establishment of rural local self-government, namely Panchayati Raj: (1) It should be a three-tier structure of local self-governing bodies from village to the district, the bodies being organically linked up. (2) There should be genuine transfer of power and responsibility to them. (3) Adequate resources should be transferred to the new bodies to enable them to discharge these responsibilities. (4) All developmental programmes at these levels should be channelled through these bodies. (5) The system evolved should be such as will facilitate further devolution and dispersal of power and responsibility in the future.

The Council also stated that while the broad pattern and fundamentals may be uniform there should not be any rigidity in the pattern. In fact, the country is so large and Panchayati Raj so complex a subject with far-reaching consequences that there should be the fullest scope for trying out various patterns and alternatives.

Thereafter, based on the broad suggestions of Balvantray Mehta Study Team most of the country was covered with Panchayati Raj Institutions in the succeeding decade.

Panchayati Raj in India was thus introduced in the early sixties with the specific purposes of accelerating the process of decentralized development in administration. This was sought to be achieved by providing an administrative structure and mechanism for delivery of services, based on the concept of popular participation. More specifically, the following objectives were kept in view while introducing the system:

1. To promote people's participation in rural development programmes.
2. To provide an institutional framework for popular administration based on the concept of 'Democratic Decentralization'.
3. To act as a medium of social and political change.
4. To facilitate mobilization process at local levels.
5. To prepare plans for development and assist in their implementation in the concerned areas.

Phases of Panchayati Raj

In most of the states, the initial start towards decentralization was promising, but it soon began to fade, either under political pressures or changes in the growth strategy of the government. There was also a trend in favour of creation of new departments for different programmes, which were intended to improve the lives of the rural poor. In the context of the country as a whole, the growth of Panchayati Raj can be divided into four broad phases:

Phase-I (1959-1966): During this period, Panchayati Raj was established in most of the states.

Phase-II (1967-1976): As a result of change in the strategy of growth, special programmes for agricultural development were given priority, while limited attention was paid to the growth of Panchayati Raj Institutions.

Phase-III (1977-1991): Steps to activate the Panchayati Raj bodies were taken up by way of institutional reforms in some of the southern states, namely, Andhra Pradesh and Karnataka. These were essentially directed towards reorganizing the structure, so that the lower tiers might become financially ad administratively viable and come closer to the people. In other states, the situation remained unchanged.

Phase-IV (1992-continuing): As a result of the 73rd Constitution Amendment Act, 1993, almost all the states have either passed new Acts or modified their existing legislations, keeping in view the provisions of the Amendment.

The Asoka Mehta Committee (1977) which reviewed the performance of Panchayati Raj Institutions vis-à-vis rural development concluded that the

PRIs in the country have passed through the phases of ascendancy, stagnation and decline in quick succession. The committee concluded "a number of developments in the past have conspired to undermine the Panchayati Raj structures and made them ineffective. In fact, except in Maharashtra and Gujarat, the PRIs have been rarely given an opportunity to take up planning or implementational work on a sizeable scale. Broadly speaking, the miniscule programmes which were part and parcel of the Community Development Programme were handed over to the newly elected Panchayati Raj Institutions.

Objectives of the Panchayati Raj

The main objectives of Panchayati Raj as laid down in Third Five Year Plan are as follows:

1. Increasing agricultural production,
2. Development of rural industries,
3. Fostering co-operative institutions,
4. Full utilization of local manpower and other resources,
5. Assisting the weaker sections of the community,
6. Progressive dispersal of authority and initiative with emphasis on the role of voluntary organization, and
7. Fostering cohesion and encouraging the spirit of self-help within the community.

The village production plans should include the following two programmes:

1. Programmes such as supply of credit, fertilizers and improved seeds, plant protection, minor irrigation etc., for which major assistance has to come from outside;
2. Programmes such as digging field channels for utilizing irrigation from large projects, maintenance of bunds and field channels, digging and maintenance of village tanks, development and utilization of local manorial resources, etc. which call for effort on the part of the village community or the beneficiaries.

Now we shall briefly summarise the main functions of the three-tier system, at village, block and district levels respectively. This being the general pattern. Minor variation in the programme of activities do exist in different states.

Functions of Village Panchayat

At village level the main functions of the Panchayat are:

(*a*) Provision of a water supply,

(*b*) Maintenance of minor irrigation

(*c*) School buildings etc.,

(*d*) Family planning,

(*e*) Development and co-operation,

(*f*) Construction of wells, latrines etc.

Functions of the Panchayat Samiti

They cover agricultural improvement, development, co-operation, sanitation, primary education, social education, cottage industries, emergency relief. It works through Standing Committees for (*a*) production programmes, (*b*) social service and finance, (*c*) taxation and administration. Block Development Officers are regarded as on deputation to the Panchayat Samiti and are liable to be transferred in consultation with the *pradhan*. The Samiti *Pradhan* exercises administrative control over the '*Vikas Adhikari*' (meaning development officer) and the staff within the block.

Functions of Zila Parishads

The functions of Zila Parishads include coordination and consolidation of the plans of the Panchayat Samiti, supervision of the activities, distribution among the Panchayat Samitis of the ad hoc grants allotted to the district by the state government etc. *Pramukh* of Zila Parishad can visit, guide and advise the Panchayat Samitis. Coordination between the work of the various departments is secured through the District Development Officer, who is normally the Collector and he is responsible to see that the amounts placed at the disposal of the Panchayat Samitis are being properly utilized and that the '*Vikas Adhikaris*' of this team are discharging their functions adequately as extension staff.

Sources of Income

The Gram Panchayats in all the states are empowered to levy certain taxes, though there are considerable variations, from state to state. The main source of income of the Panchayat are: a tax on property, cess or land revenue or rent, a tax on animals, vehicles and profession tax. These taxes are generally compulsory. Panchayats are also empowered to levy some other taxes and fees like octroi, tax on shops. Fees for the use of rest houses, drainage fee, light rate, water rate, etc. where such services are provided by the Gram Panchayats.

The Panchayats are empowered to collect land revenue only in the states of Bihar, Gujarat and Maharashtra. However, in all the states, except Jammu and Kashmir, Tamilnadu, Orissa, U.P. and West Bengal, a part of land revenue is given to the Gram Panchayats as a grant by the state government. Besides the Panchayats also get income from on-tax resources such as markets, cattle ponds, tanks, waste orchards and other remunerative assets, while generally the amount of revenue received from these sources is not very high. In the recent past the Panchayats, particularly in state like Andhra Pradesh, Orissa, and Punjab have been getting sizeable revenues from fisheries. In the states in which higher Panchayati Raj bodies have been established, all their developmental schemes and programmes within the Panchayat area usually have to be implemented through the Gram Panchayats.

REFERENCES

1. Choudhury, R.C. and S.P. Jain (eds.), *Patterns of Decentralized Governance in Rural India*, Vol. I and II, Hyderabad, 1999.
2. Desai, A.R., 2001, *Rural Sociology in India*, Popular Prakasan, Bombay Pvt. Ltd., Mumbai.
3. Ministry of Rural Development, "Renewing Local Self-Government Institution in Rural India", Occasional Papers 6, New Delhi, 1994.
4. Mukarji, N & Bandyopadhyay, D., 1993, *New Horizons for West Bengal's Panchayats*, Government of West Bengal.
5. Patel, I.G., 1994, 'New Economic Policies: A Historical Perspective', *Manthan*, January–March.
6. Vyas, V.S., 1993, 'New Economic Policy and Vulnerable Sections: Rationale for Public Intervention', *EPW*, March 6.

CHAPTER

16

Integrated Decentralized District Planning and the Panchayati Raj Institutions

Theories and Practices

—Chandan Kumar Behera

ABSTRACT

Though India is booming in its socio-economic indicators but disparity among the affluent and the oppressed is increasing. The rich is becoming rich and the poor is becoming poor. In maximum cases the disadvantaged are far away from getting the actual benefit of the development programmes run by government. Hence, creating vibrant local self government at grassroot level is becoming primary agenda of both government and non-government agencies those who are working on governance. After near about two decades of implementation of 73rd constitutional amendment effective local self governance system is still a distant dream. Except few states the objectives behind this historic constitutional amendment could not realized by its esteemed citizen. People of these states are still remaining away from taking part in development planning, monitoring and evaluating the activities. Instead of becoming active development agent they are becoming passive recipients.

This paper is intended to highlight the positive aspects of integrated decentralized district planning process by elaborating the current planning practices and the role of Panchayati Raj Institutions. It also has a focus on the pros and cons of integrated decentralized planning process and ended with indicating some ways forwards.

Introduction

73rd and 74th amendment in Indian Constitution mandates for bottom up planning and paves a way to exercise control over the basic public goods by the local people. It assumes devolution of power and authority is the key to better development. The constitutional provision of three tier panchayati raj institution is the harbinger of *Ramrajya*, the dream of the father of the nation. Gram Panchayat, the lower most tier of the PRI system at local level should be played as a role of local-self government. People at village level should be governed by themselves directly and should plan for their economic advancement and social justice. Panchayat is supposed to formulate plans and implement all poverty alleviation programmes differently to fit the local needs. Except few states the objectives behind this historic constitutional amendment is still in gloomy after near about two decades of its implementation. Even if the states those are a step ahead in its implementation, do the members of Panchayati Raj Institutions are actively formulating their plan and implementing it? In Madhya Pradesh, the Panchayat President have to depend on the Janpad and Zilla Panchayat; in Tamilnadu, the Panchayat President are too much bound by Panchayat Union officials; in Kerala, the Panchayat Presidents are very much clear about their role in providing services and developing Panchayat Plans and implementing them (Narayana, 2005). Preparing development plan in a more participatory way across the nation in a bottom to top approach is no doubt inclusive as well as comprehensive in nature. It ensures appropriate supply chain management, building up the capacity of local government, removal of the stagnation of productive sector, optimal use of capacity and existing resources.

Is the decentralized planning process a magic stick for development? Do the members of Panchayati Raj Institution (PRIs) have a key role in this process? Does the capacity of the members of Gram Sabha are adequate to run the process? This paper is intended to discuss some aspects of decentralized planning process to answer above questions.

Integrated Decentralized District Planning

A perspective approach

In a democratic self-governed country decentralization is the devolution of power as well as responsibility to the lower most echelon of the local self governance system. The process of integrated decentralized district planning facilitates the villagers to voice their preferences in a right manner. Attempts are being made for holistic development through strengthening the planning for fulfilling the constitutional directives. The most audacious strategy is the integrated decentralized district planning by empowering the panchayat institutions. But in current practice the district plans are prepared by the line departments and consolidated by the officials like District Planning Officers, Assistant Statistical Officers (ASOs) of District Planning Committee (DPC). After consolidation and preparation of district plan it is placed before the District Planning Committee, in which the district collector is the chair person.

In almost all cases the consolidated plan is approved by the committee without or with very negligible deletion or addition. Once the plan has been approved implementation of the same is again entrusted to the respective line departments. Local self governing institutions find a few opportunities (only the elected representatives in the DPC) to play in the whole process of plan preparation and implementation. Again, in this process the detail plan of all key flagship programmes are also not reflected in the district plan. Like District Project Management Unit (DPMU) of NRHM and DPMU of SSA are preparing their annual PIP separately and submitted to respective State Project Management Unit. As a result of which repetition of activities, mis-utilization of resources, mis-match of demand and supply happens. On the other hand decentralized planning process not only put a halt to these negative aspects of district planning but also leads to a new horizon of holistic development by giving an opportunity for active community participation in each step of development. Devolution of administrative and planning responsibilities from central to local governments is the key to greater development (Pal, 2001). Decentralized planning process makes the service delivery efficient by identifying more accurate beneficiaries. It ensures more democratic governance by empowering the community. So, international agencies like World Bank, UNDP, UNICEF, European Commission, UNFPA etc. are encouraging and pursuing the central government as well as some of the state governments to undertake decentralized planning process.

In this decentralized planning process the elected representatives like *Sarpanch*, Panchayat Secretaries, Ward members, *Mukhiyas* and entrusted officials should play a leadership role. By holding gram sabha the elected representatives are suppose to identify the need of the villages and prioritize it according to the people.

The entrusted officials at the grassroot level should provide technical support like linking the need to appropriate resources by identifying the developmental programmes. Decentralized Planning process has to establish effective bridge between multiple factors like linking various funding agencies (central, state, centrally sponsored, local etc.) with various developmental sectors like health, education, and livelihoods etc. It has also to eradicate the duality, existing in constitutional and legal aspects. Under an appropriate policy and directions of local administration at first the plan has to be developed by the villagers in gram sabha. After developing village plan it need to be consolidated at Gram Panchayat level to develop Panchayat plan. Like this all panchayat plan have to be consolidated at Block/Janpad Panchayat level to bring out the Block plan. Then all block plans have to be consolidated at Zila Panchayat level to bring out the district rural plan and finally submitted to District Planning Committee. In this step all the Municipalities of a district have to submit their urban plan to the DPC and at DPC all rural

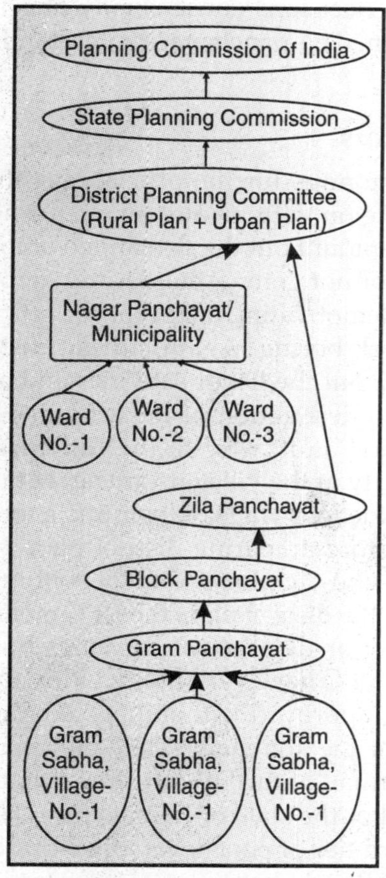

Chart 16.1: Decentralized Planning Process

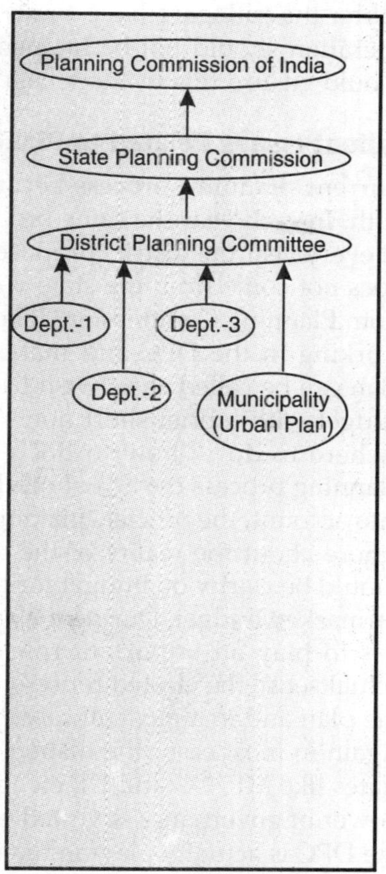

Chart 16.2: Current Planning Process

plan and urban plan have to be consolidated to bring out decentralized district plan. Finally the DPC has to submit to the State Planning Commission or State Planning Board after due approval. To facilitate this decentralized planning process in each steps a group of persons should invest their time and intellect for technical guidance. Villagers have to invest time and they should have a genuine interest for developing village plan in the Gram Sabha. Special focus should be given for inclusion of disadvantaged groups like SC, ST, women, Differently able persons and children. Women are generally interested for participating in the planning process but they feel they are not listened to and their issues are not properly addressed in the Gram Sabha. Special meeting should be organized with them before convening the Gram Sabha. It will be better if separate meeting will be organized "taluk" or "sahi" wise to identify specific needs and available resources. It helps the facilitators at village level to prioritize the need and the planning process will be more inclusive by minimizing the rigid caste dynamics. In the Gram

Sabha the villagers have to arrive at the decisions consensually and any alteration should not be happened later on. The panchayat representatives should ensure this to the villagers.

Salient Issues Related to Planning Process

Current planning process becomes monotonous for the officials involved with. In each year the same process is going on without any innovativeness. In every year the district proposes certain amount but the demanded amount does not come from the state with a plea of not getting the desired amount from Planning Commission. It becomes a demotivating factor for the officials working in the DPC and making the work boring. Again current district plan can be called as a "wish list" pointing out the list of activities and a fix budget with a brief short note. There is no description of the activities like "where to do", "how to do", "who to do" and "why to do". In current planning process the actual need and priority of the villagers are never taken into account, the officials making plans in the four walls of their office totally ignore about the reality of the villages. Before preparing district plan there should be clarity on budget for the district and the plan should be within the earmarked budget. During the approval of the district plan, the DPC member has to play an important role in addition or deletion of activities but in actual sense the elected representatives in DPC have very limited idea about the plan and in almost all cases the plan is approved without any alteration. Again in most cases the district collector or the nominated state minister (in states like MP, CG and UP etc.) is the chairman of the DPC. It shows that the power of governance is vested in the hand of the state or bureaucracy. Here, the DPC is actually playing the role of third tier of panchayat raj institutions whereas the Block Panchayat and Gram Panchayat have no role to play. Sometimes the Gram Panchayat is playing only executive role. In the whole process the community has no role to play and completely unknown about the plan. They become sidelined during implementation of the same plan and monitoring the targets. Community become passive receiver of the fruits of development programmes. History of rural development witnessed that without active community participation the development programmes has no meaning. Realizing this Constitution of India mandates for participatory district planning and initiated in First Five Year Plan (1951-56) period.

A conducive political will is essential for decentralized district planning process. The states those are pioneer in this direction are the best example. Constitution of India distributes legislative powers among the parliament and state legislatures, empowering state to organize village panchayats. Decentralized district planning process is comprised of some technical activities like visioning exercise, social mapping, resource mapping, problem identification and its prioritization, linking the need with appropriate resources require some technical expertise. Panchyat *pradhan*, *Mukyia*, and ward members, those are suppose to play pioneer role, are hardly having adequate skill to undertake decentralized district planning process. It is a tough task to gather huge number of relevant data relating to various sectors, setting of priorities by analyzing these, collective envisioning, leveraging the skills and initiatives of various stakeholders. To assemble all villagers with divergent interest of various socio-economic backgrounds in a Gram Sabha and converging their attitude and interest into a common goal of village development is a difficult task in decentralized district planning process. This multidimensional participative district planning process should follow clearly organized sequence of steps to arrive at meaningfull plan (Manual for Integrated District Planning, 2008).

Table 16.1: Decentralization – Chronology of attempts and committee reports

Year	Item	Ideas and Concepts
First Plan 1951-56	Community Development Blocks	To break up the planning exercise into national, state, district and local community levels.
Second Plan 1956-61	District Development Councils	Drawing up of village plans and popular participation in planning through the process of democratic decentralisation.
1957	Balwant Rai Mehta Committee	Village, block, district panchayat institutions established.
1967	Administrative Reforms Commission	Resources to be given/local variations accommodated, purposeful plan for area.
1969	Planning Commission	Formulated guidelines; detailed the concept of the district plan and methodology of drawing up such a plan in the framework of annual plans, medium-term plans and perspective plans.
1978	Prof. M.L. Dantwala	Block-level planning to form link between village and district-level planning.
1983-84	CSS/Reserve Bank of India	Strengthen district plan/district credit plan.
1984	Hanumantha Rao Committee	Decentralisation of functions, powers and finances; setting up of district planning bodies and district planning cells.
1985	G.V.K. Rao Committee	Administrative arrangements for rural development; district panchayat to manage all development programmes.

Source: Manual for Integrated District Planning, Planning Commission of India.

Panchayat Raj Institutions: The Prime Mover of Decentralized District Planning Process

It is crystal clear that devolution of power and authority unlocks the door to development by sharing of responsibility and accountability. 73rd Constitutional Amendment of Indian constitution introduces three tire of Panchayat Raj Institution, i.e. Zila Panchayat at district level, Block Panhayat at block level and Gram Panchayat at village level. Part IX (about the Panchayats) is the longest amendment of Indian Constitution. Article 40 of the constitution of India provides that the state shall take steps to organize village panchayats and endow them with such power and authority to enable them to function as units of local self government. Here tragedy is that the will of the state is the guiding factor for the functioning of village panchayat as a unit of local self government. Let the village panchayat free from this claw and let them plan for their economic development and social justice. The idea is to transform the community itself to self government with a hope of empowerment of people at village level. In fact, the decentralization envisaged in the constitutional amendments will erase the long-run power politics and destabilizes the hold of landlords and traders. It only needs conscious and empowered community who can be a crusade against this ill-nexus. The Village Panchayat is the lower most echelon of the three tier Panchayat Raj Institutions and should be apolitical in nature, must be free from any influence. But, in reality the political parties select candidates to contest the Gram Panchayat and Panchayat Samiti elections. Political parties bring out victory processions after declaration of Panchayat election result. There is no effort from any quarter to clean the system or ensure that Panchayat Raj Institutions remain apolitical (Datta, 2010). The reason is two fold; In one hand, the reformers (other than governance reformers) not regarded that the panchayats are relevant to them and the other is the political leaders' wants to capture the panchayat for owning vote. As a result of which the village solidarity has been replaced by the party solidarity.

The decentralized participatory planning process starts from village level with an effective leadership of the public representatives of Gram Panchayat. The *Sarpanch, Panch,* and *Mukiyas* should be pioneer and open minded inclined towards the holistic development of their village. But, in actual sense the panchayat members are more interested in power politics than the rural development (Acharya, 2002). They should strive for more attendance and more participation in the Gram Sabha. All villagers should get a chance to voice their views and all the decisions should be fare. They should facilitate the Gram Sabha in such a manner that all participants should feel they are important for the meeting. Various studies revealed that in many cases common and socio-economically poor villagers are not interested to attend and participate in the Gram Sabha meetings because they are not properly listened to and their issues are not addressed rightly. In many cases Gram Sabha happens only in papers. The Gram Panchayat is subject to convene Gram Sabha. But, the irony is that in all most all cases the date and agenda of the Gram Sabha is fixed by the state government. Hence, the date may not suitable for the villagers and local issues may not get place for discussion. For which villagers' interest for attending Gram Sabha is diminishing. In a true sense representatives of Panchayat Raj Institution are the most trusted arm of the public and they suppose to think for all-round development of their people. They are the best witness of the day to day situation of the residents of the village and can plan better in more participative way. Effective local governance is possible only when elected representatives have the full responsibility and have a genuine interest for developing their village by not only deciding what work will be done but also raising the finances. Unless and until Panchyats will become economically independent it will be hard to change and true development will be a distant dream. The sole objective behind strengthening the Panchayat Raj is to evolve a system of democratic decentralization and empowering the communities to take care of themselves by rapid socio-economic development. In a difficult budget constraint situation it is impossible to bring desired change. Each public representative should use RTI and each Panchayat *pradhan* should ask to the concern department to inform them what works they are going to undertake in his/her area with activitywise budget details.

PRACTICE IN CHHATTISGARH

"Chhattisgarh Panchayati Raj Adhiniyam, 1993" *A case study* forms the basis of Panchayati Raj System in Chhattisgarh. Devolution of powers and authority to the Panchayati Raj Institutions with respect to all 29 subjects under 11th schedule of the Constitution have been made by the state. The Gram Sabha is suppose to plan for its socio-economic development concerning to these subjects. According to Chhattisgarh Panchayati Raj Adhiniyam 1993, Article 7, it not only plan but also decides the priority of the development schemes and implement it. Seven districts of Chhattisgarh are fully covered under Schedule V, namely Sarguja, Koriya, Jashpur, Kanker, Bastar, Dantewada and Korba and another six districts are partially covered under *Schedule V*, namely Raigarh, Bilashpur, Durg, Rajnandgaon, Raipur and Dhamtari. Chhattisgarh Panchayati Raj Adhiniyam, 1993, Section 129(PESA) A-F has a provision for organizing more than one Gram Sabha in one village ensuring the participation of under privileged community living in "Tula", "Taluk" or "Sahi". Though constitutionally there are ample scope for Gram Sabha in becoming effective instrument in development process but hardly they prepare their integrated decentralized village plan. They are only implementing certain development activities decided by the district, state and center. Sometimes they are preparing programme-specific plan like BRGF plan.

Current planning process in Chhattisgarh is not a decentralized one. However, various UN agencies like UNDP, UNICEF, UNFPA and Planning Commission of India are continuously striving to initiate the process through the existing system of the state. Both five year plans and annual plans are developed by the Zila Yojana Samiti by compiling the plans prepared by various departments. In all districts there is one District Planning Committee (Zila Yojana Samiti) working according to Chhattisgarh Zilla Yojana Samiti Niyam, 1995. In which the president is, one of the state ministers, nominated by the state and the secretary is the concerned district collector. People are not aware about the plans and planning process.

Way Forward

Besides all the pros and cons of decentralized district planning we have to move forward with a positive hope for the best. There is no substitute for participative planning in holistic development process. Simultaneously we need to strengthen the service delivery system as well as service receiving system. Public as a whole should be aware about the importance of attending Gram Sabha and participating in discussion. They should be *sou mouto* interested to investing time and efforts for making planning process more effective. There is an urgent need to build the capability of the public representatives to undertake decentralized planning process in terms of conceptual clarity, accounting, budgeting, monitoring and so on. Some training programmes are organized for the PRIs members by State Institute for Rural Developments (SIRDs) and certain NGOs are certainly a welcoming steps. But emphasis is given only to train the *Sarpanch* and Panchayat Secretaries whereas more numbers of Ward Members or *Panchs* are being left or sidelined of the training programmes and unable to perform their duties perfectly. In a village Ward members are the most nearer public representatives and generally people come to them if any problem they face. At first the focus should be on ward members for building their capacity. Ward members should consult with people before deciding or planning any development schemes and beneficiaries. The capability of the entrusted officials should be build up with respect to analyzing huge relevant data, consolidating the plans, using certain software relevant to planning process. A group of volunteers should be trained in giving expert guidance in grass roots planning process to bring out a true people's plan.

Funds, Functions and Functionaries should be made available to the Gram Panchayats to be more effective and enable it to function as an institution of self government. In present context panchayats are guided by political parties, bureaucracy like panchayat executives, Block Development Officer and District Collector. In Gram Sabha the muscle power and money power are getting upper hand and the most vulnerable is neglected. Again, there is no budget envelope for the panchayats. The state should take steps to acknowledge the panchayats about sources of revenues and various funding sources by proper notification not by executive order because executive order do not have legal validity that notification have. Transfer of 29 subjects to the Panchayats mentioned in the Constitution is essential for making Panchayats more functional and vibrant. Allocations of function to the Panchayats are by an executive order, which can be withdrawn easily. The right approach would be to amend the laws relating to the 29 subjects and include them in a State Panchayat Act. Ex- agriculture including extension is listed as a function of the Panchayat but if the State Agriculture Act does not entrust the same to the Panchayat through an amendment of the relevant provision devolution of powers in respect of agriculture means nothing (Pal, 2001). According to the constitutional mandates the Panchayats should play as a role of local self government and plan for their economic development and social justice. So, it is expected that they should run the poverty alleviation schemes separately from the format set by the higher level of governments.

Strengthening the Gram Sabha, the fulcrum of the Panchayat Raj System is the most crucial step for all who believe in democratic ideal of power to the people. In spite of active and vibrant Gram Sabha the Gram Panchayat never work as a local self government. The Panchayat representatives and Panchayat executives should devote more to increase the attendance rate of people in Gram Sabha. Special focus should be given on the participation of the underprivileged especially women. Innovative ways should be followed by the Panchayat to enhance the attendance. It is no doubt, in a society where deep rooted stratification on the basis of caste, class and gender the functioning of Gram Sabha according to the constitutional provision will take time. Again this stratification coupled with the personal perception towards decentralized planning is halting the development and making it uneven.

REFERENCES

1. Acharya, P., 2002, "Education: Panchayat and Decentralization—Myths and Reality", *Economic and Political Weekly*, Vol. 37, No. 20, pp. 788-796.
2. Chathukulum, J. and John, M.S., 2002. "Five Years of Participatory Planning in Kerala", *Economic and Political Weekly,* Vol. 37, No. 49, pp. 4917-4926.
3. Datta, T. 2010, "Politics in Development" in *Rural Development in India (*Ed. by Bishnu Mohan Dash*)*, New Delhi Publishers, New Delhi, pp. 21-30.

Fernandes, A., 2003, "Aggrandizer Government and Local Governance", *Economic and Political Weekly,* Vol. 38, No. 27, pp. 2873-2879.

5. "Gram Sabha", *The Samaj (*Oriya daily*)*, 10th September, 2010.
6. *Gram Panchayat Padadhikariyo (panch, sarpanch and sachib) ke lie pathan samagri*, published by Chhattisgarh State Institute for Rural Development, Panchayat and Rural Development Department, Govt. of Chhattisgarh.
7. *Manual for Integrated District Planning,* Planning Commission of India, 2008.
8. Mishra, H.K., 2005, *Chhattisgarh Panchayat Raj Adhiniyam (Niyamo, Adhisuchanao and Durstanto*), 4th edition, India Publishing Company, Raipur, Chhattisgarh.
9. Narayana, D., 2005, "Local Governance without Capacity Building", *Economic and Political Weekly,* Vol. 40, No. 26, pp. 2822-2832.
10. Pal, M., 2001, "Decentralized Planning and Panchayat Raj", *Economic and Political Weekly,* Vol. 36, No. 12, pp. 1002-1005.

CHAPTER

17

National Rural Employment Guarantee Act

Opportunities and Challenges

—Amit Kumar

ABSTRACT

The world's biggest employment guarantee programme, India's National Rural Employment Guarantee Scheme (NREGS) has been in operation since February 2006. This scheme is a self-targeted programme designed to provide 100 days of employment to rural households and to serve as a safety net. More broadly its aim is to reduce rural poverty through the creation of sustainable rural infrastructure which is expected to foster rural economic growth. This study looks at the performance of the NREGS from two perspectives—it examines the opportunities of the programme, as well as the challenges being posed by this schemes. In terms of the efficiency impact, the analysis reveals a clear violation of the formal clauses and the spirit of the NREG Act and thereby undermining the potential of the programme in terms of providing a safety net. The estimates suggest that while the NREGS may not be creating any new employment, and may indeed be substituting for existing employment opportunities, the scheme is still considered valuable as it offers better working conditions.

Introduction

In August 2005, Parliament passed the landmark legislation, the National Rural Employment Guarantee Act (hereafter NREGA). The NREGA is a national law funded largely by the central government and implemented in all states, which creates a justiciable "right to work" for all households in rural India. Under the NREGA, rural households have a legal right to get "not less than" 100 days of unskilled manual labour on public works in each financial year.

The enactment of the NREGA in 2005 came about partly as a result of a sustained campaign by academics and activists across India. Significant efforts were made by campaign groups to highlight the crisis of food and work availability being faced by large numbers of the rural poor in India. The NREGA, as finally enacted, was a diluted version of the "citizen's draft". Nevertheless it signified a huge step forward as a social security mechanism for the rural poor.

The initial 200 districts chosen for implementation of the National Rural Employment Guarantee Act (NREGA) were the most backward districts of this country. In administrative lexicon, backward districts or remote/ underdeveloped areas are identified on the basis of a set of criteria—low agricultural productivity, high incidence of poverty, high concentration of scheduled castes/tribes, areas which suffer from isolation in demographic terms, etc. This identification process then leads to planning for development of these backward areas. The underdevelopment and neglect of these backward areas are at times reminiscent of the workings of the East India Company till 1857—"The (East India) Company which ruled India until 1858 did not make one spring accessible, did not sink a single well, nor build a bridge for the benefit of the Indians". It was also evident from the socio-economic survey that certain areas still continue to be severely underdeveloped in India, where the inadequacy of basic infrastructure and aggregate lack of development has combined with recent increases in food and employment insecurity to create conditions of rural distress that may be unprecedented. Further evidence of rural distress was found in the poor quality of housing and the lack of basic material possessions.

The current developmental indicators show very clearly that it is the states of Jharkhand, Chhattisgarh, and Orissa that lag behind on every indicator. In terms of social groups we could easily state that dalits, adivasis, nearly all backward castes and muslims are the most marginalized; women within these groups are the most discriminated. Some of these developmental woes were supposed to be addressed by the much touted government flagship programme, the NREGA. Four years since the inception of the programme, the results in these areas leave much to be desired. Additionally for the Indian state, the list of developmental woes becomes exacerbated because a substantial portion of these backward areas have also been under the influence of the Maoists.

The idea of an Employment Guarantee or the government as an employer of last resort (ELR) has been used by many governments in different forms starting with the Poor Employment Act of 1817 in Britain, New Deal Programmes in USA in the 1930s, Argentina's Plan Jefesy Jefas, Morocco's Promotion National (since 1961). During last few decades' government intervention in the labour market as an employer of the last resort has become an integral part of labour market policies in many developing countries. Recent examples of the latter include public work programmes in India, Bangladesh, Pakistan, Philippines, Egypt, Botswana, Kenya and Chile (Subbarao, 1997; Lipton, 1996). Consistent with this line of thought employment is viewed as the most important area of intervention for welfare. (Kaboub 2007: 2-3).

The basic feature of the Indian NREGA is similar to other Employment Guarantee Programmes (see Tcherneva, 2003: 2-3 for details). The Act envisages the provision of:

(*i*) Federally funded jobs to anyone who is ready, willing and able to work.

(*ii*) These jobs claim to provide a living wage and decent working conditions.

All such programmes try to tackle poverty which is experienced by those whose income deprivation and social exclusion is primarily due to joblessness. Moreover any such strategy is though primarily designed to tackle poverty but is not a "targeted" social protection programme for the poor. These are designed to provide universal "guarantee" of employment, besides fulfilling availability of guaranteed 15 unskilled manual work on piece-rate basis on demand. The employment guarantee programmes also satisfy the following conditions:

(*i*) The work which is chosen is labour intensive in nature.

(*ii*) After completion of the work under the scheme a productive asset is supposed to be generated.

The formal goals of the Act are:

1. Strong social safety net for the vulnerable groups by providing a fall-back employment source, when other employment alternatives are scarce or inadequate.
2. Growth engine for sustainable development of an agricultural economy. Through the process of providing employment on works that address causes of chronic poverty such as drought, deforestation and soil erosion. The Act seeks to strengthen the natural resource base of rural livelihood and create durable assets in rural areas. Effectively implemented, NREGA has the potential to transform the geography of poverty.
3. Empowerment of rural poor through the processes of a rights-based Law.

Salient Features of NREGA

1. Any adult members of a rural household, willing to do unskilled manual work, may apply for registration in writing or orally to the local Gram Panchayat.
2. Employment will be given within 15 days of application for work, if it is not then daily unemployment allowance as per the Act, has to be paid. Liability of payment of unemployment allowance is of the states.
3. Work should ordinarily be provided within 5 km radius of the village. In case work is provided beyond 5 km, extra wages of 10% are payable to meet additional transportation and living expenses.
4. Wages are to be paid according to piece rate or daily rate. Disbursement of wages has to be done on weekly basis and not beyond a fortnight in any case.
5. At least one-third beneficiaries shall be women who have registered and requested work under the scheme.
6. Work site facilities such as crèche, drinking water, shade have to be provided.
7. Permissible works predominantly include water and soil conservation, afforestation and land development works.
8. A 60 : 40 wage and material ratio has to be maintained.
9. Social Audit has to be done by the Gram Sabha.
10. Grievance redressal mechanisms have to be put in place for ensuring a responsive implementation process.
11. All accounts and records relating to the Scheme should be available for public scrutiny.

"Thus, NREGA fosters conditions for inclusive growth ranging from basic wage security and recharging rural economy to a transformative empowerment process of democracy." (NREGA Operational Guideline, 2008). By providing readily available employment, the program aims to put households in a better position to keep up a basic income flow when no other source of earning is available. Given the great destitution of many households, such immediate support might often boil down to mere survival aid. In addition, the NREGS also counteracts in-work poverty and powerlessness among the privately employed as, by intensifying the competition for casual laborers, it increases the pressure on employers to improve their terms of employment in the open market.

Challenges for NREGA

The current developmental indicators show very clearly that it is the states of Jharkhand, Chhattisgarh, and Orissa that lag behind on every indicator. In terms of social groups we could easily state that dalits, adivasis, nearly all backward castes and Muslims are the most marginalised; women within these groups are the most discriminated. Some of these developmental woes were supposed to be addressed by the much touted government flagship programme, the NREGA. Four years since the inception of the programme, the results in these areas leave much to be desired. Additionally for the Indian state, the list of developmental woes becomes exacerbated because a substantial portion of these backward areas have also been under the influence of the Maoists.

The main support for the Maoists, according to a report of an expert group set up by the Planning Commission entitled *Development Challenges in Extremist Affected Areas* (March 2008), comes from dalits and adivasis. The group identifies large scale displacement, forest issues, usury, land alienation, insecure tenancy contracts among other socio-economic reasons in backward areas as the main reason for the spread of Maoism. It also clearly states that for dalits, apart from sub-human poverty, there are issues of unemployment, discrimination and exclusion which are the main reasons for discontent. The adivasis, on the other hand, fare the poorest in terms of all human development indicators. The report goes on to locate the rise of Maoism in the context of the developmental paradigm of the Indian state. The field visits we undertook in these areas broadly converge with the findings of the expert group. The Maoists have been active in these areas for the past four decades and it is only recently that the Indian state acknowledges them as a potential threat to its sovereignty ("the biggest internal security threat"). The committee observed that only 71 per cent of the credit target had been achieved; 84 per cent of government funds had been utilized, and against the allocation of 10 per cent and 20 per cent for training and infrastructure, only 6 per cent and 16 per cent had been made use of. Two-thirds of the allocated funds had been used for subsidies. The allocation of central funds was more in the southern region than in the eastern when compared on the basis of the poor in either area. The credit portfolio was still dominated by the primary sector and milch cattle. A National Institute of Bank Management-National Institute of Public Finance and Policy (NIBM-NIPFP, 2007; henceforth the NN) study, showed the same scenario and it observed that credit disbursement gained pace only in the fourth quarter of the year, motivated by the aim of fulfilling the target. Governments not releasing funds and banks' indifference were the reasons for the tardiness.

Provisions like priority for women in the ratio of one-third of total workers (Schedule II (6)); equal wages for men and women (Schedule II (34)); and crèches for the children of women workers (Schedule II (28)) were made in the Act, with the view of ensuring that rural women benefit from the scheme in a certain manner. Provisions like work within a radius of five kilometers from the house, absence of supervisor and contractor, and flexibility in terms of choosing period and months of employment were not made exclusively for women, but have, nevertheless, been conducive for rural women.

Being government work, the hours of work are clearly stated and are limited to eight hours in a day (in the case of daily wage work). Fixed working hours often cannot be expected in the case of other work. This is of special concern for women who combine any paid work with household work. NREGA employment is therefore considered relatively "safe" in the sense that it is thought that there are some checks and balances in place to prevent harassment of workers.

There are, in many areas, tenacious social norms against women working outside the home. In Uttar Pradesh and Bihar, women who said that they had not been able to register as workers under the NREGA and were told that this programme was "not for them". In Sitapur district (Uttar Pradesh), there was a significant amount of hostility to female participation in NREGA, both from gram panchayat functionaries and male relatives. Names of adult women were excluded from job cards and it was commonly stated that women "cannot" work on worksites, that they are "too weak", and that it is "socially unacceptable" for them to undertake this work. The widespread prevalence of these opinions related to female labour was reflected in the fact that only 5 per cent of the randomly sampled workers in Sitapur district, Uttar Pradesh were women.

Lack of work and non-payment of minimum wages are the two different types of complaint being faced by the researcher which needs to be seriously taken care of. Though the average person-days for the job cards verified was 57 days, most labourers wanted more. Further, the daily wage earned ranged from Rs. 70-85 (the minimum wage in Tamilnadu is Rs. 100 per day). In Dindigul, main focus was on whether wage payments were being made in a timely manner and whether there was any evidence of corruption. According to the Management Information System (MIS), Tamilnadu is one of two states (along with Andhra Pradesh) where there are no significant delays in wage payments. This was indeed true, we found. None of the workers we spoke to have any complaint of delayed payment. This is a significant achievement given that delays in wage payments have caused great hardship of NREGA workers in many other parts of the country. In 2008, the central government ordered all wage payments to be made directly to workers' bank and post office accounts, as an anti-corruption measure. Tamilnadu is the only state that continues to make wage payments in cash, on the grounds that it helps to avoid delays. To see if corruption was an issue, they verified entries in job cards (downloaded from the NREGA website, www.nrega.nic.in). They verified 23 job cards (from three Gram Panchayats spread over two blocks). According to the official records, the labourers on these job cards had earned Rs. 92,050 as wages. Of this, Rs. 1,395 was not corroborated by the labourers, suggesting that only 1.5 per cent was siphoned off.

During worksite visits, they felt that, apart from increasing supervision, labour productivity could be improved by selecting works that labourers themselves perceive as being useful. When the researcher raised the question of labour productivity, a female worker's prompt answer was: "You should see how nicely we made the pond before this one. It is full of water. Now it's hot, that's why we are working like this." Perhaps the list of permissible works for GPs to choose from could be expanded. For instance, land improvement (e.g., land levelling, farm ponds) on the lands of Dalit farmers could be added to the list.

So, from the above stated we are observing that NREGA has opened a lot of opportunity for the rural poor in India. Due to strict monitoring system it is also reflecting that it will achieve almost all the objective which has already been fixed. But at the same time it poses challenges in terms of how to achieve those target and also how to keep it on right track such that it doesn't become like other poverty alleviation programme. It is not only the responsibility of the state but also the responsibility of the public in longer interest of the nation.

REFERENCES

1. Banerjee, K. (2008). "The Political Economy of Backwardness in Agrarian Systems: The Role of Social Groups, States and Markets", unpublished PhD thesis, Jawaharlal Nehru University, New Delhi.
2. —(2010): "Social Development Index", forthcoming in *Social Development Report.*
3. *Imai, K. (2007),* "Targeting versus universalism: An evaluation of indirect effects of the Employment Guarantee Scheme in India", *Journal of Policy Modeling* 29(1): 99-113.
4. *Kaboub, F. (2007),* "Employment Guarantee Programs:A Survey of Theories and Policy Experiences" Unpublished Working Paper No. 498. The Levy Economics Institute of Bard College.
5. *Tcherneva, P.R.(2003), Job or Income Guarantee?* Working Paper No. 29 University of Missouri – Kansas City.
6. *Report of Expert Committee on Development Challenges in Extremist Affected Areas* (2008), Planning Commission, Government of India, New Delhi.
7. NIBM-NIPFP (2007): "Report on Action Research Project on Gendering Microfinance under SGSY" (Pune: National Institute of Bank Management and Delhi: National Institute of Public Finance and Policy), January.
8. Khera,Reetika & Nayak Nandini, "Women Workers and Perceptions of the National Rural Employment Guarantee Act, *Economic & Political Weekly,* vol. xliv, no. 43, 20 October, pp.40-57.

Chapter

18

Food Insecurity in Rural India

Some Reflections

—Dr. Sanjoy Roy

ABSTRACT

Food security could be when all people at all times have access to enough food that should affordable, safe and healthy, culturally acceptable, meets specific dietary needs, obtained in a dignified manner and produced in ways that are environmentally sound. But food security in India raises the twin problems of uncertain food production and unequal food distribution. The impact of unequal food distribution can lead adverse effects on the rural and urban population living below the poverty line. Food insecurity is not only economic problem but also problem of non-humanity approach in India. There availability of the food grains is enough to satisfy their needs. According to the statistical data published by the Food Corporation of India and the government of India foodgrain availability is 229 million tonnes in 2008-09 which is 230 million tonnes in previous year. While it is happening because, foodgrain traders are doing speculation practice and sealing them in high prices than fair prices. Food insecurity is not only natural but also manmade. So, what is now required is a new initiative and strong National Food Security Mission and finally it is a time for a Second Green Revolution in India.

Introduction

India is second largest country in the world in the manner of population. It is most important considerable plus point of the India, because it involve large human capital. Even we all Indian are thinking that, we will become 'super power' in the world. Recently most of Indian peoples are struggling with the bread and butter due to the continuously increasing prices of foodgrain, vegetables, pulses and other cereals. India ranks 94th position in the Global Hunger Index of 119 countries in the world. While famines and starvation deaths remain the popular representation of the contemporary problem of hunger, one of the most significant yet understated and perhaps less visible area of concern today is that of chronic or persistent food and nutrition insecurity. This is a situation where people regularly subsist on a very minimal diet that has poor nutrient and calorific content as compared to medically prescribed norms. This report uses seven indicators, which directly or indirectly affect the food security and nutritional status of a person. These are based on amount of calories consumed, access to safe drinking water and toilets, women and children. On the composite index of food insecurity of rural India, states like Jharkhand and Chhattisgarh are found in the 'very high' level of food insecurity, followed by Madhya Pradesh, Bihar and Gujarat. The better performers include Himachal Pradesh, Kerala, Punjab and Jammu and Kashmir. Andhra Pradesh, Madhya Pradesh, Bihar, Gujarat, Karnataka, Orissa and Maharashtra perform poorly. Even economically developed states like Gujarat, Maharashtra, Andhra Pradesh and Karnataka find themselves in the category of high food insecurity—a reflection perhaps of the manifestation of the agrarian crisis in the states and its consequent negative impact on the health and well-being of the rural population.

Definitions

There are over 200 definitions of food security in the literature but that used at the World Food Summit in 1996 was:

> "Food security, at the individual, household, national, regional and global levels [is achieved] when all people, at all times, have physical and economic access to sufficient, safe and nutritious food to meet their dietary needs and food preferences for an active and healthy life".

According to the United Nations Food and Agriculture Organization's (FAO's) widely accepted definition:

> "Food security" means that food is available at all times; that all persons have means of access to it; that it is nutritionally adequate in terms of quantity, quality and variety; and that it is acceptable within the given culture. Only when all these conditions are in place can a population be considered "food secure."

To achieve lasting self-reliance at the national and household levels, initiatives must be founded on the principles of economic feasibility, equity, broad participation, and the sustainable use of natural resources. In recent years, most of the research initiatives for food security have focused on four key components of the FAO's definition.

- *Availability*: Providing a sufficient supply of food for all people at all times has historically been a major challenge. Although technical and scientific innovations have made important contributions focused on quantity and economies of scale, little attention has been paid to the sustainability of such practices.

- *Accessibility*: The equality of access to food is a dimension of food security. Within and between societies, inequities have resulted in serious entitlement problems, reflecting class, gender, ethnic, racial, and age differentials, as well as national and regional gaps in development. Most measures to provide emergency food aid have attempted to help the disadvantaged but have had limited success in overcoming the structural conditions that perpetuate such inequities.
- *Acceptability*: As essential ingredients in human health and well-being, food and food practices reflect the social and cultural diversity of humanity. Efforts to provide food without paying attention to the symbolic role of food in people's lives have failed to solve food-security problems. This dimension of food security is also important in determining whether information and food-system innovations will be accepted in a country, given the social and ecological concerns of its citizens.
- *Adequacy:* Food security also requires that adequate measures are in place at all levels of the food system to guarantee the sustainability of production, distribution, consumption, and waste management. A sustainable food system should help to satisfy basic human needs, without compromising the ability of future generations to meet their needs. It must therefore maintain ecological integrity and integrate conservation and development.

Food security happens when all people at all times have access to enough food that should be affordable, safe and healthy, culturally acceptable, meets specific dietary needs, obtained in a dignified manner and produced in ways that are environmentally sound. The World Food Summit of 1996 defined food security as existing "when all people at all times have access to sufficient, safe, nutritious food to maintain a healthy and active life". Commonly, the concept of food security is defined as including both physical and economic access to food that meets people's dietary needs as well as their food preferences. But food security is a complex sustainable development issue, linked to health through malnutrition, but also to sustainable economic development, environment, and trade. There is a great deal of debate around food security. If we fail to maintain above there has been food insecurity. Food insecurity exists when all people, at all times, do not have physical and economic access to the sufficient, safe and nutritious food to meet their dietary needs and food preferences for an active and healthy life.

"Nutrition security involving physical, economic and social access to balanced diet, clean drinking water, sanitation and primary health care for every child, woman and man is fundamental to giving all our citizens an opportunity for a healthy and productive life," said Professor MS Swaminathan, Chairman, MSSRF. Unless this aspect of food security is attended to with the involvement of local bodies, the food security situation in India will not show the desired improvement. To address availability, access and sustainability concerns, the report calls for reorienting India's economic policies to provide adequate support for agriculture and its vast rural population. Also, appropriate attention should be paid to conservation of common property and biodiversity resources and rehabilitation of wastelands. "We must explore a horticulture remedy to tide over this nutritional malady," noted Prof. Swaminathan.

FOOD INSECURITY

Food insecurity refers to a lack of access to enough food. There are two kinds of food insecurity: chronic and transitory. Chronic food insecurity is a continuously inadequate diet caused by the inability to acquire food. It affects households that persistently lack the ability either to buy enough food or to produce their own. Hence, poverty is considered the root cause of chronic food insecurity. Transitory food insecurity is a temporary decline in a household's access to enough food. Famines are the worst form of transitory food insecurity. They can result from several causes: wars, floods, drought, crop failures, the loss of purchasing power by groups of households, and market failures including sometimes high food prices and grain hoarding. All of these types of disruptions to food supplies can 'trigger' subsistence crises by threatening a population's access to food. They are the immediate causes of famine. But these precipitating 'triggers' lead to famine only where particular groups of people are already vulnerable to it. The most vulnerable include: small-scale subsistence farmers, landless agricultural workers, other workers who are affected by a drop in real income in famine regions, pastoralists, female-headed households, children, and the elderly. Vulnerability is complex and usually implies processes rather than events. Underlying processes 'set people up' for natural disasters or economic crises and, as 'they cause vulnerability, which is the real problem in the eradication of famine'.

INDIAN CONSTITUTION

In 1950, India has adopted a very progressive Constitution aimed at ensuring all its citizens social, economic and political justice, equality, and dignity. The Constitution of India is the parent law upon which all other enactments are legislated in the form of Central Act or State Act. Therefore any law to be valid in Indian Territory must be within the constitutional framework. Like in many countries of the World the "The Right to Food" in Indian

Constitution is not recognized as a "Fundamental Right". Hence, there is no constitutional mandate to have a claim over it as a matter either fundamental right or human right. While the Indian Constitution has recognized the civil and political rights as directly justiciable fundamental rights, the economic, social and cultural rights and thus the "Right to Food" is included in the provisions of "Directive Principles of State Policy" (Articles 37 and 38).

FOOD SECURITY: WORLD CONCERN

In recent decades, demographic and economic growth have challenged the limits of economic, social, and ecological sustainability, giving rise to questions about food security at the global level. Despite technological advances that have modernized the conditions of production and distribution of food, hunger and malnutrition still threaten the health and well-being of millions of people around the world. Access to food is still perceived by many as a privilege, rather than a basic human right, and it is estimated that about 35000 people around the world die each day from hunger. An even larger number of people (mainly women, children, and the elderly) suffer from malnutrition. Far from disappearing, hunger and malnutrition are on the increase, even in advanced industrialized countries like Canada, where each year an estimated 2.5 million people depend on food banks. About 30 million people in the United States are reported to be unable to buy enough food to maintain good health. The continuing reality of hunger and the unsustainability of current practices, both locally and globally, make food security an essential concern.

Regional and global economic crises and chronic problems of underdevelopment make the situation bad particularly in the developing world. The overall mean per capita income of so-called Black Africa, for example, is, at its best, no higher than it was in 1960, and the region has less weight in the global economy today than it did in the 1960s (Brandt, 1997). Economic informalization clearly accompanies an economy's disintegration. Real prices in domestic food markets have increased over the last few years and are set to increase further. To improve food security and global food supplies, policy scenarios of the 2020 Vision Initiative require increased exports of staple foods from industrialized countries to the LDCs. But insufficient purchasing power among the world's poorest 800 million people remains a primary obstacle to such strategies.

Multilateral agreements in trade and investment further threaten the availability and accessibility of food for large segments of the world's population. Many experts agree that the reduction in world surpluses and the increase in international prices encouraged by the Uruguay Round of the General Agreement on Tariffs and Trade pose an immediate threat to regions already suffering severe food insecurity. The duration of this threat is unknown. Global prospects for improving food security are further threatened by environmental limitations on production increases, even in Green Revolution countries, and by growing poverty. In Asia, a large share of the population will soon be without access to adequate food supplies. So, despite the technical modernization of food production and distribution, hunger and malnutrition still undermine the health and well-being of millions of people and actually seem to be worsening, particularly among low-income urban residents.

Changing Global Food System

The WTO was born into a changing food system in which there are two key trends. One is concentration of economic power into fewer, larger enterprises. These enterprises govern more and more activities in any sector of the system—from farming to catering. Increasingly, these organisations are transnational and operate in a global market. The WTO regulates that market. The other trend is control—in which organisations develop technologies and methods that increase control of the actor in question (input supplier, farmer, processor, retailer, trader, or caterer) over the variables. These methods to control may be:

1. *Environmental*, such as pesticides, varietal selection, or others affecting farming;
2. *Social and economic*, such as those affecting labour usage;
3. *Cultural*, such as use of sophisticated marketing to affect people's consumption patterns; and,
4. *Legal*, such as the rules and regulations that govern what people do and the distribution of risks and benefits.

World Summit on Food Security, 2009

The World Summit on Food Security took place in Rome, Italy between 16 and 18 November 2009. The decision to convene the summit was taken by the Council of the Food and Agriculture Organization of the United Nations (FAO) in June 2009. The Summit adopted unanimously a declaration committing all the nations of the world to eradicate hunger at the earliest possible date. It pledged to substantially increase aid to agriculture in developing countries, so that the world's one billion hungry can become more self-sufficient. The declaration confirmed the current target for reducing hunger by half by 2015. Countries agreed to work to reverse the decline in domestic and international funding for agriculture and promote new investment in the sector, to improve governance of global food issues in partnership with relevant stakeholders from the public and private sector, and to face the challenges of climate change to food security. Nations are mobilizing for action. In July, 26 countries and 14 multilateral organizations agreed to work together under the umbrella of the L'Aquilainitiative on food security. World Summit on Food Security in Rome is a further opportunity to focus on country-led and regional strategies, country-level partnerships and increased levels of assistance.

INDIAN POOR AND FOOD SECURITY

Conventionally, poverty in India has been measured through a minimum household consumption level estimated by the National Sample Survey Organisation, part of the Central Statistical Organisation, the apex statistical body. This measure was anchored in the per capita calorie norms of 2,400 (rural) and 2,100 (urban) per day.

According to the Planning Commission analysis, the number of persons living BPL stands at 36 per cent of the total population, or 65.2 million families. "These figures rise to Rs. 46,500 crore, or by 25 per cent, if we were to adopt the definition of poverty as estimated by Suresh Tendulkar," said a Planning Commission official, who didn't want to be identified. "According to his report, all-India poverty figures stand at 38 per cent."

According to the same Planning Commission analysis, the government will have to spend as much as Rs. 90,000 crore as food subsidy on BPL families, 140 per cent more than the present subsidy cost, if the Sengupta report is accepted.

Food subsidy is the largest explicit subsidy in the government's budget. The budget estimate of the food subsidy bill for fiscal 2009-10 was Rs. 42,490 crore. Apart from subsidy on foodgrains sold through the public distribution system to BPL families, the cost includes welfare programmes such as mid-day meal schemes meant for school children.

The Planning Commission official also said the Centre is continually being told by states to increase the BPL count. The total number of BPL cards, which entitle holders to subsidized foodgrains, already issued by state governments is 109 million. The existing official poverty line was originally defined in terms of per capita total consumption expenditure at 1973-74 prices; the original reference basket of goods and services was left unchanged. This is periodically updated by an expert group, using state price indices. However, the calorie count—which measures individual consumption—assumed in the original poverty line in 1973 has not changed. A true estimate of BPL families has become important for two reasons—to tackle the problem of the government's rising subsidy bills and implementation of the United Progressive Alliance's proposed National Food Security Act. Under the legislation, every BPL family in rural as well as urban areas will be entitled, by law, to 25 kg of rice or wheat per month at Rs. 3 per kg. A note for the empowered group of ministers on the National Food Security Act, a copy of which was reviewed by *Mint*, says the government will soon have to come up with well defined figures for BPL families to decide what number will be covered under the Act, besides working out a mechanism to identify BPL families in rural and urban areas.

Social worker Harsh Mander, a special commissioner appointed by the Supreme Court to advise it on the right to food, hunger and state responsibility, said a larger BPL population would reflect a "more correct scenario of the poor in India". "Spending on education, health and shelter are basic necessities, which help in capacity building and, therefore, should be included while calculating poverty," he said.

According to the government estimates approximately a third of our country's population is absolutely poor. According to the Suresh Tendulkar Committee, 37.2 per cent of Indians qualify as poor. But the Planning Commission deliberately brought the number down to 27.2 per cent. Another estimate from the state governments puts the figure at 10.52 crore or 45 per cent of the population. But if one takes other indicators that other countries take, the number will be even greater. For instance, the number of undernourished constitute over 60 per cent of the population even according to official statistics. If one takes basic housing, health care, sanitation, and other minimum necessities that are taken for granted in other countries the number of the poor goes much higher than what the government or other committees estimate. The so-called food security bill does not take these factors into consideration when calculating the BPL. Sections such as rag pickers, construction workers, street vendors, cycle rickshaw drivers, domestic workers, and several other wretched of the earth do not find a place in the BPL category of our Pranab Mukherjee-led Committee. The facts regarding hunger and poverty in India are startling and expose in all nakedness the emptiness of the innumerable promises made by the hypocritical, opportunist parliamentary parties in over six decades of rule.

According to a report in *The Hindu* of March 28, 2010, Union Home Minister Chidambaram and Finance Minister Pranab Mukherjee described as 'myth' the perception that 77 per cent of Indian people lived on Rs. 20 a day. Chidambaram said that Arjun Sengupta report had not derived such a conclusion. Pranab Mukherjee, delivering the valedictory address at the 'National Convention on Law, Justice and the Common Man' organized by the All India Congress Committee in New Delhi, said three studies conducted on the extent of poverty in India have arrived at different conclusions based on different sample surveys they have used to determine how many people were living below the poverty line. The terms of reference of these committees were narrow, affecting the conclusion. Chidambaram said the Left parties in

West Bengal were propagating the myth that 77 per cent of the people had an income of only Rs. 20 a day. No wonder, the so-called Empowered Group of Ministers (E-GOM) headed by Pranab Mukherjee had created more insecurity for the poverty-stricken masses of our country through their Draft Food Security Bill. The strong opposition from several civil society groups and social activists had prompted the Congress leadership to redraft the Bill to make it more palatable for the critics and the people at large. Even if it is merely on paper! None would believe that anything good can come out of this Bill for the vast majority of the undernourished, hungry millions who are dying like flies even as the government claims of surplus food stocks in its godowns. And stark irony is over several million tonnes of food grains rot in the godowns due to criminal apathy and neglect of our rulers who exhibit nothing short of contempt for the poor of this country in whose name they had catapulted to power. Why are these rogues maintaining criminal silence when millions of children are going to bed hungry and are dying in hundreds every day? What would make these criminals jerk out of their inertia and tale measures to distribute the rotting food grains from their godowns? And when the pathetic plight of the poor is getting worse with every passing day why are these criminals contemplating on increasing the budget for police, paramilitary forces, defence forces and spend huge sums for waging war on these very people? One has to grasp this fascist mindset, anti-people attitude and criminal contempt for the people of this country on the part of the reactionary rulers. Nothing short of a revolutionary overthrow of these criminals ruling the country in the name of the people and fake democracy can eradicate poverty and ensure food security for all.

How Effective Welfare Schemes for Poor?

The fact that 230 million people of our country virtually go to bed hungry every day shows how bogus are the so-called social welfare schemes pompously trumpeted by the successive governments. And the *aam aadmi* rhetoric brings nausea to anyone who witnesses the terrible tragedy afflicting such a huge population that is equal to the entire population of the United States or the combined population of entire Europe. Every government has introduced these schemes which mean nothing to the people of this country except death and destitution. Schemes with pompous sounding names such as Integrated Child Development Services (ICDS), the Kishori Shakti Yojana, the Nutrition Programme for Adolescent Girls, the Rajiv Gandhi Scheme for Empowerment of Adolescent Girls of the Ministry of Women and Child Development; the Sava Siksha Abhiyaan and the Mid-Day Meals Programme of the Ministry of Human Resources Development; the National Rural Health Mission and the National Urban Health Mission, Rashtriya Krishi Vikas Yojana, National Food Security Mission and the National Horticulture Mission of the Union Agriculture Ministry; the Rajiv Gandhi Drinking Water Mission, the Total Sanitation Campaign, the Swarna Jayanthi Gram Swarojgar Yojana, and the Mahatma Gandhi National Rural Employment Guarantee Programme of the Ministry of Rural Development; and the Antyodaya Anna Yojana, Annapoorna and the Targeted Public Distribution System of the Ministry of Food, and such grandiose schemes with the avowed aim of improving the nutritional status. Then why has hunger increased by leaps and bounds? And why do children eat mud in Ganne village in Uttar Pradesh as reported in the *Hindustan Times*?

Analysis of Food Insecurity in India

According to the data published by the government of India and the Food Corporation of India, total production of foodgrain was 230.78 million tonnes in 2007-08 and in recent year it is 229.85 million tonnes. There is just 0.93 million tonnes of foodgrain production decreased than last year. Hence question is that, only 0.93 million tonnes falling production of foodgrain can create such situations of food insecurity in India? When look at the statistics relating to the major foodgrain production. We found that, rice production is increased from 96.69 to 99.37 million tonnes in 2007-08 to 2008-09, wheat production is decreased from 78.57 to 77.63 million tonnes, production of coarse cereals is just decreased from 40.76 to 38.67 million tonnes, cereals production is decreased from 216.02 to 215.67 million tonnes and production of pulses is near about stable it is changed from 14.76 to 14.18 million tonnes in same year.

In the same year population growth is near about hardly 1.10 per cent and net growth of population may be 0.50 to 0.75 per cent. It is not larger growth which may become burden on food supply in India. Because, in the same period fish production is increased from 6.8 to 7.3 million tonnes, fruit production increased from 59,563 thousand tonnes and production of vegetables is increased from 115,011to 125,887 thousand million tonnes. Apart from the production of foodgrain and supported foods buffer stock of foodgrain also increase continually since 2007. In year 2006-07 buffer stock of wheat were 54.28 million tonnes and 119.77 million tonnes of rice stock. In year 2007-08 stock of wheat were 77.12 million tonnes and 114.75 million tonnes of rice and in year 2009 stock of wheat is increased to 182.12 million tonnes and stock of rice is increased to 175.76 million tonnes. There has been net growth in the major foodgrain production in India. So we conclude that, it is not economic problem it may be another type.

India's Initiatives to Ensure Food Security

1. Passing of the Essential Commodities Act in 1955
2. Green Revolution in 1960

3. The establishment of a public distribution system (PDS)
4. The Integrated Child Development Scheme (ICDS) in 1975
5. The Antyodaya Anna Yojana (AAY), in 2000
6. National Food for Work Programme (NFFWP) in 2004
7. National Rural Employment Guarantee Act in 2005
8. Sampoorna Grameen Rozgar Yojana (SGRY)
9. National Food Security Mission (2007)

In 2007, the Indian government approved two initiatives—the National Policy for Farmers and the Rashtriya Krishi Vikas Yojana—that take a holistic approach to agricultural development. It also proposes to pass a National Food Security Act in 2009 under which below poverty line (BPL families) will be provided with 25 kgs. of grain a month at a subsidised price of Rs. 3 per kg.

Demand for Food Entitlements by the Civil Society

1. The Act must hold the government accountable to ensure that no man, women or child sleeps hungry or is malnourished.
2. The Act must place an obligation on the government to encourage food production through sustainable and equitable means, and ensure adequate food availability in all locations at all times.
3. The Act must incorporate and consolidate all entitlements currently existing under Supreme Court orders and for existing schemes, especially; hot, cooked, nutritious mid-day meals in all government and government-assisted schools. Provision of all ICDS services to all children below the age of six years, Antyodaya entitlements as a matter of right for 'priority group'.
4. The Act must also create new entitlements for those who are excluded from existing schemes, including out-of-school children, the elderly and the infirm in need of daily care, migrant workers and their families, bonded labour families, the homeless, and the urban poor.
5. The Act must not abridge but only expand other entitlements such as old age pensions, maternity entitlements and work entitlement under NREGA.
6. The right to food of children in the age group of 0-6 month's must be ensured through services to the mother, including support at birth; skilled counselling especially to promote breast feeding; maternity entitlements; and crèche facilities at the work place.
7. The Act must create an obligation for governments to prevent and address chronic starvation, and reach food pro-actively to persons threatened with starvation.

8. The Act must create provisions for governments to deal adequately with natural and human-made disasters and internal displacement, including by doubling all food entitlements for a period of at least one year in affected areas; and removing upper limits to person days of employment in NREGA.
9. All residents of the country, excepting possible for categories specially excluded because of their wealth, must be covered by the Public Distribution System, with at least 35 kgs of cereals per household (or 7 kgs per person) per month at Rs. 3.00 per kg for rice and Rs. 2.00 per kg for wheat. Coarse grains should be made available through the PDS at subsidised rates, wherever people prefer these. In addition, extra provisions of subsidized oil and pulses should be made.
10. Women must be regarded as heads of the households for all food-related matters such as the distribution of ration cards.
11. The Act must seek to eliminate all social discrimination in food-related matters, including discrimination against Scheduled Castes, Scheduled Tribes, Most Backward Classes and minorities.
12. Cash transfers must not replace food transfers under any nutrition-related scheme.
13. The Act must include safeguards against the invasion of corporate interests and private contractors in food policy and nutrition-related schemes, especially where they affect food safety and child nutrition. In particular no GM food and hazardous or useless additives must be allowed in public nutrition programmes. Governments must not enter into any partnerships with the private sector where there is a conflict of interests.
14. The Act must include strong, in-built independent institutions for accountability along with time-bound, grievance redressal provisions (including provisions for criminal prosecution), mandatory penalties for any violation of the Act and compensation for those whose entitlements have been denied. In particular, the Gram Sabha must have effective powers for grievance redressal and monitoring of food-related schemes.
15. All programmes of food entitlements must have strong in-built transparency mechanisms, and mandatory requirements of social audit.
16. Within the existing PDS system, the Act must provide for mandatory reforms such as de-privatisation of PDS shops, preferably to women's groups, with sufficient capital and commissions for new owners; direct

door step delivery of food items to the PDS shop; and computerisation, along with other measures for transparency.

17. The Act must specify that no laws or policy shall be passed that adversely impact the enabling environment for the right to food.

How can India Achieve Food Security?

Now the question is how to achieve food security? The quick answers—allowing genetically modified crops, greater investment in irrigation, better economics in farming and greater government attention to agriculture—all offer short-term relief, but, unless more sustainable food systems are introduced, none will succeed in the long term. There's no doubt that something like a second Green Revolution has great potential to transform India's food production capacity and bring it up to levels that will sustain the population as it continues to grow; however, unless sustainable methods are employed—organic agriculture, for example, that feeds the soil and retains more water as crops grow—we'll be talking about another Green Revolution on the horizon in another 50 years.

Government's Initiatives

NATIONAL FOOD SECURITY ACT, 2009

Seeing the popularity of the National Rural Employment Guarantee Scheme (NREGS), which helped the Congress to win the 2009 Parliamentary elections, the newly constituted Government has thought of bringing the Food Security Act within the first 100 days of its stay in the office for the second time.

President Pratibha Patil on June 4, 2009 said that a National Food Security Act would be formulated whereby each below poverty line (BPL) family would be entitled by law to get 25 kg of rice or wheat per month at Rs. 3.00 per kg, a promise made by the Congress before general elections of 2009. Many would agree that the proposal for a Food Security Bill has come at the right point of time when the world has already witnessed food crisis in 2008 that pushed millions of people to the brink of poverty and undernutrition.

A concept note on the National Food Security Act was made available on 4 June, 2009 by the Ministry of Consumer Affairs, Food and Public Distribution. The concept note on National Food Security Act promises to ensure food security (by supplying a certain minimum quality of rice, wheat and coarse cereals) to the below poverty line (BPL) population residing in rural and urban areas. The number of BPL households would be fixed by the Central Government based on the recent poverty estimates of the Planning Commission (presently of 2004-05). As against the accepted number of 6.52

crore BPL cards, there exists 10.68 crore BPL cards by the end of March, 2009. The above poverty line (APL) population will be excluded from the targeted public distribution system (TPDS) under the new Food Security Act. Based on the recent poverty estimates (2004-05) by Planning Commission, the number of BPL households will come down from 6.52 crore to 5.91 crore and the number of APL households will increase from 11.52 crore to 15.84 crore. Only 25 kg of foodgrains to each BPL household would be supplied at subsidized rates under the new law. The validity of the new BPL ration cards issued, based on the recent poverty estimates of the Planning Commission (2004-05), would be for 5 years, after which they will automatically expire. Multiplicity of food schemes would be abandoned under the new law, which means discontinuation of a number of food and nutrition related schemes. Presently the Government provides 277 lakh tonnes of foodgrains for below poverty line (BPL) and Antodaya Anna Yojana (AAY) categories, with a subsidy amounting to Rs. 37,000 crore. Under the new Act, the government would provide 251 lakh tons of foodgrains for BPL and AAY categories, with subsidy amounting to Rs. 40,380 crore (if 25 kg of rice or wheat per month is supplied to each BPL household at Rs 3.00 a kg). Computerisation of TPDS would take place along with setting up of village grain banks and food security tribunals. The proposed Act demands for continuation of existing food related schemes such as: Integrated Child Development Services, Mid-Day Meal Scheme, Public Distribution System, Antyodaya, National Maternity Benefit Scheme/ Janani Suraksha Yojana, National Social Assistance Programme, including Indira Gandhi National Old Age Pension Scheme, Indira Gandhi National Widow Pension Scheme and Indira Gandhi National Disability Pension Scheme, National Family Benefit Scheme, and Rajiv Gandhi National Crèche Scheme. All the provisions in various such schemes have been elaborately discussed in the proposed Act. The proposed Act has asked for severe penalties against individuals and organizations/companies who are held responsible for violation of food safety norms and standards that affects the public. It may be possible to make food security in India in good manner. If we doing the proper planning of foodgrain production and fair practices in food market. There is need of strong control over the food market in India. In developing countries like India, the root causes of food insecurity include poverty, corruption, national policies that do not promote equal access to food for all, environmental degradation, barriers to trade, insufficient agricultural development, population growth, low levels of education, social and gender inequality, poor health status, cultural insensitivity, and natural disasters. If the government concentrate the problem specific it is possible by the existing majors, but there is need of implementation of that in proper manner and accurately. Public distribution system is very good way to overcome the problem of speculation by the private traders.

Another way to food security is increase in fruit, milk and fish production, Fish is not only a vital food it is also a source of livelihood for millions of people around the globe. We can solve that problem by the increase in inland and sea fish production in India. The policy of mitigating nutritional deficiencies and food security by fisheries is a pragmatic move in India, considering the fact that sea has ample scope for continuous supply of protein rich food. We need to exploit the food from sea to counter the menace of malnutrition. India, with its vast coastline and seas can use science and technology to make full use of fisheries in ensuring food security to its vast populace.

The objectives of the Public Distribution System (PDS) are good but it was failed to accomplish that objective due to the corruption. PDS is better way to tackle the problem of food speculation of private traders. If the government will succeed in the motive of PDS the intensity of food insecurity problem will be reduced in future. However, the cruel reality is that despite this huge food production, a huge buffer stock and an extensive network of PDS, millions of people are food insecure and many even die of starvation. Food insecurity and tragedy hit different parts of the country every year.

The present food crisis is due to lack of proper distribution and the trading system impeding free flow of food. Even increase in agricultural productivity also one of the solution for this problem. This should be based on integrating inputs and outputs—the supply of high yielding varieties of seeds, fertilizers, and irrigation, supported by credit alongside remunerative output prices. A second "green revolution" is essential to stimulate food production in many parts of India. It is crucial to ensure that farm and trade policies of developed countries do not artificially reduce the prices of their foodgrains. This makes it virtually impossible for farmers from developing countries to compete both in their own domestic markets, due to cheap food imports, and also in the international market.

The problem of food security comes mainly from the slow growth of purchasing power of the people in the rain-fed eco-systems. Efforts must be made to help them by developing drought resistant seeds, cost-effective dry-land farming techniques. A major challenge to food security comes from dietary diversification of the poor. If cereal pricing is left to the market forces, government playing the facilitating role, land will be released from rice and wheat cultivation to meet the growing demand for non-cereal crops such as oilseeds, fruits and vegetables in accordance with diet diversification. At the movement the problem is the problem of distribution of existing comfortable level of supply. However with increasing population combined with low agricultural productivity. Therefore we should do efforts to increase productivity and re-correct the distribution problems.

NEED FOR NATIONAL FOOD SECURITY MISSION (NFSM)

1. The growth in food grain production has stagnated during recent past while the consumption need of the growing population is increasing.
2. To meet the growing foodgrain demand, National Development Council in its 53rd meeting adopted a resolution to enhance the production of rice, wheat and pulses by 10, 8 and 2 million tons respectively by 2011.
3. The proposed Centrally Sponsored Scheme 'National Food Security Mission (NFSM) is to operationalize the resolution of NDC and enhance the production of rice, wheat and pulses.
4. The scheme to be implemented in a mission mode through a farmer centric approach.
5. All the Stakeholders to be actively associated at the district levels for achieving the set goal.
6. The scheme aims to target the select districts by making available the improved technologies to the farmers through a series of planned interventions.
7. A close monitoring mechanism proposed to ensure that interventions reach to the targeted beneficiaries.

Objective of the Mission

1. Increasing production of rice, wheat and pulses through area expansion and productivity enhancement in a sustainable manner;
2. Restoring soil fertility and productivity at individual farm level;
3. Enhancing farm level economy (i.e. farm profits) to restore confidence of farmers of targeted districts.

Components of NFSM—Rice

1. Demonstration of improved technology including hybrid and System of Rice Intensification (SRI).
2. Incentive for quality seeds of HYVs/hybrids.
3. Popularization of new varieties through seed mini kits.
4. Promotion of micro nutrients, lime and gypsum.
5. Promotion of mechanical weeders and other farm implements.
6. Integrated pest management.
7. Extension, training and mass media campaign.

8. Awards for best performing district in each State.
9. Assistance for innovative interventions at local level.

Components of NFSM—Wheat

1. Demonstration of improved Technology.
2. Incentive for quality seeds of HYVs to raise the SRR.
3. Promotion of micronutrient use in deficient areas.
4. Incentive for promotion of application of Gypsum.
5. Popularization of Zero till Machines and rotavator.
6. Providing subsidy on diesel pumpsets and community generators for irrigation.
7. Extension, training and mass media campaign awards for best performing districts.
8. Assistance for innovative interventions at local level.

Components of NFSM—Pulse

1. Increasing seed replacement rate to 25 per cent from present level of 7-8 per cent.
2. Promotion of improved production technologies.
3. Integrated Nutrient Management (INM).
4. Integrated Pest Management (IPM).
5. Promotion of micronutrients/gypsum/bio-fertilizers.
6. Promotion of sprinkler irrigation.
7. Pilot Project on tackling the menace of blue bull.
8. Extension, training and mass media campaign.
9. Awards for best performing districts.
10. Pilot project on demonstration ICRISAT Technologies.

Monitoring Mechanism

1. The NFSM will be monitored by national, state and district executive committees.
2. The Project Management Team would be constituted at district, state and national level to assist in the monitoring and implementation of the programme.
3. Mission Director at national and state level will be assisted by Project Management Team in implementation and monitoring.
4. The Department of Economics and Statistics to be involved in data collection for monitoring and impact evaluation.

Table 18.1 : Financial Outlays

During the Eleventh Plan (2007-08 to 2011-12) a fund requirement of Rs. 4882.48 crores is estimated

Year	Rice	Wheat	Pulses	Total
2007-08	70.81	234.55	96.91	402.27
2008-09	348.09	682.74	285.93	1316.76
2009-10	366.29	290.75	287.18	944.22
2010-11	428.29	341.54	286.43	1056.26
2011-12	508.79	370.75	283.43	1162.97
Total	**1722.27**	**1920.33**	**1239.88**	**4882.48**

New Initiatives by India

FCI is now Endeavoring for

1. Resource mobilisation to reduce burden on food subsidy.
2. Better Financial and Treasury Management.
3. Improved stock inventory management real time on-line system through a launched IISFM (Integrated Information System for Food Grains Management) in collaboration with NIC.
4. Creation of Profit Centres.
5. Upgradation of technology through interface with Agriculture Universities/Management Institutes.
6. Use of 'A' Twill texture gunny bags as against 'B' Twill bags as a project to reduce losses in storage and transit.
7. Multimodal transportation system through riverine/container.
8. Micro Level Inventory Management through focused weekly movement plans.

Vision 2020

(*a*) To aggressively promote Decentralized Procurement by State Governments with special emphasis in non-traditional areas and commodities.

(*b*) To initiate procurement of non-MSP governed commodities on commercial principles.

(*c*) To ensure adequate buffer for meeting requirements under TPDS and Other Welfare Schemes.

(*d*) To dispose off surplus and un-storage worthy godowns and introduce concepts of mechanized handling in the conventional godowns.

(*e*) To undertake R&D for conversion of some of the existing capacity to bulk and cost-effective utilization of existing bulk capacity.

(*f*) To optimize monthly movement programme with existing state of art of computerization within the country at various locations as per corporate policies and priorities.

(*g*) Modernization of Quality Control equipments and systems for food preservation in order to increase the shelf life of food grain.

(*h*) To venture in the fields of Forward Trading and Exports of both surplus stocks of food grains in Central Pool and no-traditional commodities.

(*i*) To introduce state of art of financial management in order to reduce the dependency on the present banking system in the country.

(*j*) To initiate systems for settlement of storage loss and transit loss through insurance coverage and revised inventory mechanism.

(*k*) To develop efficiency in human resource management both in staff/officers and workers with changed circumstances in the work approach of P.S.Us.

(*l*) To achieve state of art in computerized communication between different offices/depots throughout the country.

(*m*) Sustained corporate communication for improving image perceptions.

WORLD TRADE ORGANISATION AND ACTION FOR FOOD SECURITY

Some developing countries feel there are fundamental assumptions that need to be revised in the renegotiations to take in a broader view of food security than that driven by the market. India is foremost in this. The Indian delegate reportedly said in the May, 2010 meetings:

> "The Agreement on Agriculture is based on the rationale of open international trade in the agricultural sector. It presupposes the supremacy of an open price based system. Thereby implying that a country should import agricultural products if they are produced cheaper elsewhere. India and certain other developing countries have been stressing the need for the multilateral trading system to recognise the importance of food security. A country may not have the resources to buy agricultural products from international markets even if they are easily available. Moreover, a very large percentage of the rural population in such

countries is dependent on agriculture and any measure that has an effect on employment in this sector needs to be carefully examined. It is necessary to have a close look at the shortcomings in minimum access provisions, exemptions from the reduction commitments given for direct payments, and the issue of the possible negative effects of the reform programme on least developed and net food-importing developing countries which has not yet been effectively addressed as yet."

The creation and development of the WTO is a crucial part of this restructuring and affects the concentration of power. It is not the only factor involved. Other includes the World Bank and IMF. These have promoted policy changes favouring economic liberalisation in developing countries through structural adjustment programmes (SAPs) which have often adversely affected the poor. However, the 132 members of the WTO have agreed to be governed by its rules, to liberalise trade, open up markets and subject themselves to binding disputes settlements procedures. Unlike SAPs, these are permanent commitments, which SAPs have helped ready them for. With NGOs to provide strong civil society pressure for appropriate change in the WTO regulations and take on regional roles for specific parts of such campaigning. Specialist expertise and knowledge of assisting NGOs working in this area should be used and built on. A range of non-governmental groups are working on different food security aspects of the WTO and this work should be built upon, rather than reinvented. Both FAO and UNCTAD have produced useful detailed suggestions and these organisations are also a resource for Southern governments to use in developing their case for the next round of negotiations. This could be supplemented by work from various NGOs on different aspects of the agreements. NGOs with field level experience can also provide more case study material showing the practical effects on specific people and communities and help promote the will and capacity to negotiate within their countries of operation.

Conclusion

Though, we can say that food security problem in India is not serious if we success in the proper distribution policy. But problem is that, the government has failed to control and regulate food market in India. This problem becomes serious due to the unfair trade practice by private traders doing in drought situation and unequal distribution. The problem of hunger is due to poor economic accessibility. It is a result of poor implementation of policy measures. Systematic action along these lines would do something to level-up the grossly unequal playing field at the WTO. Currently, there is a gross imbalance in terms of power relations between the different players, their economic clout, levels of economic or agricultural development, and their capacities to negotiate such wide ranging and complex issues. So, now time for a Second

Green Revolution in India! (Farming is flagging, other industries are rapidly passing it by, and, without upgrades, technological and methodological, it is not attracting a new generation of farmers to the land. Some feel that the solution is similar, in theory, at least, to the one employed a half-century ago. It's time for a second Green Revolution. "The increase in yields in the past decades has been insignificant. India surely needs another Green Revolution," says Kushagra Nayan Bajaj, joint managing director of Bajaj Hinduthan, India's top sugar producer. But it will require a whole new set of tools, this time around. Environmental damage wrought by the first revolution, degraded soil from pesticides and fertilizers, mismanaged groundwater, make it a tougher challenge this time around.

REFERENCES

1. Amitava Mukherjee, (2007), '*Micro-Level Food Insecurity in Contemporary India: Perspectives of the Food Insecure*'.
2. Bickel, G., Nord, M., Price, C., Hamilton, W. & Cook, J. (2000), *Guide to Measuring Foodsecurity,* revised 2000, Washington,DC,United States Department of Agriculture.
3. Bhalla, G.S. (1994), *Policies for Food Security in India*, New Delhi.
4. Devereux, S. (1993), *Theories of Famine*, London, Harvester-Wheatsheaf.
5. Radhakrishna, R. (1991), "Food and Nutrition: Challenges for Policy", *Journal of the Indian Society of Agricultural Statistics.*
6. *Economic Survey of India, 2008-09* (The Government of India).
7. http://www.who.int/trade
8. http://www.foodsecuritynews.com
9. http://www.sccommissioners.org
10. http://www.nceus.gov.in

CHAPTER

19

Rural Development
Meaning and Scope

—Dr. Nagaraju Battu

ABSTRACT

The green revolution is one of the biggest success stories of India cited globally, which enabled the country to convert the nightmarish 'begging bowl' status to that of 'self-sufficiency'. It is also brought about an element of resilience in agriculture to ward off the threat of famine. The green revolution obviously ushered in an era of overall rural prosperity. Its impact was so dramatic that India became a role model for many developing nations. In this context this is an attempt to describe the rural development its meaning and scope.

Introduction

Development as a concept when applied in the context of rural India acquires a new meaning as rural development. Fundamentally, development of rural area means not only the aggregate development of the area but also development of the people living in rural areas. The objectives of development include sustained increase in per capita output and income, expansion of productive employment and greater equity in the distribution of the benefits of growth and rural development over the years has emerged as "a strategy designed to improve the economic, social and cultural life of a specific group of people living in rural areas."

The objectives of rural development are multi-directional as well as multi-dimensional. It aims at increased employment, higher productivity, higher income as well as minimum acceptable levels of food, clothing, shelter, education, health and building up of a sound value system which is in keeping with the high cultural heritage of the country. Thus rural development means all aspects of human development. Rural development must constitute a major part of development strategy if a larger segment of those in greatest need to benefit.

Meaning

Development of rural areas has been the avowed objective of planning in India. Poverty alleviation and welfare of the people, basically involves increased production and more importantly equal distribution and creating productive employment opportunities to rural people both in the farm and non-farm sectors.

With the opening of their economy, rural people have come under the urban influence and fallen victims to some of its ills. Over the years, the rural scene has seen a sea change. Under the circumstance, the concept of rural development acquires a significant meaning. More importantly the content of rural development should touch the life of all rural people. The process of development covers rural environment, rural poor and other weaker sections of the rural society.

The Tenth Plan has declared the development of rural and farm sector as one of the main objectives of the Plan and are channelising consciously physical, financial and human resources into rural development. However, rural development is fast becoming a fashionable catchword not only with government and political leaders but also with the corporate sector. The emphasis in this context is on finding what are called "approaches that work" for rural development and upliftment of the poor without disturbing property and social relations and by applications of business management methods and sophisticated technologies. The conventional philanthropic attitude of helping the poor is no longer regard as adequate. A more comprehensive approach is gaining ground in influential circles among socially and economically powerful interest groups. Recently, participants from 51 countries and several international organisations discussed their "approaches" in Delhi. The total cost of the exposition the organisers estimated to be 6,20,000 dollars (or Rs. 9.30 crores). The final achievement was the outline of a 'book' of the assembly which will be supported by an information system which, the organisers proudly claimed, included 'a computer data base'. All very sophisticated indeed very modern and very managerial. How exactly the exposition and its sponsors would be able to help uplift the rural poor in India is anybody's guess. In the backdrop of these varied interests, it is quite pertinent to analyse critically and discuss the issues in rural development in relation to rural India.

Rural Development

The Rural Development Sector Policy Paper of the World Bank observed that:

> "Rural development is a strategy designed to improve the economic and social life of a specific group of people—the rural poor. It involves extending the benefits of development to the poorest among those who seek a livelihood in the rural areas. The group includes small-scale farmers, tenants and the landless."

Again a World Bank publication defines rural development as "improving the living standards of the masses of the low-income population residing in rural areas making the process of rural development self-sustaining."

The World Bank definition of rural development is based inherently on an operational approach constrained by the practicalities of allocating loan resources over a wide spectrum of countries, ensuring maximum economic returns to them. In a seminar on approaches to rural development in Asia, discussions were centred around a definition of:

> "rural development as a process which leads to a continuous rise in the capacity of the rural people to control their environment accompanied by a wider distribution of benefits resulting from such control."

This definition is composed of three important elements:

1. Rural development should be viewed as a process of raising the capacity of the rural people to control their environment. Environment does not mean only agriculture or economic development. It includes all aspects of rural life—social, economic, cultural and political;
2. Rural development as a process should continuously raise the capacity of the rural people to influence their total environment, enabling them to become initiators and controllers of change in their environment rather than being merely the passive objects of external manipulation and control; and
3. Rural development must result in a wider distribution of benefits accruing from technical developments and the participation of weaker sections of the rural population in the process of development.

G. Parthasarathy opines that:

> "The critical element in the rural development is improvement of living in standards of the poor through opportunities for better utilisation of their physical and human resources; in the absence of this, utilisation of rural resources has no functional significance. Making the process of rural development self-sustaining not only implies the mobilisation of capital and use of technology for the benefit of the poor but their active involvement in the building up of institutions as well as in functioning of these."

Michael Todaro views that:

"Rural development encompasses (1) improvement in levels of living, including employment, education, health and nutrition, housing and a variety of social services; (2) decreasing inequality in the distribution of rural incomes and in rural-urban balances in incomes and economic opportunities; and (3) the capacity of the rural sector to sustain and accelerate the pace of these improvement."

Rural development in the ultimate analysis involves the provision of opportunities for the optimum utilisation of the human resources in rural areas. Human resource development in its turn can take place only on the foundation of adequate nutrition and work opportunities. It is, therefore, necessary to base rural development programmes with the primary aim of providing opportunities for the human population to achieve optimum expression of their physical and mental potential. Such programmes should have the following four major components:

(*a*) Economic emancipation of the family with particular attention to provision of adequate employment opportunities to women who are largely engaged at present in unpaid and underpaid jobs, often characterised by physical drudgery;

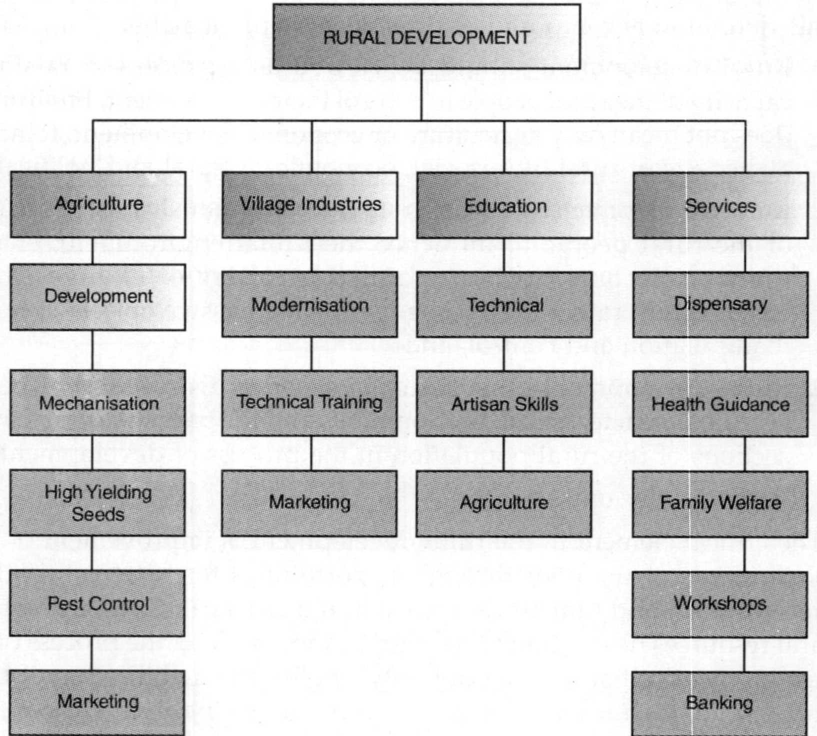

Fig. 19.1: Components of Rural Development

(*b*) Education of children and adults;

(*c*) Provision of minimum needs, such as safe drinking water supply; health care, rural communication, etc.; and

(*d*) Promotion of a small family norm through social and health education.

Rural development has been accorded a priority by the government and rightly so. The emphasis placed on rural development is not new. Even prior to independence, Gandhiji had succinctly pointed out the importance of developing villages, if India is to develop as a whole. No doubt, substantial efforts were made in the past to develop rural areas and yet the rural poor continue to live in abject poverty. Independence and the Five Year Plans have fetched little benefits to them and meant little change in their age-old ways of living. The major shortcoming of the efforts made to develop village was that they were piece-meal in nature and did not take into account the kaleidoscopic difficulties of rural areas varying in pattern from region to region. Rural development is not an easy job as not only economic problems are involved but also the social and psychological issues are inter-mingled with stagnant agriculture and lack of allied activities. The caste problem is again a major issue as about 23.6 per cent of the rural population (15.64 crores) comprises scheduled castes/tribes. Consequently, inertia and indifference have taken deep roots giving rise to suspicion and the lack of urge to develop.

Scope

The scope of rural development is very vast. Yet, an attempt has been made here to indicate some of the broad areas of rural development which needs an integrated approach.

1. Developing social consciousness of people about rural development and its lasting benefits.
2. Solving the basic needs problems by collective decision-making and collective action.
3. Building up dedicated village leadership.
4. Use of science and scientific knowledge to devise appropriate technology for improving productivity at all levels.
5. Development of agriculture and allied sectors.
6. Improved water management by building tanks, small dams on the nullas and building canals etc.
7. Creating new employment opportunities by subsidiary occupations.
8. Developing cottage and village industries based on local resources.
9. Developing non-farming skills to promote and sustain service sector.

10. Developing an efficient delivery system, leading to easy supply of inputs, credit and good outlet for their products.

REFERENCES

1. APO, 1994, *Rural Development Policies and Strategies; Report of an APO Seminar 14-22 September 1993, Islamabad, Pakistan.* Tokyo, Asian Productivity Organization.
2. Bendavid-val, A., 1991, *Rural Area Development Planning, Principles, Approaches and Tools of Economic Analysis, Vol. 1&2,* (27/1 & 27/2). Rome, Training Service, Policy Analysis Division, Economic and Social Policy Department, FAO.
3. Bhargava, B.S., Jos, C. Raphel, "Miorking of Grama Sabha in Karnataka: A Study of Macro-Level", *Journal of Rural Development,* Vol. 13(1), 1994.
4. Chambers, Robert, Rural Development: Putting the Last First, Addison Wesley Longman Ltd., 1983.
5. KKU, 1987, *Rapid Rural Appraisal—Proceedings of the 1985 International Conference, Khon Kaen, Thailand,* Rural Systems Research and Farming Systems Research Projects, Khon Kaen University.
6. Mukherjee, A. ed. 1995, *Participatory Rural Appraisal Methods and Applications in Rural Planning,* New Delhi, Vikas Pub. House Pvt. Ltd.
7. Mishra, S.N.,1983, Kaushal Sharma, *Problems and Prospects of Rural Development in India,* Uppal Publishing House, New Delhi.
8. Nooij Ad. "Rural Development: Comparative Perspectives" *Sociologia Ruralis* 23(3-4) 83:199-203. (Eastern and Western Europe).
9. Thekkamalai, S.S., *Rural Development and Social Change in India,* New Delhi, D.K. Publications, 1983, p. 208.

Chapter

20

Diversification in Agriculture

A Key to Rural Development in the Perspective of Globalizing India

—Prasanta Bauri

ABSTRACT

India is a land of villages and agriculture is central to rural livelihoods. So the need for rural development is essential. Indian rural economy has witnessed remarkable changes in the era of globalization. The most striking impact of globalization on Indian crop economy has been in the diversification in agriculture. It is the diversified cropping pattern that is inevitable in the era of globalization as a route to development of crop and as well as rural economy. The present paper tries to focus on the impact of globalization on development of rural economy of India through diversification in agriculture.

Keywords: *Crop Diversification, Globalization, Rural Development.*

This paper consists of four sections. In Section I we deal with the inevitability of agricultural development as a route to rural development. Section II makes a focus on globalization keeping in view that how diversification in Indian agriculture is triggered by the process of globalization. In Section III we highlight on the relevance of crop diversification in agricultural development, thereby, in rural development in India. Finally, Section IV makes concluding observations.

I

> "My vision for the future? ... a world where nobody has to suffer from poverty—a world completely free from poverty."
>
> —*Dr. Muhammad Yonus*

The dream of Nobel Laureate Dr. Yonus will come true if the rural poverty and its consanguinary income inequality is subdued. Since an overwhelming majority of world's total poor population lives in rural areas so the rural development is very much crucial to make a world completely free from poverty. The expression 'rural development' is a multi-dimensional concept which denotes all aspects of development including not only economic but also social, cultural, infrastructural, political and organizational development that occur in a rural society. The World Bank (1975), however, defined rural development as

> "... a strategy designed to improve the economic and social life of specific group of people—the rural poor. It involves extending the benefits of development to the poorest among those who seek a livelihood in the rural areas. The group includes small scale farmers, tenants and the landless".

It is well-known fact that for proper rural development, agriculture should act as a driving force.

The history of the world provides overwhelming global evidence that general economic growth of any nation must be preceded, or at least accompanied by, solid agricultural growth. Agriculture has played central role since the English Agricultural Revolution which paved the way for the Industrial Revolution. This process still applies today, and poor countries in Africa, Asia and South America will be no exception (Rukuni, 2006). The significance of agriculture in the economic development of any country, rich or poor, is borne out by the fact that it is the primary sector of the economy which provides the basic ingredients necessary for the existence of mankind and also provides most of the raw materials which when transformed into finished products serve as basic necessities of the human race. Early theoretical literatures on the responsibility of agriculture in the economic development can be traced as far back as to the eighteenth century in the writings of the physiocrats. According to physiocrats, it is only in agriculture that nature labours along with the man farmer consumer, but also a surplus which nourishes the other classes of society. Importance of agriculture in economic development as recognized by the classical writers too. Adam Smith's basic growth model refers only to the agricultural sector. In his model, technical improvement in agriculture is the pivotal point for sparking off development in other sectors of the economy.

In India, vast majority of the people lives in rural areas and engaged in agricultural earning directly or indirectly. In pre-independence period, Mahatma Gandhi emphasized the role of youth in rural upliftment thus "Go to the villages and busy yourselves, not as masters or benefactors but as their humble servants. Let them know what to do and how to change their modes of living from your daily conduct and way of living". *Kabiguru* Rabindranath Tagore also, took steps to develop villages around Shantiniketan. Efforts were made by others also. In post-independence, several schemes have been taken up since the beginning of the fifth plan (1974-78) in the matter of rural development with a view to diminish rural poverty. In spite of having different approaches to rural development the successfulness of these is dependable on the development of agriculture. The process of globalization plays a significant role in regard to this. Diversification in agriculture or crop diversification being a universal phenomenon of raising alternative high value crops instead of traditional crops which is triggered by the process of globalization has emerged as a key to agricultural development.

II

In today's era it is held that globalization is *sine qua non* to growth and prosperity of an economy of any country. The Government of India has made some radical changes in its policies regarding foreign investment, trade, exchange rate, industry and fiscal affairs etc. These various elements taken together constitute an economic policy, which marks good-bye to the earlier. Since July 1991 when the rupee was devalued, the Government of India has announced several new policies under the name of new Economic Reforms. The main features of the new economic reforms or policy are liberalization, extension of privatization, globalization of economy, market friendly state etc. (Lekhi, 2001). Globalization implies opening and liberalizing trade in capital and technology and is emphasized as a strategy of development, even in the rural areas while we come across the concept of global village. It emphasizes the functioning of the market and positive gains from trade, which may be shared by all sections of the society. Besides providing an outlet for the surplus produce, globalization widens the extent of the market and scope of the division of labour. It also encourages technical innovations and overcomes technical indivisibilities besides generally enabling trading country to enjoy increasing returns and faster economic growth. Therefore, globalization seems to be an opportunity and not a threat to the countries of third world (Pandit, 2007). Neo-classical economists argue that benefits of economic growth resulting from globalization would trickle down to the poor and therefore economic growth would be inclusive, not exclusive (Sau, 2007).

Liberalization of world trade in agriculture has opened up new vistas of growth. India also seems it as an opportunity for export promotion. Agriculture is one of the areas in which India has an inherent strength to dominate the global markets. As we have moved away from an economy of despair and food shortage to self-reliance and exports, it is imperative to look for vast opportunities in export markets which are possible only when commercialization of agriculture through diversified cropping pattern takes place. Economic reforms with accent on market economy functioning have led to the accelerated commercialization and diversification in agriculture in India. Food habit across the globe is now changing with faster pace and due to liberalization in agriculture trade the demand of diversified food materials (beside rice and wheat) like cash crops viz. sugarcane, coffee, tea, fruits and vegetables is increasing. Adverse agro-climatic conditions in other countries does not permit them to grow all these crops, therefore, they depend on import. However, in contrast to this, India having diverse agro-climatic condition make them potential candidate to raised diversified crops. No country grows such a wide range of fruits, vegetables and flowers and in such abundance as India. Results revealed that the establishment of WTO and GATT in 1994 has brought drastic changes in Indian cash crop export[2] through progressive reduction of trade restrictions. Shivay and Kumar (2007) observed, changes in food habits of our rural people are also responsible for crop diversification in globalizing India. This show that the crop diversification from traditional rice-wheat system is the need of hour for India and diversification towards high value crops is being considered a way to increase agricultural growth rates (Bhattacharya and Chatterjee, 2007). Moreover, tariff reduction and import liberalization have reduced the cost of imported materials and make them easily available to the Indian farmers. Therefore, it is fact that diversification in Indian agriculture is triggered by the process of globalization.

III

In the post-independence periods remarkable changes have been witnessed by Indian agriculture. The most salient aspect is the massive production of foodgrains making the country from a deficit prone to a situation of plenty (Ananta, 2002). The substantial investment in irrigation, rural infrastructures, research and extension has helped to attain remarkable growth in agriculture leading to self-sufficiency in production of foodgrains (Roy and Pal, 2003). The development of Indian agriculture is characterized by the process of crop diversification over time. Our crop economy has faced the change in farming trend from subsistence to commercial (De, 2003). There has been a significant increase in the percent of gross cropped area under fruits and vegetables (Jha *el al.*, 2009). The crop sector depicted a steady diversification in India with replacement of foodgrain crops with non-foodgrain crops (Joshi, 2005).

A desirable process of crop diversification or changes in cropping pattern would be one which favour crops which are either labour-intensive or import-substitute or exportable or ecologically sustainable along with their role in accelerating agricultural growth (Roy, 1994). Agricultural diversification is considered to be the most appropriate strategy that augments growth, stabilizes farm income especially of the small and marginal farmers, generates full employment, protects natural resources and attains the goals of food security (Bathla, 2006). It can be used as a tool for income augmentation, employment generation, poverty alleviation and export promotion. Diversification towards high value crops is being considered a way to increase the contribution of non-rice crops to agricultural output to attain higher agricultural growth rates. Besides enhancing growth, it is felt that diversification will also be able to contribute towards a higher nutrition level, poverty alleviation, employment generation and sustainable natural resources management (Bhattacharya and Chatterjee, 2007). The level of diversification of crop enterprises reflects the extent of economic development in the rural sector. For the rural economy in general and small and marginal farmers in particular the crop diversification has been considered a ray of hope for their economic upliftment. The average earning per unit land area is observed to be higher in the diversified cropping system, particularly in betelvine cultivation, flower and horticulture. The demand for crops like cashewnuts, flowers and fruits is high enough in the international market, particularly in the era of globalization to help us earn substantial amount of foreign exchange (Sau and Pathak, 2007). Crop diversification is effective in minimizing the risk of the peasants as the Indian farmers face problems due to vagaries of monsoon.

The relevance of crop diversification on rural development is also empirically proved. Reduction of rural population below the poverty line[3] is significantly explained by the farm incomes. According to Shariff (2001), the farm income in rural India constituted two-third (65.65%) of the total rural households during the globalization period which is no doubt a mark of significance of the farm sector while the growth rate of rural non-farm employment reduced from around 3 per cent to 2 per cent. So, the strategy of crop diversification is exceedingly relevant to the Indian crop and rural economy.

A CASE STUDY OF WEST BENGAL

In West Bengal during globalization era the role of crop diversification in the reduction of rural poverty and income inequality is commendable. In West Bengal both the Entropy and Berry measures of crop diversification shows the increasing trend of agricultural diversification following economic reforms (Table 20.1). We observed that Entropy crop diversification index alone has explained 61 per cent and Berry's crop diversification index has explained 60 per cent of the variation of the index number of agricultural production.

Table 20.1: Extent of Crop Diversification in West Bengal for different years

Year	Entropy Measure	Berry's Measure
1990-91	0.44	0.54
1996-97	0.46	0.58
2000-01	0.50	0.63
2003-04	0.48	0.62
2004-05	0.47	0.62

Source: Sau and Pathak (2007).

Agricultural growth through crop diversification in the state created relatively low growth rate of consumer prices. It is clear that the growth rates of consumer prices for food, non-food and total groups in West Bengal are lower compared to other major states, even to all-India average. Since most of the poor are net purchasers of food, relatively low growth rate of consumer prices for food provides them necessary nutrition status to get lift from below poverty line (Himanshu, 2007). From Table 20.2 it is crystal clear that poverty has declined during the globalization period in rural Bengal.

Table 20.2: Comparable Estimates of Rural Poverty and Inequality in West Bengal

Techniques of Estimates (in Percentage)	1983	1987-88	1993-94	2004-05
Headcount Ratio	63.6	48.8	41.2	28.5
Poverty Gap	21.06	11.58	8.3	5.4
Squared Poverty Gap	9.46	3.99	2.45	1.42
Gini Ratio	30.0	25.8	25.4	27.4

Source: Himanshu (2007).

Dev and Ravi (2007) also support that absolute number of poor in rural Bengal perceptibly declined to 19.4 millions in 1993-94 from 26.15 millions in 1983 and further registered significant reduction to 17.58 millions in 2004–05 (Table 20.3).

Table 20.3: Absolute Number of Poor and Percentage Distribution of Poor in Rural Bengal

	1983	1993-94	2004-05
Absolute number of poor (millions)	26.15	19.40	17.58
Distribution of poor (percentage)	10.47	8.04	7.80

Source: Dev and Ravi (2007).

IV

Hence, the strategy of diversification in agriculture is relevant to rural development in globalizing India. Getting lift the rural masses of India from the situation pinched with hunger and want, thereby transformation of rural economy require the growth path of the agriculture sector to be accelerated. Poverty remains a predominantly rural problem and agriculture is generally central to rural livelihoods. Therefore, steps for improvement in agriculture have a major impact on poverty. Growth of the agricultural sector of an economy depends considerably on the process of agricultural transformation, which is in turn well connected with sifts in production pattern, i.e., on the extent of crop diversification. Therefore, efforts should be made in having greater degree of crop diversification in the sector. So, in the Tenth Five Year Plan "the thrust is on diversification towards high value of more remunerative crops considering the agro-climatic conditions, endowment of land and water resources and the market demand both within the country and outside. Emphasis would be on production of fruits, vegetables, flowers, agro-forestry, tree farming, animal husbandry, dairy, aquaculture, etc." The Approach Paper in the Eleventh Five Year Plan (2006) has also suggested for raising agricultural output, the strategy of diversifying into high value outputs, fruits, vegetables, flowers, herbs and spices, medicinal plants, bamboo, bio-diesel, but with adequate measures to ensure food security.[4]

ENDNOTES

1. There are a number of approaches to rural development, namely Tagore approach, Gandhi approach, general economic development approach, neo-classical approach, structural approach, integrated rural development approach, participatory decentralized planning approach, target group approach, system approach etc. For the details, see, Sau (2006).
2. **Table 20.4: Export of Selected Agricultural Products before and after WTO ($ million)**

Commodities	1992-93 to 1994-95	1995-96 to 1996-97	1997-98 to 1999-2000	2000-01 to 2003-04
Basmati rice	297	354	443	416
Spices	171	319	384	330
Tea	328	383	447	351
Coffee	213	436	334	224
Tobacco	131	212	210	306
Cashew	320	370	468	390
Floriculture products	7	20	26	37
Fresh fruits		71	73	115

Source: Chand (2005).

Table 20.5: India's Agricultural Trade ($ million)

Year	1990-91	1995-96	1999-2000	2003-04
Export	3352	6098	5842	8029

3. **Table 20.6: Percentage of Rural Population Below Poverty Line**

Year	Percentage
1983-84	45.7
1993-94	37.3
1999-2000	27.1
2004-05*	28.3
2004-05**	21.8

Note: * As per Uniform Recall Period.
** As per Mixed Recall Period.
Source: Planning Commission, GOI (2007)

4. For the details, see, "Approach Paper to the Eleventh Five Year Plan", Planning Commission, Government of India, June 14, 2006.

REFERENCES

1. Ananta, T.C.A. (2002), "Institutional Reforms for Agricultural Growth", *Indian Journal of Agricultural Economics,* Vol. 57, No. 3.
2. Bathla, Seema, (2006), "Regional Dimensions of Inter Crop Diversification in India: Implications for Production and Productivity Growth", *Agricultural Situation in India*, December.
3. Bauri, Prasanta, (2008), "Issues of Agricultural Growth and Crop Diversification in the Era of Globalisation – A Study of Purulia District of West Bengal", an unpublished paper presented in the National Seminar on Issues of Development in Developing Countries organized by the Dept. of Economics with Rural Development, Vidyasagar University, West Bengal during 19-20 March, 2008.
4. Bauri, Prasanta, (2009), "Relevance of Crop Diversification in Rural Development in the Era of Globalization—A Study with Special Reference to West Bengal", *Vikas Vani Journal,* Vol. III, No. 4.
5. Chand, Ramesh, (2005), "Global Trade Scene, WTO and Indian Agricultural Issues and Experience", *Agricultural Situation in India*, Vol. LXII, No. 5.
6. De, U.K. (2003), "Changing Cropping System in Theory and Practice: An Economic Insight into the Agrarian West Bengal", *Indian Journal of Agricultural Economics,* Vol. 58, No. 1.
7. Dev, S. Mahendra and Ravi, C. (2007). "Poverty and Inequality: All-India and States, 1983-2005", *Economic and Political Weekly*, Vol. XIII, No. 6,
8. Himanshu (2007), "Recent Trends in Poverty and Inequality: Some Preliminary Results", *Economic and Political Weekly*, Vol. XLII, No. 6.

9. Jha, Brajesh Kumar, Nitesh and Mohanty, Biswajit (2009), "Pattern of Agricultural Diversification in India", Working Paper Series No. E/302/2009, Institute of Economic Growth, Delhi.
10. Joshi, P.K. (2006), "Crop Diversification in India: Nature, Pattern and Drivers", Report prepared for the Asian Development Bank (ADB).
11. Lekhi, R.K. (2001), *The Economics of Development and Planning*, Kalyani Publishers, Delhi.
12. Pandit, M.L. (2007), "Globalization and the Third World: An Opportunity or a Challenge", *Vidyasagar University Journal of Economics*, Vol. XII.
13. Roy, S.K. (1994), "Availability of Institutional Finance and Changes in Cropping Pattern: A Preliminary Study", *Vidyasagar University Journal of Economics*, Vol. III.
14. Roy, B.C. and Pal, S. (2003), "Investment, Agricultural Productivity and Rural Poverty in India: A State Level Analysis", *Indian Journal of Agricultural Economics*, Vol. 57, No. 4.
15. Rukuni, Mandivamba, (2006), "The Growing Business", *Our Planet*, special edition, published by United Nations Environment Programme (UNEP). Also available on the internet at *www.unep.org.*
16. Sau, S.N. and Pathak, Sarat, (2007), "Diversification of Agriculture Rationale and Determinants—A Study with Reference to West Bengal", *Indian Journal of Regional Science*, Vol. XXXIX, No. 1.
17. Sau, Sachinandan (2006), "Approaches to Rural Development and Theoretical Bases of Rural Development Pogrammes in India", *Vidyasagar University Journal of Economics*, Vol. XI.
18. Sau, Sachinandan (2007), "Globalization, Economic Growth and Exclusion: The Indian Experience", *Vidyasagar University Journal of Economics*, Vol. XII.
19. Shariff, A., (2001), "Indian Human Development Report—A Profile of Indian States in the 1990s", Report No. SEO10008, National Council for Applies Economic Research, Delhi.
20. Shivay, Yashbir Singh and Kumar, Dinesh, (2007). "Crop Diversification and Change in Food Habits of Rural India", *Kurukshetra*, Vol. 55, No. 12.

CHAPTER

21

Globalization

Global Economic Crisis and Rural Development

—Dr. M. Trimurthi Rao
—B. Prathima

ABSTRACT

Rural Development in India has witnessed several changes over.the years in its emphasis, perspectives, approaches, strategies and programmes. As a consequence it has assumed a new dimension during the past four decades. In the light of experience gained by following a particular approach, a new approach has been followed for the forthcoming development programmes. The shift in emphasis is intended not only to accelerate the pace of growth in the rural sector but to ensure to social justice by reducing social and economic inequalities in rural areas. In spite of the implementation of various development programmes, the vast number of people in rural areas still living below the poverty line. They have been subjected to economic deprivation, exploitation, discrimination and oppression of the worst kind. Even after sixty-two years of Independence the rural poor do not have access to quality education, quality health care facilities, protective drinking water facilities, good sanitary conditions, and proper employment opportunities etc. Especially in the era of globalization the income inequalities are increasing between the rich and poor. There was a wide gap between the rich and poor. The process of globalization and liberalization has further marginalized the poor and weaker sections of the society. Keeping in view the above aspects this paper reviews the existing rural development programmes, changing perspectives of rural development and emerging challenges in the context of globalization and also suggests alternate strategies for the development of rural areas.

Introduction

Rural development as a concept is not a new one. It had received the attention of great personalities like Mahatma Gandhi, Rabindranath Tagore and many others much before Independence. *Gandhiji's* concept of rural reconstruction and Tagore's Shanthiniketan were perhaps the first systematic attempts in this direction. Gandhiji said "India lives in villages". This is true even today also. According to 2001 Census report nearly 72 per cent of Indian population lives in the rural areas. According to the World Bank definition "Rural Development is a strategy designed to improve the economic and social life of a specific group of people—the rural poor. It involves extending the benefits of development to the poorest among those who seek livelihood in the rural area". The group includes small and marginal farmers, tenants, landless labourers, artisans and weaker sections of society.

Rural Development implies both the economic betterment of people as well as greater social transformation. Alleviation of rural poverty and generation of employment opportunities were the primary objectives of planned development in India. Ever since the inception of planning, the policies and the programmes have been designed and redesigned with this aim. The problem of rural poverty was brought into a sharper focus during the successive plans. Later on, the focus has been shifted to growth with social justice. It was realized that a sustainable strategy of poverty alleviation has to be based on increasing the productive employment opportunities in the process of growth itself. Increased participation of people in the rural development process, decentralization of planning, better enforcement of land reforms, maximum utilization of natural and human resources, development of skills of rural people, and greater access to credit and inputs go a long way on providing the rural people with better prospects for economic development. Improvements in health, protective drinking water, housing, sanitation, energy supply coupled with attitudinal changes also facilitate their social development.

Katar Singh (1999: 20), defined the term "rural development" connotes overall development of rural areas with a view to improve the quality of life of rural people. In this sense, it is comprehensive and multi-dimensional concept and encompasses the development of agriculture and allied activities, village and cottage industries and crafts, infrastructure, community services and facilities and above all the human resources in rural areas. In fact, rural development is the end result of interactions between various physical, technological, economic, socio-cultural and institutional factors. Rural development is a strategy to improve the economic and social well-being of the rural people in general and rural poor in particular.

The main objectives of rural development in all societies, irrespective of their economic, political and socio-cultural systems are: (*i*) to increase the availability and improve the distribution of life-sustaining goods, such as food, clothes, shelter, health and security; (*ii*) to raise per capita purchasing power and improve its distribution by providing better education, productive and remunerative jobs and cultural amenities; and (*iii*) to expand the range of economic and social choices to individuals by freeing them from servitude and dependence (Katar Singh, 1999: 53). So, rural development is the process leading to sustainable improvement in the quality of life of rural people, especially the poor.

Tapan Kumar Shandilya (2005: 339) drawing from the experience of large number of experiments in the rural development involving local communities, the Government of India soon after Independence launched the Community Development Programme (CDP) to rejuvenate economic and social life in the rural areas. The emphasis was on infrastructure building at the local level and investment in human resource development through the provision of education and health services. The programme was implemented in well defined geographical area or blocks.

By the late 1960s the second phase of rural development programmes started with measures that promised to address directly and exclusively the poor in the rural areas. This target group-oriented approach started with the programme for the development of small and marginal farmers, landless labourers etc. and finally culminated in the Integrated Rural Development Programme (IRDP). Serious efforts for poverty alleviation were initiated during this phase. The distinguishing feature of the poverty alleviation programme during this phase was the emphasis on creating employment opportunities and distributing renewable assets among the poor.

Objectives of Rural Development

Rural development programmes in the Indian context have been framed to achieve certain specific objectives. They are:

- Social transformation and social development in the Indian villages and to change the attitude of rural people towards development.
- Creation of infrastructural facilities and generation of employment opportunities for the rural people.
- Providing basic amenities to the rural people such as protective drinking water, better housing facility, better sanitation, proper health care facilities, and quality education.
- Improving infrastructural facilities such as transformation and communication facilities, irrigation, school buildings, health center etc.

- Improving the quality of life of the rural people by providing nutritional food, health care facilities and better education.
- Promotion of democratic leadership at the grassroot level by setting up local self-government.
- People's participation in decision-making and development activities.

In order to achieve the above objectives national level rural development policies and strategies have been formulated and implemented in India since 1952. Some of the important rural development policies are National Water Policy, Agricultural Price Policy and Rural Credit Policy (Katar Singh, 1999: 121-127). All these policies have been formulated for the development of rural areas in India.

Strategies for Rural Development

A review of various rural development programmes and policies followed in India reveal four strategies of development (Katar Singh, 1999: 134-136). They are: (*i*) Growth-oriented strategy, (*ii*) Welfare-oriented strategy, (*iii*) Responsive strategy, (*iv*) Integrated or holistic strategy.

(i) Growth Oriented Strategy

According to this strategy the state has to play a vital role in building infrastructure and maintain favorable climate to stimulate the growth of rural enterprises. The critical assumption of this strategy is that the benefits of increased production will gradually trickle down to the poor. Based on this strategy the programmes like Intensive Agriculture District Programme (IADP), Intensive Cattle Development Programme (ICDP), and High Yielding Varieties Programme (HYVP) were launched.

(ii) Welfare-Oriented Strategy

The critical assumptions of this strategy are that people are not competent to identify and resolve their problems and that the government specialists can identify their needs and meet them with the financial and administrative resources available with the government. Based on this strategy the programmes like Minimum Needs Programme, Applied Nutrition Programme, Mid-day Meals Programme etc., were launched. The primary means used in this strategy are free distribution of goods, services and civic amenities in rural areas.

(iii) Responsive Strategy

The critical assumption of this strategy is that the rural poor will identify and resolve their problems if provided with minimal support and otherwise left to their own devices and initiatives. This is aimed at helping rural people help themselves through their own organizations and other support systems. Its concern is with responding to the felt needs of the rural people, as defined by them. The role of government is to facilitate the self-help efforts of villagers by providing technologies and resources that are not locally available. Based on this strategy the programmes like Operation Flood, DWACRA were launched.

(iv) Integrated or Holistic Strategy

This strategy combines all the positive features of the earlier three strategies and is designed to simultaneously achieve the goals of growth, welfare, equity, and community participation. This paradigm takes a very comprehensive but integrated view of the basic problems of poverty, unemployment and inequality and seeks to address the physical, economic, technological, social, motivational, organizational and political bases. Based on this strategy the programmes like the Integrated Rural Development Programmes (IRDP), National Rural Employment Programme (NREP), and Training of Rural Youth for Self-employment (TRYSEM) were launched.

India has gained vast experience in the implementation of rural development programmes. The perspectives, strategies and approaches to rural development have changed over a period of time. In the light of experience gained by following a particular approach has been evolved in the course of time and such new approach has been followed for the forthcoming development programmes. The shift in emphasis is intended not only to accelerate the pace of growth in the rural sector but to ensure social justice by reducing social and economic inequalities in rural areas and also minimizing the wastage of natural resources. During the post-independent period rural development programmes have shifted in its emphasis from the 'target area approach to target sector approach to target group approach'. In the initial stages especially during the first two decades of Indian Planning the strategy seemed to be production-oriented than welfare-oriented. In the seventies and eighties onwards it has shifted more towards welfare-oriented approach. During nineties the rural development has taken a new approach due to the influence of globalization and liberalization. During this period it has shifted to technology and market-oriented development approach (Chinta Ganesh, 2006).

Rural Development in India

In spite of the implementation of various rural development programmes in India for the past six decades, still the rural areas are at great disadvantage as far as provision of basic infrastructural facilities and services such as roads, drinking water, electricity, schools, hospitals, transport, communications and social security are concerned. Not only these public facilities and amenities in rural areas are inadequate, but they are also very poorly organized and undependable. As a result, poor villagers are forced to suffer generation after generation with poor education, poor health, unemployment and poverty. So, improvement of their flight requires intensive government intervention with strong political will. In fact, during the post-independent period the successive governments have initiated number of development programmes for rural areas in India. But there are clear indications of the solving down and malfunctioning of many of the programmes undertaken over the years by the central and state government of the rural areas and poverty alleviation.

Rural development under diverse nomenclatures during the past six decades has been an adventurous effort with various policies, strategies, and models involving policy makers, planners, administrators, scientists, technologists, academicians and social workers. It is a programme of developing rural communities with a network of organizations and institutional linkages from the national level to the village level with several layers of administration in between. It is multi-faceted programme initiated and launched with great hopes and high promises. The perspectives and strategies of rural development have been changing from the past two decades. Especially in the context of Globalization the nature and content of the development programmes are undergoing tremendous changes. In spite of the large amount of budgetary allocations still number of problems are persisting in rural areas.

The experience in India so far has been that the benefits of development have not been equitably shared by all. This has aggravated the problem of poverty, which has manifested itself in various forms, including rising unemployment, malnutrition, growth of slums, fall in real wages, and impoverishment of marginal and small farmers. The growing poverty in rural areas undermines the principal objective of planned development, which is improvement in the standard of living of the masses. It has been acknowledged that a high rate of growth is not a substitute for deliberate policies to ensure equitable distribution of the gains of development. Therefore, there is a need for public policy to ensure growth with social equity or social justice. Rural development policies need to be designed to improve the conditions under which rural people work and live. The goals of policies must be governed by what people desire, and the measures of policies by what people think the government can and ought to do bring about the desired change.

According to the report of National Sample Survey Organization (NSSO), nearly 48.6 per cent of the 90 million farm households are caught in the debt trap. In Andhra Pradesh, 57 out of 100 indebted households are beholden to moneylenders. Although there has been much effort to increase and streamline institutional credit, small farmers still depend upon moneylenders for a variety of reasons (M.S Swaminathan, 2005: 10).

The workers in the unorganized sector constitute 93 per cent of the work-force in Rural India. Workers in the unorganized sector have low earnings and poor working conditions, and lack of social security. It is being realized that there is a need for social security programmes, particularly for neutralizing some of the negative consequences of the liberalization reforms. Besides, the case for any sort of changes to labour laws can be strengthened if all workers have at least minimum wages and minimum of social security. The state has a role in helping the poor in times of insecurity and in ensuring minimum security for those unable to gain from the post-liberalization economic growth process (Mahendra Dev. S, 2005).

Rural Development is a prominent and integral part of social development. It implies redistribution of excess-cultivable land to landless and the small farmers and other measures to remove inequalities among rural people. It will not be of the type, as in earlier notion of the Green Revolution that led to increase in food production without alleviating the hunger of the masses. Rural development for the welfare of the masses should prevent hunger and proletarianization.

Rural Development in the Era of Globalization

The term Globalization has become a popular term in recent years. It has attracted the attention of the intellectual community and social activists both at home and abroad for over two decades. Globalization denotes an economic process of integrating county's economy with the world economy, through free enterprise and free trade. Globalization is termed as market population or neo-liberalism. It means 'privatization, deregulation, and liberalization' of the national economies in order to promote the allocation of resources by the market. Globalization is a process by which the events, decisions and activities in one part of the globe have significant consequences for the other parts of the globe. It represents a closer integration of the world economy.

In the Indian context globalization implies relaxation of restrictions on participation of foreign direct investment, multinational corporations, foreign collaborations and liberalization of imports and exports. The trust of globalization has been provided since the new Industrial Policy Resolution and Trade Policies of India in July 1991. Globalization in India will continue to be subject to the democratic process.

Globalization has far reaching social, economic, political, cultural, environmental and technological consequences. Global forces play a much greater role in the determination of the price structure, level of investment, quality of product, occupational structure and direction of economic activities.

Globalization releases enormous opportunities and challenges for developing countries like India. Globalization is bound to affect the employment of labour. Some economists argue that globalization would block the employment opportunities in the agricultural, industrial and service sectors of the developing countries like India mainly due to their inability to compete with developed countries and imposition of the issue of labour standards in the international trade.

Like any other economic phenomenon, globalization is based on set of values, such as competitiveness, efficiency, wealth accumulation and the free play of market forces. Globalization of business and trade without a global view of the society as a global family would lead to social tensions and economic strife, and this is what happening today in many developing countries which have adopted the structural adjustment programmes. In the paradigm of globalization, there is no place for such values as sympathy, kindness, compassion, world-brotherhood, cooperation and so on. Because of relatively easy flow of capital internationally as compared to labour, capitalists/portfolio investors would benefit the most from globalization. This would aggravate the problem of disparities in income and wealth between the rich and the poor. Further globalization would also engender corruption, black money and other social evils. As portfolio investors would like to keep the bureaucrats and politicians on other side by bringing them. Besides powerful and rich countries define and redefine the rules of the game of globalization to suit their own national interests or the vested interest of their capitalist investors. This leads to clashes of interest and financial instability, as has been recently experienced in several East Asian Countries (Katar Singh, 1999: 131).

Globalization has created two distinct classes of 'haves' and 'have-nots'. When economists and sociologists are one in saying that the palpable effect of globalization has to be seen in the provision of employment, water supply, sanitation, health, education, purchasing power, housing and the like, we have to ask ourselves whether globalization has helped us meet the basic needs of the people. The answer is an emphatic 'No'. The plight of women and the rural masses is as bad as ever before. We need bottom-up development and not top-down policies that take us nowhere.

The Nobel laureate Amartya Sen says "despite unprecedented increase in overall opulence the contemporary world denies elementary freedom to vast numbers—perhaps even the majority of people". There is a growing volume of opinion in the World Bank that its policies should reflect the aspirations of the poor rather than the narrow western interests. The negative consequences of adopting the western models of growth have already been demonstrated in the recessions in Africa and Latin America. The future of millions of poor across the world will be determined by the way institutions such as IMF, World Bank and WTO function with the set mind to serve the US business interests or change the mindset to serve the larger interests of the world.

Due to globalization large section of Indian society is feeling insecure. Hence, the government has a crucial role to play in providing social and economic security to the people in general and poor people in particular. In this context, the issues that needed greater attention are education, basic health care, land reforms, development of micro-credit, employment generation, and empowerment of rural poor and women. Keeping the negative consequences of globalization in view, the government should strive to minimize the demerits of globalization. Government as well as the people at the helm of affair should play a more responsible and constructive role for the protection and the improvement of living standards of the rural poor.

Effective Measures to Implement the Rural Development Programmes in the Context of Globalization

Globalization is the process by which the world economy is transformed from the set of national and regional markets into set of global markets without regard to national and regional boundaries. In order to reap the benefits of globalization, the government of India has to adopt the following effective measures to achieve the national rural development objectives:

- Awareness Camps
- Changes in the Cropping Pattern
- Technological Transfer
- High Yielding Varieties (HYV)
- Commercial Crops
- Hoarding Facilities
- Marketing Facilities
- Skill Development
- Rural Industrialization
- Empowerment of Women

Conclusion

Globalization is a process of interaction and integration among the people, organizations and government of different nations, process driven by international trade and investment and aided by information technology.

This process has effects on the environment, on culture, on political systems, on economic development, prosperity and on human physical well-being in societies around the world. The current wave of globalization has been driven by policies that have opened economies domestically and internationally. Advances in information technology have dramatically transformed economic life. It has given valuable tools for identifying and pursuing economic opportunities, including faster and more informed analysis of economic trends around the world, easy transfer of assets and collaboration with far flung areas.

Globalization is deeply controversial. Proponents argue that it allows poor countries and their people to develop economically and raise their standard of living while opponents claim that creation of an unfettered international free market has benefited multinational corporations in the western world at the expense of local enterprises, local cultures and common people. Resistance on globalization has taken place at popular and governmental levels, as people and governments try to manage the flow of capital, labour, goods and ideas that constitute the current wave of globalization. We are passing through a stage of uncertainty about the future possibilities.

In order to find the right balance between benefits and costs associated with globalization, people of all nations need to understand how globalization works and the policy choices facing them and their societies. Globalization can also be profoundly enriching process opening minds to new ideas and experiences and strengthening the finest universal values of humanity. Every country has to learn and qualify itself for the global relationship. Similarly India has to continue with the pace of globalization. In fact, it is not an easy task. Things are really bad in the country side. If we do not improve our agricultural sector, we will be jeopardizing our national economy. "Synergies need to be developed between the technological advancement and problems to ensure a sustainable agricultural growth for the economy".

Hence, the government has a crucial role to play in providing social and economic security to the people in general and poor people in particular. In this context, the issues that needed greater attention are education, basic health care, land reforms, development of micro-credit, employment generation, and empowerment of rural poor and women. Keeping the negative consequences of globalization in view, the government should strive to minimize the demerits of globalization. Government as well as the people at the helm of affair should play a more responsible and constructive role for the protection and the improvement of living standards of the rural poor.

REFERENCES

1. Chinta Ganesh (2006), *Rural Development in the Era of Globalization*, (Ed), Osmania University, Hyderabad.
2. *India Rural Development Report (1999)*, National Institute of Rural Development (NIRD), Hyderabad.
3. Katar Singh (1999), *Rural Development—Principle, Policies and Management*, Sage Publications, New Delhi.
4. Maheswari, S.R. (1995), *Rural Development in India—A Public Policy Approach*, Sage Publications, New Delhi.
5. Ministry of Rural Development (GOI), *Annual Report for the year 2008-2009.*
6. Mishra, S.K. and Puri, V.K. (2008), *Development Issues of Indian Economy*, Himalaya Publishing House, Mumbai.
7. Mahendra Dev. S, "Social Security for Unorganized Workers" in *The Hindu* Daily Newspaper, Sep. 26, 2005.
8. Satyanarayana G. and Reddi Ramu M. (2006), *Rural Development Strategies in India in the Context of Globalization*, Ed), Osmania University, Hyderabad.
9. Somasekhar K. (2006), *Changing Role and Strategies for Strengthening Khadi and Village Industries Sector in the Context of Liberalization*, (Ed), Osmania University, Hyderabad.
10. Swaminathan, M.S., "Rural Knowledge Revolution: A Road Map" in *The Hindu* Daily Newspaper, July 9, 2005.
11. Ramesh Chandra (2008), *Globalization, Liberalization, Privatization and Indian Policy*, ISM Books, Delhi.
12. Ruddar Datt and Sundaram K.P.M. (2008), *Indian Economy*, S.Chand & Company Publications, New Delhi.
13. Tapan Kumar Shandilya, "Poverty Reduction: A Long View from the 1950s to the Millennium" in *Poverty and Sustainable Development* (Ed), R.K. Singh, Abhijeet Publications, Delhi.
14. United Nations Development Programme (UNDP), *Human Development Report*, (2008), Oxford University Press, New Delhi.

Index